Sunspot Literary Journal

2020

Laine Cunningham / Editor, Publisher
Angel Leya / Graphic Designer
Morrow Dowdle / Poetry Editor
Rich Ehisen / Advisory Board Chair
Marion Grace Woolley / Advisory Board Member

Writing a New World

Sunspot Literary Journal 2020
Volume 2 Issue 4
Writing a New World

Published by Sun Dogs Creations
Changing the World One Book at a Time
Print ISBN: 978-1-951389-19-2
eBook ISBN: 978-1-951389-25-3

Cover Image *Gaslighting* by Johnson Bowles
Cover Design by Angel Leya
Sunspot Logo by Timothy Boardman

Copyright © 2020 Laine Cunningham

All rights reserved. No part of this book may be reproduced in any form or by any means, electronic, mechanical, digital, photocopying or recording, except for the inclusion in a review, without permission in writing from the publisher.

TABLE OF CONTENTS

Tonight I Can Write / Diana Raab 1

Promises / Dave Malone 2

Equal, Opposite / Jerome Berglund...3

The Trees / Mitchell Nobis...4

Sierra Leone Poem / Renee Elton..6

Saturday in the Park / Melanie Martinez 10

Holidaze / D Fulford..11

They Say / D Fulford..13

After the Journey / Esther Sadoff 14

HC1 / Alan Lyons 15

The Point Is / Candice Kelsey 16

Shilo Inn / Tessa Ekstrom..17

Elected and Necessary / Valyntina Grenier 18

If I Were a Fish / Walter Weinschenk..20

Rumble / Pasquale Trozzolo..21

Afterimage Man / Silas Plum 22

The First Giant / Silas Plum... 23

Open House at a Paper Mill / Jennifer Judge 24

Drive / Jennifer Judge...26

A Glimpse / Debbie Robson 27

Unrequited by the Sun / Stella Hayes 28
Ladybug Eclipse / Ernst Perdreil 29
Saguaros / Ann Howells 30
Tristness / Gabrielle Vachon 31
l'étrangeté / Alena Marvin 33
Bright Lights Big City / J. Ray Paradiso 34
Salvage / Mickie Kennedy 35
Gone Outranks Broken Every Time / Samantha Madway 36
Indelible in Absentia / Samantha Madway 37
Incomplete / Nam Nguyen 38
IN 204 / Nina Wilson 39
A Life in Four Operations / Kim Waters 40
Still Life with Poppies / Chukwuma "Chuks" Ndulue 42
Five Major Ideas with Flat Design / Susan Landgraf 43
Gary Copeland Lilley's Recipe / Susan Landgraf 45
Elephant in the Room / Susan Landgraf 46
Sea Vision Part 1 / Ernst Perdreil 47
Sea Vision Part 2 / Ernst Perdreil 48
An Origami Girl / Charlene Stegman Moskal 49
The Swimmer / Anton Franz Hoeger 50
In Lovely Blueness / Anton Franz Hoeger 51
Refraction / Heikki Huotari 52
My Treat 2 / Heikki Huotari 53
Kitchen Closed / kerry rawlinson 54
Wooden Muse / kerry rawlinson 55
The Man Who Misspelled God / Mekiya Walters 56
In Avalon We Continue / Haolun Xu 74
Self-Portrait / Josie Del Castillo 75

Mom / Josie Del Castillo	76
The Letters / Victoria Shannon	77
Must Love Bernie / Kimberly Diaz	82
Face to Face 1 / Jack Bordnick	84
Face to Face 2 / Jack Bordnick	85
Demolition / Lenora Steele	86
Slices of Life / Susan Bloch	89
Forever Dream / Ping Wang	96
The Eternal Shine Room / Ping Wang	97
Discrete Infinity / Cassandra Moss	98
In Defense of My Stories / Roeethyll Lunn	114
Looking for Love: To-Do List of a Lake Monster / Marilee Dahlman	116
Villainy 04 / Nicole Foran	118
Villainy 09 / Nicole Foran	119
Heat / Rayne Debski	120
The Heated Mission / Laurence Williams	123
Color Burn / Hayley Patterson	130
Quilted Landscape / Christina Klein	131
The Tower Bells / Alli Parrett	132
The Jellyfish / River Elizabeth Hall	133
Is This the Ritz? / Doley Henderson	135
Chebyshev Spectral Overcast / Ryota Matsumoto	143
Recursive Topography of Uncertainty / Ryota Matsumoto	144
Swimming Lessons / Virginia Watts	145
Burning / Robin Bissett	149
Untitled Zone Plate Photograph 1 / Robert Oehl	150
Untitled Zone Plate Photograph 2 / Robert Oehl	151

The Other Margot at the End of the World / Zach Sheneman..152
The Bridge / Hediana Utarti 167
Trevor in Tenby / Penny Jackson 168
Come Live with Me and Be My Love / Michele E. Reisinger.........169
On No Account Should You Shout "Fire!" / Mary Byrne 170
Out to See / Valyntina Grenier 189
Uprising / Valyntina Grenier 190
We Make This Wind It's Wrath / Valyntina Grenier 191
Alternate History / T.B. Grennan...192
Miscellaneous / Samantha Schlemm 198
A Certain Perspective / Marjorie Tesser...200
Drop / Tonissa Saul 210
Leaving the Farm / Elizabeth Gauffreau 211
Paradises / Lara Chapman... 234
Chasing the Dragon / Kathy Hoyle..235
Michelin Boy (With Rabbit Ears) / Gabriel Embeha 264
Review of *Idiot Wind: A Memoir* by Peter Kaldheim /
    Neal Lipschutz 265

2019 Inception Contest Winner & Finalists

    The Lungs are the Seat of Grief /
        Elizabeth Marian Charles..268

    Citrus Sinensis / Cynthia Belmont 269

    Magnets / Barb Reynolds..270

    Cheonjimun / Kat Lewis..271

    The Mad Scientist's Husband / Eric Roe.....................................272

    Before and After / J Brooke 273

    Maddie Wants a Man / Kim Diaz...274

Single Word Contest 2020

- Aloha / Stephanie Launiu 276
- You're Mine You / Valyntina Grenier 278
- Burning / Olga Gonzalez Latapi 279
- Self-Quarantined / C.W. Buckley 280
- The ה Meanings / Omer Wissman....................................282
- Viral / Claire Lawrence 285
- Ubuntu / Ethel Maqeda 286
- The Meaning of Free / Hannah van Didden 289

$100 for 100 Words or Art 2020

- In These Uncertain Times / Alice Dillon........................ 292
- Willow Widow / Karen Walker...293
- Time a Grand and Final Judge, Grow Bravely in Love / Church Goin Mule 294
- Guernica / S.T. Brant 295
- Tilting Towards Self-Annihilation / George L Stein 296
- Rescue / Charlotte Wyatt 297
- Keep Those Hard Times Away / Benjamin Malay 298
- Red / Jacqueline Schaalje 299
- Resident Light / Louis Staeble 300
- No Rest for the Weary / Craig Anderson........................... 301

Young Authors and Artists

- Trailing Childhood / Sidney Muntean 303
- Untitled / Weatherall Crump-Kean 306
- The Haunted Asylum / Robert Fitzgerald Beavers Jr. 307

Contributors 308

Sunspot Literary Journal
Writing a New World

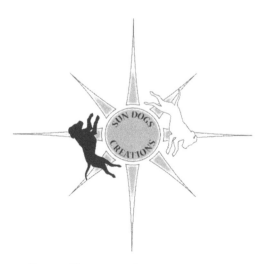

Sun Dogs Creations
Changing the World One Book at a Time

Tonight I Can Write

Diana Raab

(After Neruda *Tonight I Can Write the Saddest Lines*)

I thought he would be with me
until our end. I had to say goodbye
to him who rests, now, six feet above,
six feet below a night we only knew.

I wanted to be who he awakened to
each morning, not who he waved
goodbye to across our ocean
or those stars which lit only
our shadows.

He named me to her, his wife:
she tied his hands, in prayer
behind his back, resigned, exhausted
to what was to be his fate.

I am left an orphan by a love
which promised to give—
shattered now—rich only with
imagined memories, the oceans
and its stars my only light.

Promises

Dave Malone

> *You made me promises promises*
> *You knew you'd never keep.*
> Naked Eyes

Your red hair thick as bisque
smelled of bourbon and smoke
in our hangover mornings,
the breeze through the Indiana corn
snuggled your bedroom window
at dawn. We held each other
ladled in cream sheets, burning low.
Once, we pinkie-promised to shave our heads
as the wind picked up and tossed your curtains,
radish and arugula onto the chopping block
of your nightstand. The cold front
slipped into the barber's chair beside you
later that morning. While I, I kept a silence
in my palm. And curls to my shoulders.

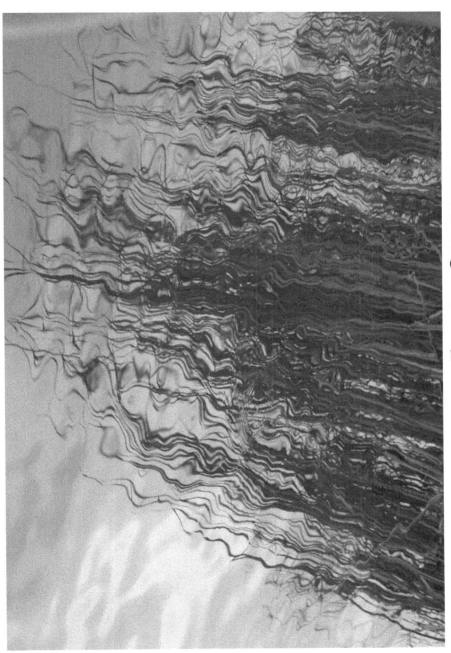

EQUAL, OPPOSITE / JEROME BERGLUND

The Trees

Mitchell Nobis

America,
I've been trying to write a poem
about trees for three days, but
America, you keep shooting
people. I want my boys to
appreciate the trees too, but
how am I supposed to teach
them about the trees when I
don't even know how to keep
my boys alive?
I do my part.
I feed them. Hug them.
Teach them how to treat
others with love.
I play basketball with them. Snuggle them.
Teach them the difference between right
and wrong. And America, you make that
last one hard. I want my boys to know the
woods, to know some rivers, to have some
favorite books, but America, it's awfully
distracting that you keep shooting people.
I've been trying to write a poem about
trees for three days, but I can't, America,
when you shoot up another school &
show a Black man getting shot live
online by an officer but let his killer
go free— both of those in just this
week.

Someone said "what is it when a death is ruled a homicide but no one is responsible for it" and America, that's a helluva good question. How do I teach my boys about trees when we don't have an answer for that.

I want my boys to know right from wrong, and most of us have a good grasp on what that is, but America, why don't you? I want my boys to know that they matter. I want my boys to enjoy this life too. And that's easy right now when everyone thinks they're cute, but what happens when they're taller than you, America, and need deodorant and their skin becomes a weapon and their hair becomes a threat to you. I want my boys to solve problems with thinking and words. I want my boys to love you.
America, I've been trying to write a poem about trees for three days, but you keep shooting people. America, you keep letting people shoot people.
I want my boys, America.
Leave me my boys
I want my boys
I want my boys

Sierra Leone Poem

Renee Elton

The Village of Waiting

Kpekelei a vala ngi gowui-huvei ma lo,
a kpangui lalewe

---

1. **White** Light

No bird as beautiful as its song, no woman singing
Early in the harmattan, November morning
A memory of music, raining
Showers of silence on rice fields, dancing
Slowly arms bent to skim the ground first
With one hand then the other, swaying
Bodies sway. Perhaps it was the chief who gave
The signal, I did not see. We sat on mats, drinking
Palm wine and eating salted mangoes.
Ngi pimbili gaa, ngi pambala gaa, ngi tea fee, ngi gbahanga...
We sat for hours, until Sentu took my hand
And led me toward the river.
In the water you are formless, weighted
Only by feathers of hair.

The casualties are not only those who are dead. Gutters
Of grief flow through the village, sewage washed
From a common wound. The clamor of flies in torn

Flesh, we cannot hear each other speak. The fleeing soldiers burn
Forty homes, killing fifty people, raping girls between
The ages of fifteen and twenty. I will show you fear
In the eyes of this child, stripped from her mother's breast.
I will show you fear in a handful of rice.
> Ngewo calls us
> Amma calls us
> Soko calls us
> Nyame calls us
> And we do not hear.

Are you looking into the same dim, green
forest light, are you looking for me?
I waited by the road-block, the menace of bright
Day clear as the blade of a knife piercing brilliance.
You did not come.

Grown old without wisdom, generations of dire disconnection.
Sacrificial yam in villages of night-singing and night dancing,
Who creates the symmetries here? What beast
Devours the children? Bintu dances in the red dust, reads
The night sky. "It is all the same," she tells me, "the world
Is not good for anybody."

Preponderance of acacias
Hart's-tongue fern on oil palm
All sorts of lovely things whose
Motions of fluency speak
Through tongues of claret
Orchid, voices of river grass,
Lively young crocodiles playing like kittens,
Words seep from the color of things,
And we wait for just the right dim shade of twilight,
To strip off dusty lappas, and pour
The murky brown river water over our heads.

Chrysalis of vermin my sweet malarial nightmare lioness of palms
Sande woman Bundu woman your dancing initiates white with kaolin
Bleed in imitation of climax onto the soapstone fertility heads of the dead

II. Black Mask

"Lie down!" cracks the order, and the uniformed
Arms descend. Dove gray walls, dove gray days,
Broken slate that gravels the floor, prisoners'
Soles dripping red strands, uncoiling from a skein
Of terror.
      The snake was wrong.
      The chameleon was wrong.
      The spider was wrong.
Kerosene smiles, Kofi is not properly dead, the dog's
Teeth still embedded in his neck, saliva of confident
Dogs. White Master.

The thigh should be round,
A bit fleshy;
The calf should be long, drawn out, and shapely.
It is the duty of the mother to ensure that her child's legs are straight.
A major concern about a female's legs is their position—
They should be as close together as possible,
With no space between the thighs.
Little Mende girls go about nearly naked, so they must learn
To protect their modesty by keeping their thighs closed.

Village of memory, murmur of mothers'
Songs—"buy you one cup sugar, buy you
One cup ginger, make you ginger beer sweet,
So town boy go buy em."
Lead me to the river, Bintu, lead me
To the water, daughter of the river,
Your watery tongues welcome my legs,
My arms, my outstretched hands.

Twin mask of the *Sowo*
Carved of bombax
Shiny black spirit
There is no woman here
Who does not love your cut neck
To have such a neck

Ringed in flesh, when all
Your charms have faded,
Tell them to look at the back
Of your neck, old woman,
Tell them you danced the *Sowo*
Mouth of silence
Eye sleeping in the head, dulled
Eye and mouth of the blind,
Bird and snake,
Melody and poison, birds
Are speaking, calling us
To the river, *Sowo* is a woman
Black as cooking pots
Wet jet to the eye

Bintu, the village dead are calling us
Bintu, Nyame calls us to the river
Bintu, Soko calls us to the river
Bintu, Amma calls us to the river
Bintu, Ngewo calls us
Calls us
And we do not hear.

Notes

Epigraph. "Man-of-the-town, you must be very sure of the strength of your legs before you knock at the door of a *Sande* shrine." *Sande* saying.

Line 10. "I have danced far and wide, I have danced round and round, I have leapt into the air, I have sunk onto the ground—I give up. I have done my best but failed." *Mende* proverb of *Gonde*.

Ngewo/Amma/Soko/Nyame. African deities.

Bintu. Woman's name in West Africa.

Mende. Ethnic group in Sierra Leone.

Sande/Bundu. Female secret societies in West Africa.

Sowo. Spirit of Sande-female God.

Saturday in the Park / Melanie Martinez

Holidaze

D Fulford

We were never sans xmas quirks and messy like
Reverend Bob's passive aggressive requests for

root beer tale-telling of mountain crags and
spamming the night with German expletives

we just hoped he would never hug Mom again
ill-conceived boner package in tan polyester

all the pets snagged on Grandma's oxygen lines
while she beckoned us claws sharpened to whisper

a pithy reminiscence or insult, coaxing smiles
or telling me she hated my hair choices, tattoos

sometimes Pop would show up for a few minutes
soused weepy, feeling in the way needy and

Mom, then, never sat down the entire long night
bustling in gravies, chopping, sipping Coronas

the expensive bourbon or cheesecakes Casey brought,
and you, without question, would be late so

everyone would have to wait too long drinking a
little too much snacking showing off for each other.

You're gone, now, so it's easy to keep on feigning
we're all vexed your belated throws the evening

cadence into tailspin of memory and Mom sits too
much, Pop and Grandma died, Bob's German now

tucked into mothball-painted thrift store suits, Casey
still brings cheesecake cooks the ham and even though I

quit drinking years ago I'll raise up at 7:00 because
Mom sent your letter saying we'd think and drink

to you right now and instead of the dark place you
today live we all pretend you're late, as ever, but

we know you'll be there when you arrive.

They Say

D Fulford

They say that everyone who alights at life's doorstep
will somehow influence it—this takes varied forms
depending on who you are and what you need from

> the moment and the other, too, who might blow in
> discretely, supplicating or maybe they tiptoe across
> your face in steel-toed stilettos of ardor and it will be
> all you can do to tell them you need some time to think.

You, brother, never asked permission came screaming
into my life abreast your mellow twin and from the very
moment we met were akin but wildly dissimilar as

> siblings habitually are, and though I did not enjoy the
> inborn knowledge of your distresses roiling internally
> your own twinges I also never assumed you would be the
> one to knock everything down with a mere swipe of hand.

After the Journey

Esther Sadoff

My hands are two pilgrims
praying and everything
becomes an oily skin of water.
When push comes to shove,
everything collapses into water.
Forgive my bones as I press
them back into the ground.
Forgive the ridge of my spine
floating in the side of a tree
downing sheets of rain.
The words in my head will
hum like bees without me,
tiny orbs of water tucked
behind their eyes.
This ship will sail on,
its captain crashing about
in the waves and never
knowing the journey is done.
Some days, a fleet of boats
will congregate like fish
in a column of light,
looking for a westerly wind,
and taking off again.
My smile, like the sun,
will hang from an
unbreakable string.

HC1 / Alan Lyons

The Point Is

Candice Kelsey

for Michelle McNamara

I sleep with
a knife under my pillow
fingers gripped on the camel bone handle
ready for anything
I sleep with that knife

perhaps you should have one
under your pillow too

we could be weird and knifey together
we could cringe when the housekeeper finds it
we could both feel safe finally

fighting each other's demons
protecting each other's bodies
burrowing each other's fears
like termites in the wooden beams
like mice beneath the floorboards

like cancer in the marrow

I know you probably won't but
still under my pillow sleeps a knife
that can speak for both of us—

Shine a light in my face at 3:00 am
Golden State Mother Fucker or some copycat killer
and you'll bleed the rage
of a thousand sleepless women

Shilo Inn

Tessa Ekstrom

If his breath didn't smell so bad
I could disappear into this moment
Turn this bed into the ocean
Try to drown in it.
I could get lost in the small parts of my mind
Where old memories reside
Or use the sharp edges of the blinds
To carve forgiveness down my spine.
Put my trust in a glass jar
Watch flowers and bees and
The secret life of your daughter
Rot beneath my feet,
Paint pictures with my menstrual blood and other fluids.
But his breath reeks with a liar
That begs me to build bonfires in his skull
A hymn so deep, deeper than my hymen knows
And I am wrung out by the fire,
A heat with the desire to determine
The roots of entire weeks of my life.
But the burn can only hold so many shots
Of whiskey before a quiet and retrospective
Fight or flight leaves nothing but the wish
That I was anywhere but at this Shilo Inn.

Elected and Necessary

Valyntina Grenier

One woman operates the Da Vinci Robot
another woman oversees
its insertion and removal
from my body

They deliver my cervix
uterus
poly cystic ovaries
endometriosis

Irrational fear conceived
a still life continually
attempting to abort
primordial punishment
as crippling pain

I don't want to bear this
I can feel myself slipping
back to the day

another surgeon laid photos along the desk
from my laparoscopy
I received them with a sense of violence
like being slapped with the replicated objects
of my wounded organs

It was strange
being alone with him
shocked to see
inside of my body
I imagine being at the surface of my skin
My body doesn't know
my *psyche doesn't desire*
to make another person

I lay my hands over the most painful spots
to feel myself as the surface of a sea
minnows feeding on roots of pain/ healing
healing a healing body

My grinding figure
all those eggs
phantoms for a page
I blow my brain to bliss

I turn to face
lemon and butter cream
chrysanthemums and carnations

The yellow ribbon
tied around the waist of the vase
reminds me of shoulders
and evergreens

If I Were a Fish

Walter Weinschenk

If I were a fish (and it may yet come to pass),
I would consign my soul to the water
And wear it like a linen shroud
That moves with me in cool continuum.

I would split the water with my lip
And, with my tail, I'd sew it up;
I'd venture forth as I see fit,
Silver in the morning,
Bloody gold at night.

But never would I break the plane
Of the silver ceiling overhead
(Unless, of course, a fly flew by,
Low enough to snap it up).

For if I were to pierce that mirrored veil
For more than just a moment,
I simply couldn't bear to see
A world that wasn't meant for me,
A world too cruel for piscine eyes:
I'd be overcome by the sorry sight,
Upon the shore, of elderly trees
Enslaved by wind, made to dance,
Their limbs pulled back and snapped
Like whips, and I'd see, as well,
The desperate flight of fathers and mothers
Along the beach, screaming names
Of sons and daughters,
Plucking up children on the run
Before the rains arrive.

Rumble

Pasquale Trozzolo

Like a ship at sea
She has a melody.
A low rumble
Echoing off waves
As if fog were in the air.
She pulses taking
Oxygen as she moves.
Barely glancing.
Hardly noticing.
As if alone.
First I was insulted, but
Who am I kidding?
This is meaningless
At its best.

Afterimage Man / Silas Plum

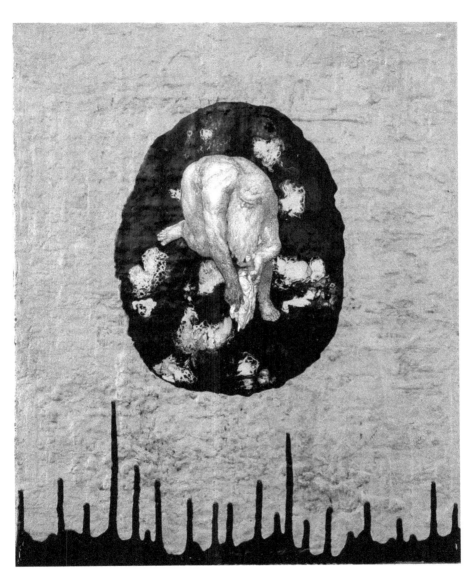

THE FIRST GIANT / SILAS PLUM

Open House at a Paper Mill

Jennifer Judge

      I was embarrassed of it all then—
      the Hane's pocket t-shirts, the steel-toed boots
      that smelled of leather, sweat, and
      sickening sweet paper pulp.

      My father's world was
      white and beige, dull steel
      of machinery, the color of gloom,
      miles of life walked away on concrete.

      I saw it once, open house
      day, families crowded into lookout rooms,
      paper cups of orange
      drink and powdered-sugar donuts.

      Outside, tractor trailers held
      their loads of trees, long pines,
      all their limbs removed, just
      waiting to feed these machines.

      After 25 years, I try to wear
      his life like a badge, like
      his suffering has earned me
      an identity, working class status.

      The dumb luck of prosperity:
      my grandmother writes to say she
      is so happy that we have what they

could never get—the house of our dreams.
That's the hope of immigrant life—
black lung and alcoholism,
poverty and welfare checks—
it ends up here: new cars, college degrees.

We can't surrender it all
to future generations and smile.
The shoulders we stand on
ache with a knife-digging hurt.

Drive

Jennifer Judge

1.
My daughters will never be babies again—
the dresses long gone, the dolls mildewing in boxes.

I watch old videos—a younger self lifts the slight toddler heft
to hip, spider legs cling instinctively as a closed fist.

Mommy, a apple, a apple, a apple, again and again and again,
a kitchen we don't own anymore, a voice I don't recognize.

2.
In a dream, I am in our car. I am trying to steer,
but the rain is so hard, washes the windshield to gray.

I cannot see, no matter how hard I peer into it.
I am in the passenger seat.

I realize that my husband is in the car,
wheel useless in his hands. I am forced to steer.

A Glimpse

Debbie Robson

I read once that a woman walking in
her local park encountered a pixelated
fall of light separating her from the other side
—the rest of the park, people and the houses
on the street. Suddenly miniature stars
imploded and fell, the filament drapery
twinkling and revealing a slightly different
but not completely other world.
Familiar houses in unfamiliar colors,
strange cars, the fabric of people's clothes
unrecognizable. People going about their
business in a completely natural way despite
her observation. Another dimension it seems.
But had she crossed over or merely glimpsed?

I'm glimpsing all the time. No torn curtain
just old houses that call to me and turn
their normally implacable faces my way.
Front doors, brick porches, windows, eaves
a grinning fenestration. Oh yes, my paint
wasn't always peeling. You see he's twenty-
one again, leaning on the porch with his
slicked back hair and tight jeans. Her skirt
ruffles as she leans to kiss him. Frangipanis
reappear in front yards, curtains billow
from paint stuck, card-boarded windows.
Young people, three abreast, run laughing
down that overgrown path to a backyard.
And my house on Cypress Street has
reappeared and with it a new alternative.

Unrequited by the Sun

Stella Hayes

    I stare into the sun without protective eye gear,
Gearing up for high risk

    The doom taking me on a carpet ride   circling around loss's motion

    It receives me in a half-hush,
Like when you decided that love couldn't support air

    The sun is as bright as the sun,
Arriving at a close   an eye to shun the sun beneath a closing eyelid

    What if we feed spoonfuls of sugar to each other under the stare of the sun?
We would go to dig the fields, sowing our dreams for the next generation

    The deflating atlas filling up with sun rays
Children at play with decay,

    If silence had a sound, it would sound like loss without a heartbeat
A ghost moving in for good,

Time, a strand in travel

LADYBUG ECLIPSE / ERNST PERDREILV

Saguaros

Ann Howells

rule rock-strewn mountainsides,
godfathers, *padrinos*,
towering some fifty feet
as they survey their domain.
No sissy succulent could survive here
where daytime temperatures
reach 120 degrees.
But saguaros flourish; May's flowers
lead to June's red-fleshed fruit.
Upstarts, young ones no taller
than a hitching post, dot the terrain
among scattered cholla, organ pipe,
and *ocotillo*, like stumps
after cutting saws thin the forest.

They must reach fifty years, you know,
and some approach a hundred,
before they sprout those stubby arms,
pose like mugging victims, hands up –
though some are one-armed,
and a few wear ringed appendages
like Elizabethan collars. Erect.
Taciturn. Seemingly omniscient.
Like Grandfather they are
self-made and self-sufficient.
Sharp spines and thick-ridged skin
protect. Well-adapted to hardship,
these crusty old hermits
may even prefer it.

TRISTNESS

Gabrielle Vachon

I am the brunch spread
on this beachside restaurant in Florida.
My mother spills syrup on my
tongue and asks me why I am so sad. She
laps up my nervous sweat with big
delicious bites.
She uses the word: triste.
In French, it belongs to the
mimes, and their frowning affectations
*Triste*ness smudges an upside-down
smile on a clown's boorish red lips
Old movies about the war are triste
Painting a gazebo blue overlooking the sea
is peak triste, it is the address on the mailbox
My mother drinks me, a large pulpy glass of orange nectar,
like she pressed me herself between the palms of her manicured hands

Like the Sun first pressed me into jet fuel
when I stepped foot in the sunshine state
I ran miles and miles on the beach
with my bikini top falling down,
but even the sand scratching my nipples could not convince
me my breasts weren't gifts to this world
I told the snowbird her husband was gay,
and laughed so hard to match her wails that I could not believe
my lungs never ran out of air
Mania never runs out of air,
like my spine never runs out of coconut sunscreen applied
in the shape of a toothy grin between my shoulder blades

Alas,
I watched one too many episodes of TLC's excellent programing in the hotel
    room,
and the 6$ minibar skittles weighed my tongue down
till it was numb and sour.
The sailor's rope in the lobby décor rung round and round my throat
like an untimely umbilical chord. I wept until the ocean spat me back out,
    and the foam carried me to the early bird special,
where my mother rips into my ribs like bacon.
I say to her, while she swirls my hipbones in gummy fruit jam,
that I am not sad, but simply depressed.
What's the difference, she asks, triste is triste.
I cannot see her through the Aunt Jemima in my eyelashes.
The waves of the ocean pounding onto the shore remind me I will never
    escape its currents

L'ÉTRANGETÉ

Alena Marvin

Who else could have glittered under the sun
Like a diamond?
Across the garden, among the browning roses,
With those poor big eyes that burned.

His hair a web of cornsilk, he beckoned,
So I followed.
Into the orchard, where the shade and tall grass hid every sorrow,
Silent, he pointed upwards.

I wondered then if it happened often.
He shook his head.
The sky like a bruise, the sun low in the valley, it was then
That I saw what he cried for.

An oddity, only now visible.
Our hearts, pounding.
He shone like the stars, yet he was hidden from the world,
But that was what he prayed for.

The tall steeple, beyond the green hill,
The blue cornflowers.

When will I get my chance, I asked,
To be a ghost like you?
I'm not a ghost, I'm from outer space.
I nodded, as if I'd known.

The pendulum rushed over the sea,
Our eyes swung lazily,
And my hand fumbled over his
In the flickering shadow of the eclipsed sunset.

To see him cry was stranger than to see him at all.

Bright Lights Big City / J. Ray Paradiso

Salvage

Mickie Kennedy

A stay of leaves,
a coherence of tree and path.
Splice of salt among a stumble of stone.
The thrash of doors unhinging at the rust.
At the pry of youth a proxy of fruit.
The wound of absence proceeded
by the constellation of touch.

The slender killing of a deer.
Horsehair plaster succumbing to a century of leaks.
The disregard of hand-cut nails.
The punctuality of a porch dissembling at dawn,
the memory of one plank at a time.
The blue orchard rounded to the nearest acre.
Burn barrels along the rows to smoke out the blight.

A larder of bustle reduced to a rounded fist.
A bottle of the half-turned wine.
A summoning of cardinals.
An eclipse of reds and grays.
The dialogue of months
against a scatter of squirrel and moss.
What catches in the throat?

Gone Outranks Broken Every Time

Samantha Madway

    All systems firing, frenetic, watching me
                                                       tick-tock
  till the countdown clocks in at
  single digits and
  I detonate,   birth a blast area,
                                 auto-irradiate.
Inner peace apostate,
transfixed by all that powder on my plate,
stage whisper *mirror, mirror, on the floor,*
who's the saddest and is there more?

Morning opens,
                            different level of
worse, follow my nose, embrace the accursed.
Another disaster, another pyre, another
incident report in my file.

Didn't we already arrest you?
                                  None of this is new.
And I'm repeating the very worst part, eternal false start.
But I can still deploy all the right lines,
swear
                I too feel The Change
                this time. (I do, I really,
                really do, and now
                I'm fine.)

But I'm just pacing, craving, prearranging, plotting
my next mistakes—
                    all I am   is what I chase.

Indelible in Absentia

Samantha Madway

you never brought flowers,
but still broke my vase

I made you make me cry

you ran my mind across a washboard, later
reminisced about the day we went antiquing

I said less

you were the mudslide, but I caved me in

I lost an extra winter
watching the floor

you kangaroo courted me, smiled at
seeing me chased for days by your screams

I said less

you accused me of being nothing
more than a metaphor

I said *this isn't what I'll remember*
because you made me promise to forget

INCOMPLETE / NAM NGUYEN

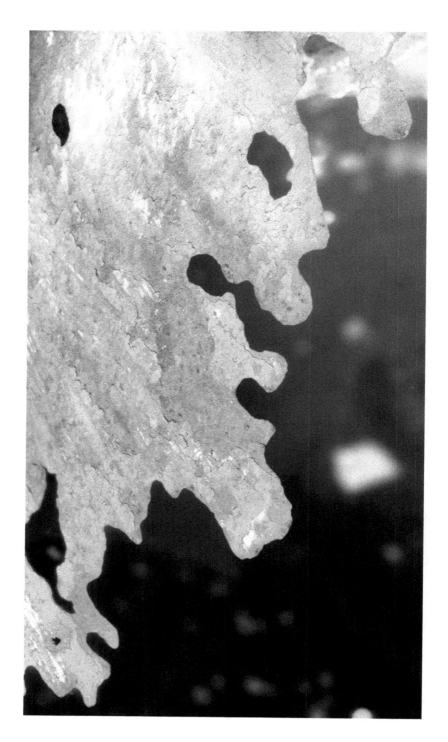

IN 204 / Nina Wilson

A Life in Four Operations

Kim Waters

I Addition

It begins
in the classroom heat
of a late August afternoon,
a lead pencil lagging
on your tongue
as the numbers squelch
under your squint
because at that age
you're growing flesh,
gathering
what's around you
and trying to make sense
of a Cuisenaire box set
of Panglossian colored columns.

II Subtraction

No longer satisfied
with what's presented
on the paper before you,
rebellion
kicks its heels in
and like an unhung handset
in a public telephone booth
you're an adolescent
hovering in space,
counting backwards
in a minor chord,

thinking you know best,
even though
what you're left with
is less than before.

III Multiplication

With two x chromosomes
you're going to need
a bigger house,
more garage tools
and kitchen utensils
for the children
who have begun
to appear
in your own image
and suddenly life
becomes a tic tac toe,
a cross-stitch
with your family name
embroidered
in the hallway.

IV Division

Finally,
it comes down to this,
time reversing
in on itself,
downsizing
to a nursing home,
belongings gone,
a morse code
of dots and dashes,
the SOS of death
until you're gone
and an obelus appears
in the partition
of your estate.

Still Life with Poppies

Chukwuma "Chuks" Ndulue

Trees are more vicious
in their lean, the whinnies
of road dogs, more menacing.

You offered a swollen hand,
on a corn moon night and
the night turned in on itself.

Summer is gone now.
No more beach front
swilling, or casual palmistry.

The forecast is cloud-cover,
dry embraces, looming hours,
square shouldered shaking.

We count telephone poles,
plan discount pyres, talk of life
under a skimmed layer of creosote.

Five Major Ideas with Flat Design

Susan Landgraf

1. Equal Surfaces

Skin, sermons, songs.
Ideas lined like trees.
Watch for birds and the next
full-color catalogue to come.

2. Buddhist Space

Everything is here.
Eggs and the wombs that hold them.
Eggs and snakes to eat them.
The mouths of bullhorns and trumpets.
Pockets with keys and coins
and their owners whose mouths
choose *joy or fuck.*

3. Constructed, measuring space

Rulers and lines with scales
and mathematics. Tools of the creator
looking inside the void. There angles,
there the idea of door in a context
of walls and rafters where a woman's breath
can steam the windows.

4. Light

Cataclysms – leaves burnished, grief
brought out and laid to dry. Peach
on the sill. Shadows struck dumb.

5. Expressionistically

Time on fire.
Space an iceberg, double-minded,
sequoias the same and mountains.
Space shouts out dimensions
through the telescope,
an invented eye.

Footnotes:
There is no equal surface.
A Buddhist Space holds air space.
Breath is always in a context.
Headstones throw shadows.
You can't breathe fire.

Gary Copeland Lilley's Recipe

Susan Landgraf

Keeping wickedness from your door
is magic you can count on:
a haint blue bottle tree.
Fill the bottles with the blessed earth –
stones, bones, old letters, and prayers.
Against the curses of certain
ancestors and practitioners
of blame and shame this invitation
for ancestors that have your back.
If you don't have an oak or pine,
build a facsimile. Pour a shot
of good whiskey and baptize
the ground under your tree.
Pour a second shot and bless yourself.

Elephant in the Room

Susan Landgraf

She will adopt this white elephant,
this mended chair
sit for awhile and dream a mirror
that doesn't produce poisoned apples.

Seeing the horse-child reminds her
of an upside-down question
under glass. It can't speak.
It can't wither or sprout.

Even under the brightest sun
and oddly shaped shadows
the first word in her dream
was "o." The second "no."

There is this chair
her father made
that no one wanted
because of the memories.

She will put it, too, under glass
where the moths can't go, where
except for the elephant
it has lost memory.

SEA VISION PART 1 / ERNST PERDREIL

SEA VISION PART 2 / ERNST PERDREIL

An Origami Girl

Charlene Stegman Moskal

expert at elusive
folds in on herself,
hides in the empty paper,
creates whatever
one needs to see;

is a shape changer,
a box, a bird, a basket,
both opened and constrained –
illusory, absent, a cipher
who hides in blank spaces.

I never hear her walking,
silent, sliding steps, soundless –
tissue paper that floats on air;
there are no footsteps.

Her voice quiet, paper thin
she sings comfort songs
written for someone else.

She is secure in two dimensions
flat as the family photographs

sealed flat in a yellow clasp envelope.

THE SWIMMER / ANTON FRANZ HOEGER

IN LOVELY BLUENESS / ANTON FRANZ HOEGER

Refraction

Heikki Huotari

  Jacob, seeing Rachel, husbanded his mother's brother's sheep. I knew the minute I ran into it it was a wall and not a well. Disturbances of atmospheres restricted me to hallowed ground. Penultimate? Is that your final interjection? An objection asked and answered interfaces in a cloud. Exceptions may be made for seven or more chickens or
  a road is long and winding or a type is strong and silent so with Gertrude Stein I beg to differ. Father Nature loved a vacuum, a parade. I called the one who stayed a lazy bones, the one who took the special breakfast lightly and the one who wanted to be left alone. I shall continue contemplating peer review or quantum blue until I have a quorum or
  I'm slowing photons and remotely diagnose the alien with schizophrenia, advise the alien to be in limbo only with the nonjudgmental alcoholics or the outer measure of the apparition may be smaller and the inner larger but by god that apparition is no plaything. Contraindicating popular opinion, you may have your thorns and thistles without bells and whistles, your goats neither fainting nor in trees. It is when midnight light breaks into prison that refraction happens.

My Treat 2

Heikki Huotari

Give me a sidewalk to sit on and I'll connect the dots or equally improbably be written off. This cubic corner is a cubic corner spiders might belie. It's only an electric eye, it's not an outrage what Bob Dylan's done, that's not Bob Dylan's name and those with real names, those whose needs to eat and sleep are in remission, seek to simultaneously eschew and consume. The human form is taken–do you, unborn, have a backup plan?

We called it beauty rest and in the colors of a second sunset we were two thirds of a person and one third of us would storm a barricade if there were further innocence to lose and in my ice age I'll grow into your opinion, your solution, even as a worker ant, when given insulin, becomes a queen.

You wonder where that phantom hand has been, in what repose. Your marching orders include humans left and right. The scissors put their teeth in and the scissors sing. The branches meet above your street, the roots below. It's out and back and there's a hairpin turn. Because your name is on a list no one will talk to you but if you tell me what your optics are, I'll see what I can do.

Kitchen Closed / Kerry Rawlinson

WOODEN MUSE / KERRY RAWLINSON

The Man Who Misspelled God

Mekiya Walters

I'd never heard Paganino Paganini raise his voice before the day that Gabiano's letter came. Alessandro, his only son, had taken over the printing business years before I came onboard, but Master Paganino still involved himself when his health permitted, reviewing accounts and editorial decisions, sometimes touring the workroom, reprimanding a man or two for shoddy work or laziness; but he never spent his passions on us. He had a jagged face and a rigid spine and more commitment to the ideal of *mediocritas* than any patrician, breaking fast each morning with the same dry crust, the same handful of olives as a poor man, unmoved by the mercantile world's vicissitudes.

And yet his voice rose now behind Alessandro's study door, and fell, and rose again, and all motion on the press floor slowed as the sound of unfamiliar fury drew us from our work—all but Lorenzo, the *battitore*, who continued swabbing ink onto the block of type that he and I had just maneuvered onto our press's carriage, his rhythm stoic and unbroken, for he was hard of hearing.

It was a humid day in spring, a few weeks after the Feast of the Ascension, when we and every other printer in Venice had set up open-air booths in St. Mark's Square. Meager profits, but that was how the fair went every year. Since then, things had been looking up. In the front room, elaborately clad men perused the catalog by the window and the second-hand books in the shop's northwest corner, some looking over the unbound volumes heaped along the walls and on the outdoor tables, shielded by an alabaster awning from the sun. A breeze fingered the unbound pages, mixing the smells of Mercerie Street—perfume and sewage and flowers and sea—and bearing them back to us in the workroom, through the cracked-open door, along with the customers' voices. We had our own damp miasma on the work floor—sweat and moist paper and the mineral-sharp bite of tincture—as did the slave quarters at the back of the shop: spice, shit, cooking oil, and whatever garbage had been dumped in the alley the night before. Alessandro's study and the servants' rooms were on the ground floor, too. The Paganinis lived above us, and only with permission did any of us ascend the stairs. I imagined that they kept their windows open.

Through the door to the front room, I could see Pietro, the compositor, doing his best to maintain his composure, running a delicate finger down the ledger as a gray-voiced man I couldn't see struck him with question after question, quick as a jouster, not waiting for an answer to each one before delivering the next: "How much will the binding cost?" and, "How many days?" and, "You know, the prices aren't as good here as what I've seen in Bavaria."

This was Pietro's first time behind the counter. Alessandro had pulled him from the work floor while he and his father retreated to the study to look the letter over. This had never happened before.

My attention was still on Pietro when a thud came from the study. I turned. A savage yell, and then the heavy walnut door crashed open and disgorged Alessandro, who stumbled into the nearest press—mine—and jolted loose the paper I'd been securing to the gauge pins. A slash of crimson above his eye. He raised an arm to deflect a second projectile: a bone-sharp crack, and something rattled across the floor. Alessandro clutched his arm. Enough flesh, I couldn't help thinking, to protect him from everything but a bruise. Over the years his robust appetite and taste for wine had stripped him of his father's visage, softened his edges. He reminded me of a sea urchin I'd once found as a boy washed up on the Ifriqiyan shore, so thoroughly encrusted in algae that its spikes were nearly hidden. Even then, I'd known better than to pick it up.

Master Paganino stood in the doorway, emotion sewing up his silver brows and rutted cheeks, looking like nothing so much as a wooden pillar eaten through by termites, about the crumble. Had the breeze from the street not abated, I'd have feared it would disperse him. On again, off again since 1509, he had been ill, as if the defeat at Agnadello, the loss of so much land from the Republic, had effected in him an equivalent diminishment of spirits—but I'd never seen him look so frail as he did then. Perhaps he knew, as animals do, that he would be dead within the year. Or perhaps fury had blasted all thoughts, even those of mortality, from his brain.

"You've ruined us," he said.

"For God's sake," Alessandro hissed, "not here."

Even Lorenzo had turned to watch the drama, quick, dark eyes following our employers' lips, an ink-stained leather paddle forgotten in each hand.

"Why not here?" Master Paganino demanded. "These men, Alessandro—" and with a twitch of his arm, he brought us all into the fold, "—till their contracts expire, they're your flesh and blood."

Alessandro, terse, resentful, nursed his arm.

"You can lie to your betters," Master Paganino pressed on, "hide from your peers, but don't think you'll deceive your servants. They feed on secrets as we feed on bread."

I glanced at Alessandro, expecting indignation—he thought well of himself as a man of the people: what could his father tell him of the working class?—but his pride had been shattered. I could see it in the slump of his shoulders. I didn't like witnessing this confrontation, though I'd developed no great affection for either of the Paganinis while in their employ. Like Master Paganino, my father had been a frugal man, and pious as Abraham, and because decades had passed since we'd parted, and his face had faded in my mind, it was the elder Paganini's that came before me sometimes when I tried to call it up. Alessandro's impudence irritated me as it irritates me to see a man toss a perfectly good crust in the gutter—a precious paternal resource squandered.

"My son," Master Paganino declared, raising his voice to make us all his audience, "knows nothing of prudence. How many times, Alessandro, how many times did I tell you—that book—that goddamned book—"

Only a fool would have to guess which of our books he was referring to.

It was only then that I noticed Caterina in the doorway to the slaves' quarters. A tall girl, sinewy, but something less than sturdy-looking, and a few shades darker yet again than me. She'd once been attractive, I imagined, or nearly so, but now her cheeks bore pockmarks, and her hair had grown prematurely gray. She'd been with the Paganinis longer than any of us, traveling with Master Paganino when he visited Venice or Isola del Garda while his wife Christina stayed behind in Toscolano to oversee the paper mill. Caterina was the only woman in the house this year, for Alessandro's Daria, too, had stayed in Toscolano to look after the mill and her mother-in-law. Were it not for Caterina's childlessness, she would most likely have been ejected from the household long ago. As it was, Christina tolerated her.

Master Paganino looked about to lay hands on his son again. Then he swayed, barely managing to catch hold of the doorframe. He'd forgotten his silver-tipped cane.

In an instant, Caterina was at Master Paganino's side, ducking under his arm and taking his weight with a grimace.

"You've gambled away these men's bread," Master Paganino said, hardly aware, it seemed, of the woman supporting him. His eyes never left Alessandro's. "When they starve, who do you think they'll turn on?"

I felt as if, halfway through stepping into a boat, a wave had come along and set it rocking beneath me.

Caterina leaned her weight into her charge, and like a horse guided by a skillful rider, he acquiesced and shuffled toward the stairs. I'd once overheard her trying to convince him to take a room on the ground floor, but he'd refused. The ground floor was for servants, he'd insisted, and Jews. Even Alessandro's friend, the polyglot Jew with the lazy eye who came to stay with us last autumn, had slept on a bedroll next to mine, despite the precious service he was rendering at no cost but room and board. No exceptions to the household rules.

Caterina had relented, had not brought it up again.

We all watched them climb the stairs, Caterina's whole frame angling to bear Master Paganino's weight. Only when they'd reached the first-floor landing did Alessandro turn to us.

"Well?" he demanded. As if we were the ones obliged to explain ourselves. A tremulous note rang in his voice. "His mind is going," he said. "I can assure you, it's not as bad as he thinks. He sees mountains, I only see small stones. He hasn't got the energy—but do I look worried? No. You shouldn't be, either." His hand fluttered to his forehead absently. He glanced at his fingers as if distracted, then wiped the blood on the pleat of his giornea. "We only go hungry if we stop the presses. Let's not let that happen."

He retreated into his study and shut the door.

Lorenzo's eyes met mine across the bed of type. The sheet of paper that I'd let slip had folded over onto the inky bed. It would have to be discarded. I removed it gingerly, carried it to the short stack of rejects in the corner, and returned with a fresh one.

"What the hell's going on back here?" Pietro's head poked in from the front room. He eyed the study door. "Is he in there?"

Nods all around the work floor.

"Master Alessandro!" Pietro called. When no answer came, he crossed to the door and rapped hard on the walnut with his knuckles, ignoring the knocker in the shape of the Paganini family seal. "A customer wants to speak to you, sir. He's asking about prices. What should I tell him?"

Lorenzo caught my eye and gave his head a little shake, as if to dislodge water from his ear. I shot back something that would have liked to be a smile.

"I haven't got a clue where anything is," Pietro muttered, to us, it seemed, "or how much he's asking for it. And I can't read his handwriting." He glanced at the door as if hoping to find instructions scrawled there in a legible hand. "If he doesn't come out, we might as well close the shop."

"Should we shut the presses down, too?" This from Matteo, the second *tiratore*.

"No," I said.

There was no clear chain of command in the printing house beneath the Paganinis. Normally in their absence, authority fell to whomever they explicitly left in charge. As a journeyman and first *tiratore*, though, I thought I had a fairly strong claim to seniority. And my gut told me that shutting down the presses would mean more than half a day of lost profits—would mean acknowledging that something had begun to shift beneath our feet, something none of us could control. That our livelihoods here at the press were in jeopardy.

"You heard Alessandro," I added. "Do you want to go hungry?"

Pietro jabbed a thumb over his shoulder. "Do *you* want to get out there and manage the mob?"

"Close up the front, then," I said. "We'll keep the presses running."

Sometimes men want nothing more than to be given clear instructions. This was one of those occasions, evidently.

The creak of wood, the scrape of paper, the squalling of ungreased screws resumed. Lorenzo and I folded down the frisket and the tympan, rolled the carriage under the till, and I took hold of the iron bar and heaved to turn the screw and drive the platen down so that the ink would kiss the paper. In the background, Pietro attempted to maneuver confused customers out of the shop, announcing that the backroom had flooded, that we would need a day to clean up, maybe two.

He returned a few minutes later, looking a bit calmer, though no less haggard, and took a seat on the edge of the nearest workbench. "What do you think he's gone and done now?" he asked, his voice low enough that it wouldn't reach the study.

"God only knows," said Giorgio, Matteo's *battitore*.

Lorenzo made the sign of the cross, eyed me sardonically, and stuck out his tongue. I stuck mine out, too.

"Something's gone wrong with the Koran," Matteo said. "It's got to be."

I did my best to look as if I hadn't heard, but anyone could have seen the hairs on my neck standing.

Pietro, sardonically: "And what could possibly have gone wrong with that?"

From the beginning, Master Paganino had disapproved of Alessandro's ambition to print the Qur'an—never mind that it was Paganino's friend Gregori's *Kitab Salat al-Sawa'i* that had inspired the enterprise, and that Gregori's Arabic typeface had served as Alessandro's first model. Gregori had been the first printer in Venice—in the world, as far as any of us knew—to solve the principal problem in printing Arabic, that of joining up the ligatures. Alessandro had always fancied himself a visionary, ready to shatter all the staid conventions to which his father cleaved—also a cosmopolitan, at ease with Jews and Muslim, sheikhs and slaves—and Arabic printing was the sort of thing he would have liked to put his name on. It galled him that someone else had gotten there first. But Gregori only intended to sell the book of hours that he'd printed to Arab Christians in the East—a niche market. Alessandro had hatched a grander plan.

Since I'd entered his employ, Alessandro had developed a habit of pulling me aside at odd hours—sometimes after the work was finished, sometimes in the middle of a print run—and interrogating me about my upbringing in Ifriquiya, trawling for exotic details with which to enrich his vision of the world. He liked extracting stories from travelers, too, and from his many business connections, and from all this, he'd gathered that most Muslim households couldn't afford a Qur'an and depended on the copy available at the local mosque. He understood that the book could not be printed except by hand, and that this was an expensive undertaking, and he'd probably assumed that this owed solely to the technical challenges of joining ligatures and juggling a multitude of contextual letterforms. Maybe I should have corrected him. But I was only a machinist. This wasn't my job. And anyhow, it had seemed possible at the time that I might be mistaken. The Christians, after all, saw no sin in mass-producing holy books, and besides, I'd come from the countryside, an olive farm on the outskirts of Tunis. I knew little of the Eastern cities. Maybe Ottoman buyers *would* take interest in a printed Qur'an.

Master Paganino didn't trust Saracens, wanted nothing to do with them. He'd already handed the reigns to his son, though, and went months sometimes without leaving his bed. He'd had no choice but to trust Alessandro. I'd done the same.

And so Alessandro had hunted down Gregori's typeface and bought it off him in 1515. But he hadn't been satisfied. The following year, the Genoese Giustiniani published a polyglot Bible, partly in Arabic, using a different typeface, which Alessandro had also moved to purchase; but this one, too, had failed to meet with his approval. In the end, he'd gone and engraved his own elaborate set of punches and matrices, spending a small fortune on lead, steel, and copper, smelting and chiseling all through the dawn and midnight hours, stomping around the workshop in a short-tempered haze while discarded prototypes piled up in waste bins. What flaws a man who read no Arabic could have found in the first two sets, I'd never fathomed, but at a certain point, one learned not to question Alessandro.

"He's always been a gambler," Matteo said. "And his father can go on about prudence all day, but they caught him minting counterfeit coins once." He took a sheet of paper from the workbench and set about securing it to his press. "In my opinion, the apple doesn't fall far from the tree."

"That's only a rumor," Pietro said. "And Mamádo's right. Let's finish the run, at least. No point speculating."

Alessandro had always refused to call me by the Tuscan name I'd received from my first and only master, an apothecary, years ago. When he hired me, he'd insisted that I tell him my given name, Mamdouh. He hadn't much appreciated my attempts to correct his pronunciation, though. And so, I'd become Mamádo.

A second passed, and then another, and I realized that at the mention of my name, uncomfortable stillness had descended on the workroom. Nobody was looking at me.

"Once we've got something done," Pietro said, "we can close up shop, even if it's a bit early. I could use a drink."

My authority seemed to have slipped away as easily as it had come, yielding to an unspoken agreement that I should be excluded from any further discussion of the Qur'an.

Work resumed. I understood my colleagues' desire to mull things over privately without having to guard their tongues, but that did not dampen my frustration. In all my years as a *tiratore*, I'd spoken of my faith to no one except Alessandro, and then only under duress. I had not held myself apart, even when the other men tossed back drinks or mumbled prayers, though I hadn't partaken, either. Most days, my fellow printers treated me no differently than any other *tiratore*. Still, they knew I wasn't Christian.

"Should we be wasting our money on wine?" I heard Matteo murmur to Giorgio at the other press. "If our salary's in question?"

"Have you got something better to spend it on?" Giorgio shot back.

"I have, as a matter of fact. I've got my family to feed."

I tried to focus on the rhythm of the work, the resistance in the bar. I felt a kinship with both, and neither. I agreed that wine seemed foolish, but I had no family to feed. Which was to say that I no longer knew if I had a family, or if they needed feeding. Which was to say that I'd had a family, once, that I'd once fed them, and that as a consequence, I was here. No idea if they'd survived the droughts or the Hafsids' ousting, stayed in Tunis or sought shelter among the Amizaghs in the hills. Sometimes I wondered. Sometimes—but what kind of workingman has time for such thoughts? Wasn't I stockpiling coins in my mattress, just in case? And wouldn't I send that money back to them if ever an opportunity came? Did any day contain enough hours to do anything more? How many thousands of times had I thrown my weight against the bar? How many tens of thousands of times had I raised the platen, rolled back the carriage, extracted the glistening, neatly printed sheets, and carried them to the workbench to stack atop their fellows? How many millions of pages had the workbench borne? On a good day, we could average three thousand, the evidence of our labor piling up around us. This day, though, was not a good one.

For the first time in years, I began wondering how many more pages I would have to secure. I'd grown adept at ignoring the ache in my shoulders, but I couldn't prevent my mind from flitting to and fro, alighting on discomfort first, then curiosity, and then unease. I would have food and shelter that night, and perhaps the next, but for how many more thereafter?

Quite some time had passed since Caterina had helped Master Paganino up the stairs, and no one had come back down. To distract myself, I resumed a familiar habit: entertaining suspicions and dismissing them. Some women never could bear children, after all, no matter what was done to them, and Master Paganino would be an unusual man indeed if he'd never taken advantage of what was his. Yet I found I had little difficulty believing that he was, indeed, an unusual man. There was something about the sheer indifference that he showed her, unmarred by any trace of embarrassment or contradiction—this from a man who'd built his reputation on Christian books and narrow scruples. A Cypriot who used to serve the Paganinis had told me once how he'd entered Master Paganino's room and found him stretched on the bed and Caterina at the bottom of the bedroll, his feet in her hands, working over the callouses with her strange, stubby thumbs as he'd stared heavenward, utterly distracted by nothing at all, his face blanker than paper. Caterina, for her part, never showed any outward sign of love or hatred, disgust or affection: just a sort of ritualistic devotion, not unlike that of old women in prayer, arthritic limbs creaking with the effort of prostration, unaware that not everyone endured this pain.

It would have been different with Alessandro as head of household—Alessandro, who never missed an opportunity to get his hands dirty. More than once, I'd watched him strike up conversations with riffraff and beggarmen, servants and slaves, pursuing one-sided discourses with half-savage domestics ignorant of his language and indifferent to his company, and, when the objects of his interest ignored or rebuffed him, becoming impatient and venting his anger on them, or on whatever other unlucky man happened to be standing nearby, with blows. I found so many of his habits irritating, and so little in his nature to redeem him, and yet as night began to fall, my thoughts returned to him like blackbirds circling back toward a chimney. Whatever had gone wrong with the Qur'an would land on both of us, after all, and such circumstances have been known to effect bonds between men where none would otherwise exist. It was such a bond, such a concern, that I felt forming then.

We finished the run just as the lamplighters came along Mercerie Street, nimbly wielding their unruly poles. A Tartar boy, a new slave whose name I didn't know, came around the work floor, scaling stools and benches to reach the lamps and light them. Lorenzo and Giorgio took their beaters into the alley behind the shop to clean them, while Pietro set about disassembling the type that he'd set that morning, removing the sorts one by one and rinsing them in a pan.

As *tiratore*, my responsibilities included ensuring that my press was properly greased and readied for the next day's labor, but I struggled to concentrate on these tasks, my attention hovering by Alessandro's study door, which had remained shut all afternoon, silence piling up behind it like dark clouds on the horizon.

I scoured the workroom, peering under benches until I came upon the object that Master Paganino had thrown at his son: an oversized leaden sort, slightly deformed, but clearly an attempt at the medial form of ba'. Unlike the rest of the rejects, which Alessandro had relegated to the waste bin, this one had been promoted to paperweight.

I carried the ba' to Alessandro's study and knocked, and when no answer came, I pushed the door and found it yielding. I went in.

Alessandro sat with his legs stretched out beneath his desk, a hand over his mouth and chin, gazing into the middle distance. He might have been sitting there for days or decades, a statue carved to capture every facet of despair. The darkness in the room was nearly absolute. An unlit lamp sat near at hand.

"Sir," I said, placing the ba' on the desk and taking a seat across from him, "if I may ask, in the event that there's a problem—that the press—" I couldn't decide how to phrase the question. After a long hesitation, I asked, "What will happen to my contract?"

Alessandro looked at me as if the act of recalling my name would have taken more effort than remained to him. "I don't know," he said. "I don't know what will happen to any of us."

This uncertainty, the cracks branching out through the floors of the future—it occurred to me that this was more or less what Caterina had been living with for years. Since 1509, at least, and probably much longer. I couldn't quite imagine Master Paganino ever putting her up for sale, certainly not unless he fell into a truly desperate situation, and yet I also understood, as every slave understands, that this is the one way in which our masters can deceive us. And themselves.

Perhaps I could consult her. Learn how she readied herself each day for the unknown future. But no. She was one of those slaves who'd made an art of bondage, who let slip nothing that the masters wouldn't want to hear, whether or not they were listening. Even if I approached her as a fellow who'd once worn chains, I knew that I would get no more from her than I could from a cobblestone.

"This mountain," I said to Alessandro, "that you say is merely stones. What is it really?"

Alessandro rubbed his mouth and drew his hand down to his chin. I couldn't tell whether he was looking at me or into some abyss. "Gabiano's man's been taken into custody," he said. "The Sultan wants his head. They've scheduled him for execution. And his ship's been scuttled. All the type and printed copies, all at the bottom of Constantinople's harbor."

I shouldn't have had to ask the next question. I should have known. But the longer I'd lived in this city of Christians, the muddier things had become. I'd been a free man and a slave in Tunis and in Venice, a farmer and a merchant, a treacherous domestic and a loyal apprentice and, finally, a trusted journeyman, and I'd encountered so many peculiarities along the way that I no longer felt capable of either surprise or intuition regarding what was right or natural for men. These days, I needed things spelled out for me.

Besides, if I didn't ask, my silence might arouse Alessandro's suspicions.

I heard my voice in the darkness: "Why?"

"For blasphemy," he said.

A weight settled on me, then—as if I'd lain down between the platen and the paper. My mouth grew dry, and all through my body, an ache struck up its steady drum, part hunger, part fear, part weariness.

"The envoy's Gabiano's cousin," Alessandro said. "He intends to lobby for his release. He's demanding that we send a thousand ducats."

"A *thousand*?" Surely, any man worth such a sum should never have been sent behind enemy lines. But perhaps not every coin was meant for Constantinople.

Alessandro nodded, grave.

A thousand ducats would ruin the press. A great deal had already been spent on printing Holy Book. In addition to purchasing the two sets of type and engraving a third, Alessandro had sunk a truly magnificent sum into setting up a branch of his printing house in Constantinople—without, as far as I knew, ever securing permission from the Sultan or any other authority. Now the raw materials for that enterprise lay at the bottom of a Levantine harbor.

At the very least, I thought, he'd saved money on proofreaders.

"Mamádo," Alessandro said, sitting forward suddenly, hope lighting up his face, "Mamádo—these Turks. You're familiar with them, aren't you? They're more or less your countrymen. Perhaps you could draft a letter on my behalf, and Gabiano's. Surely you could reason with them more effectively than a Christian."

I shook my head. "I know nothing of the Turks, sir. Their homeland's nearer yours than mine."

"But you're from Ifriqiya, aren't you? They own Tunis."

"They took it four years ago," I said. "I've been here for more than twice that."

"No matter." Alessandro waved away the minor inconveniences of time and geography as if swatting at fruit flies. "You worship the same God. Perhaps you can make them understand that we meant no offense. Smooth things over."

"I know nothing of the arts of persuasion," I said. "I'm just a *tiratore*."

In truth, I had no desire to get mixed up in these negotiations. Far from lending weight to my words, I suspected that my being a Muslim would invite the wrath that only a traitor can earn. I knew, after all, or should have known that even if every line of type was rendered perfectly—a standard that very few compositors had ever achieved—God's word still deserved better: the painstaking, hands-on, years-long labor of hunch-backed scribes and rubricators, the enduring human touch, the dedication and the sacrifice. And yet I'd given my labor to the Paganinis and, for room and board and a handful of ducats every month, sanctioned their irreverent undertaking.

The Sultan probably wouldn't bother sending agents as far west as Venice in pursuit of a *tiratore's* head. Probably. But it wasn't impossible.

"Please, Mamádo," Alessandro said. "I shouldn't have to remind you what this means for all of us. If the press goes under, your contract's void. I can't help that. But maybe you can."

His fears, of course, were rational—more rational than mine. The future of the press was the immediate thing. All else was hypothetical. But another, awful thought had squeezed into my mind: that at any moment, Alessandro, possessed by fear and by the thought that I might save him, would leap up and bolt the door, light the lamp, place pen and stationery before me, and demand that I compose a letter to the Sultan. And I would not know what to do.

I'd never told him outright that I read or wrote classical Arabic—never lied. But neither had I corrected him. I'd learned the alphabet, of course, as a child, cross-legged on the floor of the kuttab with the rest of the boys from the outskirts of Tunis, filling our tablets with copied-out letterforms, but I'd been a poor student, always tired, mind occupied by matters of soil and sun and how to pack as many olives onto a cart as possible without any escaping. My father had shown me how to keep accounts and records, and I felt certain that if Alessandro were to set an invoice or an order form before me, all these years later, I could have completed it with ease. But there'd been no treatises on my father's shelves, no poetry. In Venice, years after leaving his drought-ravaged farm, I'd acquired a passing familiarity with the Latin script, but upon gaining freedom from the Tuscan apothecary, I'd sought apprenticeship with a printer not because I'd considered myself a man of letters, but only because their elaborate machines, replete with bars and central screws, had looked, to me, like olive presses.

When I'd learned, soon after Alessandro hired me, that he had designs on printing the Holy Qur'an, it had dawned on me that he might have brought me on specifically to help with this project. If I proved useless, I might soon find myself back on the streets, replaced by some more knowledgeable man. And so I'd suppressed my unease, though deep down I'd sensed the disaster that mishandling the words of God might bring. Alessandro's friend, the Jew he'd picked up from the ghetto who claimed to speak fifteen languages, though he begged most days for food, had stayed with us during the Qur'an's production, standing over Pietro's shoulder as he'd arranged the Arabic type in mimicry of the hand-printed manuscript that Alessandro had obtained at auction, occasionally making corrections, pointing out subtle distinctions between the letterforms. Once the first copy of each page was done, it had been passed to me, and at Alessandro's orders, I'd run my eyes from top to bottom, right to left, and, only half comprehending the intricate script, declared their work sound.

It came to me then that I, not Alessandro, was responsible for our situation.

"I wish he were dead," said Alessandro. I could no longer see his face in the darkness. "He could've had the decency to pass before the letter came," he added, "but no. He's hung on for years just so he could see me run the press into the ground. He knows I've got more vision in my little finger than he could ever dream of. He never could stand it. He's always wanted to see me fail. I bet he's up there working over a speech right now, dreaming of putting me in my place when I go up to see him. Well—I won't go. He can rot there!"

Quick as an insect, Alessandro flung the ba' I'd recovered so hard that stone chips from the wall behind me stung my neck and arm.

I flinched. "God will hear you."

"God can hear my thoughts, and his. He'll decide who's the bigger prick."

I imagined my own thoughts running into God's ear alongside Alessandro's and his father's—languages mixing, a muddied stream, a Muslim prayer wafting up from this Christian city like a lone white dove amid a flock of sparrows—and it was as if a stopper had been removed and all the Venetian words had gone swirling from my mind and down a long, dark drain. I opened my mouth, and darkness, thick and bitter as tar, flowed in. Never before had I been so evacuated by language, so full of night, as I was then. A single thought blossomed at the center of my mind: that I must remove myself from the study as quickly as possible, before I was called upon to speak.

But my limbs refused to answer.

Perhaps if I held my breath, Alessandro would simply go on talking, requiring nothing but that I listen. Perhaps he would even forget that I sat there, hidden by darkness, my presence increasingly irrelevant to his soliloquy. I knew I'd already faded into the background as images of his father swam before him. Then again, he never really saw anything but his own reflection.

I lost the sense his words as my mind twisted around itself, a serpent snapping at its own tail. I could no longer hear anything but my own echo.

When the lean season had come, when my father had realized that our debts had swollen too large and that we would not turn a profit that year or the next, an agreement had been reached between us, and we'd made a journey to the slave market in Tunis, a journey from which only he'd returned. That morning has faded, dispersed like dust, but I remember the night before with vivid clarity. In my mind, it's the same night that we reached our resolution, though in truth, a week or so probably passed. I still recall the way he watched me without turning to face me as we sat side by side against the earthen wall of the family room, a dinner tray on the floor between us, our fingers still glistening, trading a few words now and then, sounds that meant less than the silence between them, both of us knowing that we were equals, finally, men. I've always felt certain that no matter how desperate our family became, he would not have forced me into bondage had I not agreed. I couldn't explain where this certainty came from. Perhaps from the look in his eye, the set of his jaw, half in shadow as the lamplight flickered on him—but the eyes, the jaw, the silver brows and rutted cheeks, are Master Paganino's.

I'd entered Venice on a slave ship, knowing that my family would live for months on the sum I'd fetched, and that all in all, I was lucky: we'd done business with Venetian merchants back in Tunis, and I could survive with their tongue. From there I'd fallen into the hands of the apothecary, who'd done me a great service without knowing it by concocting illicit substances, which he'd peddled in the alleys. I'd reported his activities to the authorities, and the city had rewarded me with manumission.

But with liberty had come a new disease. As long as I'd labored in bondage, I'd found it possible to put thoughts of my family from my mind. Of course I missed them, but it was a simple, selfish yearning. I'd already sold my flesh that they might eat: I owed them nothing more. But once I apprenticed myself to a printer and started ferreting liras away, a strange and unexpected feeling—guilt, or one of its toothy cousins—had begun to gnaw. All through the days and restless nights, I'd told myself conflicting things. That as soon as I had a few hours to spare, I would go to the harbor and find a traveler willing to carry a message to Tunis. That I would wait until I'd saved enough to purchase property, then mount my own expedition. That resenting my family for what they'd done, hoping the Turks had enslaved them, or maybe just run them off into the hills, could not be excused, and so must be atoned for. That no matter how I felt or what I did, we'd parted ways till heaven.

Yet as my years in the lands of the Christians piled up, as my own faith grew ever more confused, as I forgot which way was East, as I forgot my father's face—my mother's, brothers', sister's, too—as the Traverse shrank before me, even the prospect of posthumous reunion grew dim. I recalled the mendicant Sufis who used to shun the mosques and preach instead in city squares, proclaiming that no coin compared to the treasure of God. My father used to echo them whenever his children complained of hunger. But the droughts had lengthened, and God's treasure couldn't purchase poultry in the markets, and a false note had crept into his voice, a fearful one. Eventually, I would hear the selfsame tremor in my own. I'd never felt myself to be a greedy man, but as years passed, I began to fear that, somehow, I'd gone astray, thinking of olives when I should have been studying, sewing man's coins, not God's, into my bedroll. On both sides of the sea, I heard men talk of poverty as if the purse weighs leaden on the soul, and the only way to Heaven is to cut them free. On this point, it seems, if on no other, Christians and Muslims can agree. And yet time and again, despite this consensus among holy men, I'd seen want lead only to baseness and misery.

But perhaps the fault lay with the men and not the principle: my father, who'd sold his flesh and blood; Master Paganino, ready at any minute to humiliate his son; and myself, of course, with my excuses.

Then and there, in Alessandro's study, I resolved that I would correct the error of my ways. I would go in search of a religious teacher. There were other Muslims in the Republic, after all. I would find them. I would find out how they got along, would start to pray again, would make a ritual of attending the public debates between the monks and Sufis. I would educate myself until I could scour every page of the Qur'an and understand where I'd gone wrong—if not to secure my place in Heaven, then at least to ensure that my punishment would not be in vain. I would bury myself in scripture until I could debate the most respected 'ulamas, the most learned imams—until I could write my own eternal sentence in Arabic if need be.

Then a knock came at the study door.

Alessandro raised his head.

Ochre light fell on the limestone floor around the shadow of a woman as the door creaked open. "Master Alessandro," Caterina said. "Master Paganino wants you."

I couldn't see her face because the light was behind her. I doubt that I could have deduced much from it even if I had.

"Tell him he can have his business if that's what he wants," Alessandro said. "I'm not going up there."

"He's weak," Caterina said. "He spent too much of his strength today. He wants to see his only son before he sleeps. He'll wake tomorrow, God willing."

A muscle worked in Alessandro's jaw. He looked about to cry.

"I should go," I said, rising from the chair. The heel of my sandal hit something on the floor—the ba'—and sent it rattling into the shadows.

"Mamádo," Alessandro said, leaning forward, elbows on his desk, "Mamádo—" but then he stopped, as if he'd spoken without knowing what he meant to say.

I felt drawn, as if by a powerful ocean current, toward Caterina and the door, but I held myself there for a moment, suspended between opposing forces, waiting for Alessandro's command.

"Go," he said, and put his head in his hands.

I left the study, slipped past Caterina, and went to my room.

Had someone asked me then, I could not have explained what I was doing. I moved as if God Himself had taken hold of my limbs, steering me to the corner and guiding the blade as I slit open the bedroll and pulled out handfuls of coins without bothering to count them, enough that despite my clumsy clutching, they ran through my fingers. I went back out onto the empty work floor. Stacks of black paper lay on the workbenches alongside beaters and sorts left out to dry on rough gray cloths. Caterina had just shut Alessandro's door. She looked like a tree growing up through the limestone, ancient and lightning-struck. I closed the distance between us so swiftly that her eyes widened and she seemed to shrink from me. I tried to press the coins into her hands.

She wouldn't take them. She looked down at them, then up at me, her eyes two blunted iron nubs. A hint of a curl crept along her lip.

I pushed the coins against her breast so hard that she staggered half a step. A few of them clattered to the floor. She caught my hands and accepted the rest, for the sake of silence, I think, eyes flicking to the study, to the stairs, then back to me. For a few seconds we stood like that. I could feel a vein in her cold wrist pulsing. Then she turned and vanished into the slaves' quarters.

I stood in the deserted workroom. A terrible exhaustion swept down on me and stole the strength from my limbs. The flickering lamplight breathed life into the grain of Alessandro's door and set it writhing.

I went back to my room, lay on my back, and shut my eyes, but I couldn't sleep. Pious, tempestuous thoughts assailed me. I shivered from head to toe, though the night was warm, shot through with a strange and zealous fury, certain that it would stay with me for years to come, sustaining me—that soon I would neither eat nor drink, that I would grow hard and lean and certain where I had always been opportunistic and not quite generous enough, and not quite kind. I would reform myself so that no disaster like this would ever again have reason to befall me. Any other end to this turbulent day seemed impossible.

How easily we deceive ourselves.

In the years to come, I would not find a religious teacher. Nor, I must admit, would I devote myself in earnest to the search for one. I would move from press to press—the Paganinis', in fact, did fold—and here and there, when I found time between mechanical duties, I would pray. But the passion that seized me that evening would dissipate as quickly as it had come—as if it had been necessary for one thing and one thing only, and, with the completion of that task, it was allowed to fade.

Except that if my short-lived revelation really achieved its purpose, then how to square it with what happened a few days later, when I retired to my room and found my bedroll stuffed again with coins?

For a few brief hours, I let myself imagine a miracle. My good deed had been acknowledged and paid back in kind. The treasures of man and those of God were not so different after all. So I told myself. So I believed. But after some time, my mind began to clear, and I saw myself, and Caterina, and the world once again for what we were. My assaulting her with coins began to seem a very Alessandro thing to do.

To this day, I can't explain why she returned the money. Perhaps, all along, she was more a slave in spirit than in body. Or perhaps her faith was simply stronger than mine.

Three months later, the elder Paganini died. Word reached me that he'd willed Caterina to one of his associates. I would never see her again after leaving the press. I do not know if she was ever freed.

On Alessandro's orders, all the Qur'ans not sent to the East were burned except for two galleys. I don't know what happened to those. Nor do

I know what befell Alessandro's Arabic punches and matrices. Countless men would have paid no small sum for them, perhaps even enough to let the press limp along for a few more years, but I doubt that they ever went to auction. Alessandro was an all-or-nothing sort of man. He never printed another book. His father's will named him sole heir to the estate in Toscolano, but as no rumor of disaster there has found its way back to me, I can only imagine that Daria runs the mill now.

Hour by hour, day by day, I train myself to do the work before me as I did those first few months in Venice: to finish tasks and take my pay with no thought squandered on the past or future. I know only what is in my hands, beneath my nose, or on my tongue. To quiet my thoughts, I count the pages, count the pages, count the pages passing through my hands, but morning after morning I toss the last day's numbers out like swill from a chamber pot and start anew. Morning after morning, day after day, the world shrinks a little more, a little less space in the mind for burdens. My employers are pleased, but their pleasure means nothing to me. I know that what I'm striving for is possible, for I did achieve it once, though under different circumstances: chains around my body, swaddling clothes around my mind, serenity in knowing that I could neither owe nor be owed.

A free man, but I'm learning, day by day, to be a slave again.

Once in a while, though, something happens—a wanton thought, a careless word, an odor wafting on the street—that catches at my memory as rough-hewn brick might catch at a thread from an old wool coat. Like the last thing Alessandro said to me, the day he ordered the back stock burned, servants flowing like ants around us, bearing equipment and stacks of black paper, dismantling our lives. He leaned on one of the presses as I'd once seen his father lean on Caterina. His eyes alighted on me as I passed and followed me until I hesitated, turned.

I, for one, have never learned to expect the tactlessness that misery brings out in men. Somehow, I always imagine that pain will conjure decency, not spread itself like plague.

For my simplicity, I have no excuses.

"You're lucky," Alessandro told me, "not to have a father." Then he turned and vanished into his study, pulling the door behind him.

In Avalon We Continue

Haolun Xu

No, I don't think I'm ready yet,
    even with my body refusing to regenerate stating that this is a warning, a lamp lit against the cramped spaces of possibility,
    Spring filled the air with the sound of infants. I forgot the shrillness, their bicuspid throats still those of a bicuspid. I think they are most realistically our parallel to dinosaurs. Blameless, pure, unable to grow hair.
    I haven't forgotten the season of pollen, and they haven't forgiven me,
    the pressure of both light and degeneracy tumbling into the smallest crevices. I can find the seedlings underneath my fingernails. I cannot exclude myself from the ceremony of earth.
    But I can try. I shower five minutes later than the rest of my family. I sleep three hours more than the rest of my friends
    (Only I can give myself the nickname Farmland, but just for today) I reflect on the decorum of the natural order. This is a new social rule, because I am not close to myself anymore, but I am formal.
    At night, I peer out of my night-dark room, and into the blue lights of the world. I take my fingers and replicate the pollen. I pretend to weave honey to the dawn. When I wake up from this, I am legally purified, by an invisibility I dreamed visited me the day before.

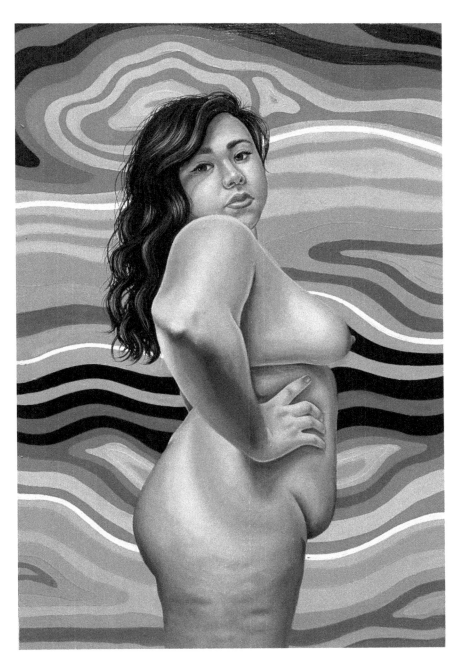

SELF-PORTRAIT / Josie Del Castillo

Mom / Josie Del Castillo

The Letters

Victoria Shannon

Sheila sent me back all my old letters, the ones I wrote from my college to hers, back when we were each learning about tequila shots and how cool we looked under party lights. The letters came to my office last week in a big manila envelope. I didn't know what to do with them.

We had become friends in high school, validating the maxim that opposites attract. Her auburn curls, flowing saris, and boho style all reeked to me of antiestablishment intellectual. A radical and free thinker: That's what I wanted to be. But I also wanted to be a horse trainer, a playwright, a passenger on a houseboat floating through Europe, a folk singer, a habitué of the West Village, and a helicopter pilot. I wanted to be anyone but myself, whoever that was.

Sheila and I were both sixteen going on twenty-five like the wind. We were trapped in 1990s suburbia, salivating for the day we could leave home and get on with our lives. But Sheila always seemed older, more sophisticated, more knowing. She would wax on about Susan Sontag, Naomi French, and Mother Jones, lecturing me on the perils of capitalism and patriarchy. I was caught up in Salinger, and suddenly embarrassed by it.

"Religion, property, and government enslave us," she'd wag at me as we sat by the creek in the woods behind her house. "It's obvious this political system doesn't work, but our parents are blind to it. We need a revolution."

Sheila had her nose straightened that year. I had never noticed anything wrong with it. Before the operation and after, I stared and stared. It was a nose, for crying out loud, and it looked fine, even on her slender frame. "Just because," she smiled at me. "I just wanted to, you silly. It'll make a difference later on."

She talked me into cutting class one afternoon, promising a surprise. We ended up in my parents' basement, and she pulled out a plastic bag of white powder and a ten-dollar bill. I'd never seen cocaine before.

"Oh my God! You brought this to *my* house? Sheila! How could you?" I was panic-stricken. I was sure my brothers would come home and find us.

"Oh, Peaches, don't agitate. Just go find us a mirror," she laughed.

My heart thudded in my chest even before the first snort. Still, I managed not to breathe too much of it away. Afterward, I felt like an adult, smug and experienced. But the power trip and the paranoia canceled each other out, leaving me too scared to ever try it again.

Her parents were divorced, a novelty for me. I met her dad one weekend, and he seemed like a perfectly fine father specimen: balding, glasses, sociable, professional. "What's it like?" I asked her later. "Not having your father around?"

"Like all men," she said, fixing her scarf into a chic double knot in front of her dresser mirror, "my father is an oppressor. He's an embarrassing role model. Darling, I'm not missing anything without him." I'd never heard a father so reviled. It made me rethink my entire, normal relationship with my own.

I was a bit crushed when I found out Sheila was a good student, a hard worker, and aiming to graduate from high school early so she could start accumulating college credits. Her manifest-destiny mindset made me wonder why she wanted to hang with me – me with all my loose ends and hers tighter than a drum. I didn't know what drove her, but I wanted some of it.

Toward the end of our senior year, I saw her less often; she had graduated that winter and was taking classes at the community college. But we were both still in a hurry. I couldn't wait to stand in the middle of a sidewalk, any sidewalk, anywhere, and scream, "I'm here!" She was racing toward something, too, but I couldn't fathom what it was.

"We are going places, girl!" she crowed as we sat on her front steps a few days before the senior prom.

"Yeah," I said. "You sure are."

"Oh, come on, Peaches." Her big, rust-colored eyes flashed with excitement. "Big stuff coming. You'll be there for me, yes? We'll take on the world. We'll show them how it's done."

I nodded obediently. What was she seeing in our future, and why was I so deprived of vision? *Baby, we were born to ruuuuunnn!* she scrawled across the inside cover of my yearbook.

At Sheila's graduation party, I marveled at her ability to acquire people; I didn't know a soul there except her and our history teacher. But I met a guy. At eighteen, Cary was super serious and way above me. He was practically a political consultant already, working on campaigns and planning his next steps up through the ranks. Still, he thought I was "interesting," and we played at dating for the summer.

Sheila outdid me, as usual. Her boyfriend was older, a teaching assistant at the community college with a receding hairline and his own apartment, where he lit incense and let us drink beer. He nodded a lot and spoke philosophically, warning us often that "life is short and time is swift." I felt like we were actors on a set.

And then, in a flash, high school was history. Sheila went off to Berkeley, and I went to a land-grant college in the Midwest, the farthest place from home that would accept my rotten grades. We charged ahead like racehorses without a bit, heading toward a finish line hidden in mist.

That's when we started writing letters. Hers made fun of what she called Moo U., and mine sagged with jealousy over Berkeley and tried to make my life interesting.

It wasn't, no matter how much I yearned for it to be. I went with the flow, did what my roomies did, tried to follow the classwork, found little that engaged me. What had I expected from college, from life on my own? Romance, stimulation, and adventure, for starters. I looked for them under a few rocks and came up with nothing but dirt.

Sheila met a guy, a native of California, an egghead getting his PhD in transportation engineering. I spun through Mark, then Jimmy, then Joel, then a guy whose name I can't remember, and I think there was another Mark. My letters must have burbled about boyfriends and tequila, while hers interpreted Rothko and Emma Goldman.

Something changed when I fell into an intro-to-architecture class. I sat up straight. Even the tools of the trade turned me on. Vellum and Mayline straightedges. Pen plotters and 3-D software. Rules that must be followed, yes, but creativity, too. Oh, my. I could do this. And I did, obsessively. I became fixated on Gehry. I felt purposeful.

Sheila dropped a bombshell one day, by telephone. She would be getting married to her egghead as soon as she got her degree, and she wanted me to be her maid of honor.

I hung up the phone in a stupor. It was bad enough that she couldn't come up with someone better than me, among her wide and eclectic group, to stand by her side. No, what kept me awake that night was the idea that Sheila, my radical sophisticate, my free-thinking Sheila, was getting married at all. Marriage was what our parents did. A wedding belonged in the pages of a fashion magazine. It was as if Marco Polo had opted out of that trip to

China; he'd rather stay home and mind the books, thank you very much. *Is Sontag married?* I wondered. Our furious charge into the unknown was faltering. The mist had cleared, and…it was this?

I went along with it, like I always did. I have some adorable photos from the reception: me in a lavender floor-length country dress mock-punching her groom; an arty shot of Sheila reaching out to stop me from spilling a glass of champagne; the bride and myself, with the cute best man between us, dancing our version of the hora. Her husband was sane, even ordinary, she was blissful, and I never asked her what the hell she was doing. When I come across the photos from time to time, I shake my head. Who *were* these people? What *were* they thinking?

Getting a degree took me a couple of semesters longer than planned. Outside of drawing classes, I never became much of a student. Afterward, I took design jobs on the East Coast, first Boston, then New York, then Washington. Sheila stayed West, doing some Silicon Valley marketing thing, got her master's. We still wrote letters, but my heart wasn't in it. It dwindled into Christmas cards, clipped and routine. "Chica! How's the Left Coast?" I wrote. "Miss you! Talk soon!" Every one was a lie, and I hated doing it.

Then I stopped even that. I still got postcards from her trips to Europe, her son's birth announcement, then one for her company's I.P.O. I read them, threw them out, felt terrible, and went off to my pen plotter. My latest prophet was the Irish landscaper Mary Reynolds, and I was percolating new ideas for melding stone buildings with earthen berms. I had clients who saw value in my vision, and I had a budding reputation.

When we were in our thirties, Sheila finally quit writing. I was relieved, more relieved than I thought possible. For almost twenty years, I had been supportive and agreeable. I shared secrets and Springsteen and first-time everythings. But my heart sank with the weight of the truth. It was never real. We were never really friends. I was just a groupie, a parasite.

Last week, that fat package postmarked California appeared on my desk with Sheila's return address scrawled in a familiar handwriting. Our letters. Scores of them. All wrapped in youth, energy, desire, and anarchy. How naïve and pathetic and hollow they must sound. It had been years since Sheila had even crossed my mind. I circled around the envelope on the kitchen table, wondering what to do with it.

On a whim, I made an excuse to visit a prospective client in San Francisco. Yesterday, after my meeting, I rented a car and drove to Walnut Creek. My curiosity was vague, not malevolent, neither bold nor fearful.

Her neighborhood was on the grand side, with sprawling acreages, double garages, a backyard pool visible here and there. Number 225 was on a large corner lot, not far from an office complex. I parked in the shade across the street and rolled down my window. A leaf-blower droned in the distance. Her yard was a mess of bright orange dirt, obviously under repair, with the outline of something like a rock garden taking shape in the middle. A Subaru with mud on its flanks was in the driveway.

Another SUV pulled in next to it as I sat there. Sheila emerged in a tight black skirt. Standing for a moment with her hands on her hips, she surveyed the yard work. She'd straightened and streaked her hair, but I easily recognized the languorous pose and spare proportions of two decades ago. She turned halfway in my direction, shielding her eyes against the sun. I didn't duck or flinch, but neither did I consider approaching her. Maybe the letters were her way of sealing the past, closing the circle on something that had never ended agreeably. My need was visual: to see her, to absorb the aura of her life, to prove to myself that she had lost her way. Or maybe that I had found mine.

She turned back to the yard, kicked the dirt, and headed inside, no doubt to open the mail and peel the carrots. The door clicked shut. I started up the rental car and headed to the airport.

When I got home today, her manila envelope was gleaming on the table, caught in a ray of the mid-morning sun. I tossed it in the trash without a second look. There was nothing more I needed or wanted from Sheila. I have a trip to Dubai coming up, a big project at work, and my partner's birthday to plan.

Must Love Bernie

Kimberly Diaz

In 2015, I had two major goals.
1. To find a guy to partner up with for the rest of my life.
2. To get Bernie Sanders elected President of the United States.

But maybe not necessarily in that order, so I placed this ad on a popular dating site.

USER ID: MustLoveBernie
HEADLINE: I Love Bernie but I Might Like You

MustLoveBernie is a non-smoker with a thin body type, Libra with mixed color hair and a bachelor's degree, nonreligious and a free thinker. MustLoveBernie is looking for a relationship but seeking a man for dating. Interests: concerts, movies, tennis, dining out, traveling, bicycling and Bernie Sanders for President!

About Me:
Right now I'm really focused on getting Bernie Sanders elected but I like to have other kinds of fun too. And I really could not seriously hang with anyone who is not committed to voting for Bernie Sanders. In Florida, you have to be a registered Dem to vote for him in the primary. I will ask to see your voter registration. GO BERNIE!

First Date:
Meet for a drink, talk to the bartender about Bernie Sanders, if we hit it off, maybe dinner some other place, talk to the server about Bernie Sanders, etc. . . . For more information about Bernie Sanders go to www.BernieSanders.com. Or take me out . . .

Afterward, I received a few I love Bernie too messages, but mostly angry ones. Are you looking for a date or what? You're alienating half the men out there. That's okay, I said, I'm only looking for one.

Then the unthinkable happened—Trump in the White House, I took the ad down. Dated a couple of guys I met out in the real world. No luck there either. Now as 2020 approaches, I have two major goals.
1. Get Trump impeached.
2. Get Bernie Sanders elected President of the United States.
Go Bernie!

FACE TO FACE 1 / JACK BORDNICK

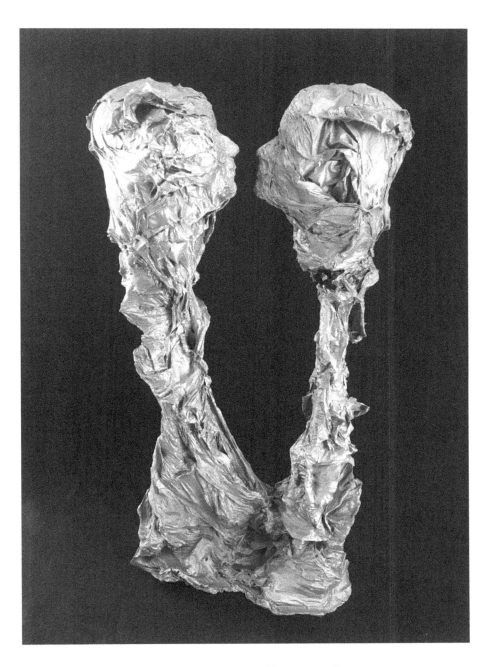

Face to Face 2 / Jack Bordnick

Demolition

Lenora Steele

The filling station at Esplande and Inglis is coming down today. The one with the turret that doubled as a taxi stand. The one with the hardwood bench where a little girl waits for Daddy.

I am stood across the road with a little gang when the excavator's claw scrapes the cedar skin looking for a place to catch hold , a place to begin. Its end has come.

He had a Brownie, my father, so my first six years are documented with frills and frocks, gloves and curls; after he died no one could find it or no one wanted to. As if whatever was left would not warrant any pictures. The excavator slows; I hear a phone, stalled on the landing I hear my mother at the foot of the stairs. Something has changed.

Now!

The excavator lowers its bucket pulls back, quiets. I am six. I don't want to be in the way. I turn, go back to my room. Wait. But it takes forever, what's coming, so I am crouched now on the landing in a corner when the men come in. The scent of the oven's bread explodes when the draughts of January enter; the stretcher is catching in the door jam, a bitter cold is flooding the hall, the bread makes it smell like any other day.

The gang has grown to a crowd. Extras, cast for effect; they pull their breath in unison. The belfry made this place a landmark. They are telling stories. I move out of earshot. I can't bear their anecdotes.

I am alone as I watch the men struggle to get into Daddy's room, the place he hasn't left now in weeks except on Christmas morning when my oldest brother lent himself a human crutch and ferried him to the living room. And there it is, one final picture; my oldest brother is behind the lens so he is not caught in the frame. Soon, when it is over, he will quit his job in the woods and leave for Toronto. He will send money home. The brother between us will turn sullen. He will never reconcile the coming loss.

The motor fires up again. The crush of spectators stir as the operator levers the bucket this way and that until it catches hold and sinks its claws through a wall, razing a century's old labor. It's operator grows more sure of her target. The clapboards moan and like human skin after a burn, easily peel away. A part of the roof collapses, the people cheer. The shattering lead pane can be heard above the din.

Cancer left him with part-time jobs—A Fuller Brush case, filled with everything a wife could want and then some and he'd wink and to give my mother a break on her nerves my father would take me along. I remember the women at their backdoors; molasses cookies and milky teas and the way they smiled down on me like they knew more than they should. Their hands felt like tiny prayers when they patted my head. I loved those women in their aprons and their backdoors. I planned to be just like them.

And we kept hens. And gardens. Sold eggs and carrots. Charged with dusting the red soil off the root vegetables and collecting eggs, I grew important. I became necessary but then not really. When the time came, I was sent to my room. Goodbyes are not for little girls. There are no words small enough to fit. At the hospital, they said. Another day, they said.

The wrenching continues, the splintering wood, the breaking glass, the moaning hemlock timbers. The crowd swarms and the engine roars with resolve.

It had a crinoline, the dress I was wearing when the hospital called. There had been a mistake, only six, it could not be allowed. I have to say I love you I said but no one heard.

They said, funerals aren't for girls, little ones. Be brave, they said, for Daddy, they said . . . .

The operator, returned from a break, climbs up into her cab. The engine revs. The onlookers brace themselves, take pictures. They want to show their children, their grandchildren what it was like, what this corner was before progress took hold. How this town once held something different. How time cannot hold anything for long. They want to say, we were there. And so was I.

He drove taxis from here, my father and sometimes long into the night I would hear the back door open and my mother's rocker squeak as she moved to meet him in the entry. Some nights I would creep down to the kitchen where they sat with tea and rice that he'd bring home from the Chinese restaurant right next door. Spoiled, my brothers said but I didn't mind for that made it so I could have some on a little Melmac plate.

The crowd flares up and the last standing wall is exposed and there along the spent wainscoting, on a battered hardwood bench a little girl, watches her Daddy lift his hat from the stand, wills him to turn, to notice, to wink.

And it's down. A ruinous pile of timber and glass. The crowd sputters and breaks apart. A bulldozer roars into motion.

There will be no taxis dispatched today.

Slices of Life

Susan Bloch

I'd like to say it began with the magic of yeast. That sour aroma takes me straight back to my childhood in Johannesburg when I sat on the Formica kitchen counter watching Mom's nimble fingers rolling and folding the raw dough. She gave me a lump to work on too. I squished it and prodded it and stuck my finger into it. Soon I was talking to it. Telling it to behave itself.

Mom wore a pink-and-white checkered apron tied around her back into a bow; a sprinkling of flour dusted her black patent stilettos. She often leaned over to kiss my forehead. For days after those kisses, I didn't wash my face. That was when it all began. My relationship with food and love.

Decades later I realize that when I write about food, I'm hiding behind a facade. I'm really writing about love—wanting love, losing love, and simply loving.

When Dad, a partner in his accountancy firm, came home from work after days studying figures, he poured himself a glass of Ballantine's Scotch and sank into his green-and-ochre floral armchair. I sat on his lap breathing in the oaky fragrance. Ice clinked against the sides of his cut-glass tumbler. He opened a hinged cedar flat-topped box, cut the tip off a Bolivar Cuban cigar, slid off the paper ring embossed with a picture of a man wearing a blue jacket with gold epaulets, and placed it on my thumb. Snuggling against his chest, I giggled under a cloud of cigar smoke. As a kid, these were the only times I spent alone with Dad. Now, on those evenings I miss him, I pour myself a tot of single malt, inhale the aroma, and imagine Dad's arms around me.

In the kitchen, Mom allowed me to stand next to her on a stool with my own piece of dough to knead, smell, poke, and taste. I didn't know then that I was absorbing the unspoken secrets of baking—how to crack the eggs cleanly, separate the yolks from the egg whites, sift the flour to eliminate lumps and tiny mites, and knead the mixture to the right podgy consistency—pushing and stretching, pushing and stretching, until my arms ached and the dough softened. I copied her every movement and measurement, learning exactly how thin to roll the dough; how much butter, sugar, and cinnamon to brush over the pale pastry; and how to twist it into a braid.

"Without the yeast, this would be like a brick," Mom told me. Her upper arms quivered while she worked. "The secret is to make the mixture elastic."

Mom would place the spongy lump of dough into a large bowl and wrap it in a blanket to keep it warm while the yeast fermented overnight. As if a magician cast a spell while I slept, the dough rose to a huge balloon, to be kneaded again. Mom showed me how to roll out the dough to exactly the right thinness, spread it with strawberry jam, and sprinkle cinnamon, raisins, and cocoa powder on top. We rolled it into a crescent shape, carefully lifted it onto a baking tray, brushed the top with beaten raw egg to brown the crust, and popped it into a four-hundred-degree oven. An hour later the aroma of a moist, sweet, brioche-like cake filled the house. We ate it warm with slivers of butter that melted on the pastry. The babka took hours to make and no time to vanish.

I had to eat all my breakfast before I went to school. Even though I showered teaspoons of brown sugar and dollops of butter on top of the oatmeal, the thick goo would stick to the roof of my mouth and refuse to slide down my throat. To Mom's despair, it sometimes took me half an hour to clean my bowl. Eventually, she gave up nagging. I got my way—munching Rice Krispies while I read the cartoons on the Kellogg's box. Snap, crackle, and pop tickled the inside of my mouth.

As a kid, my favorite birthday treat was to go to the Doll House Drive-in Restaurant in Johannesburg. When the waiter clipped a tray onto the top of Dad's window, I breathed in the aroma of a grilled cheese and tomato sandwich on white bread. My teeth crunched the crusts and the gooey cheese stretched like spaghetti in long lines to my lips. Dessert was mixed canned fruit salad layered with Wall's vanilla ice cream and decorated with swirls of whipped cream, chocolate gratings, and a maraschino cherry with a stem. Using a long-handled teaspoon and my lizard-like tongue, I licked the tall sundae glass clean. Even though we had an abundance of fresh papaya, bananas, grapes, mangoes, and passion fruit in South Africa, it was the sugary syrup coating soft chunks of pineapple, peaches, cherries, and grapes that made me ooh and aah. Now my stomach sours when I think of eating that soggy, greasy sandwich, flabby fruit, and synthetic-tasting ice cream. But I continue to celebrate my birthday with a grilled cheese and tomato panini on focaccia bread—and a scoop of rum and raisin Haagen-Dazs on warm apple pie.

When Mom baked a chocolate cake, she always left some raw batter on the beater and in the bowl for me to lick and scrape. It was as good as the cake itself. Sixty years later when I bake, I stick out my tongue to lick the batter at the end of the spatula. I close my eyes and can almost breathe in her fragrance: Chanel N° 5.

My mother's babka recipe was famous in Johannesburg's Jewish community—and that was saying something. There was fierce competition as to who made the best apple pie, cabbage salad, and cheesecake. But there was no arguing that Mom's babka was the best. Now long gone, she is always beside me when I stretch and tuck the mixture, whispering her secrets.

"A little more water, just a drop . . . don't knead so hard . . . gentle as you flip the dough."

The dough sighs as I push it down. I hear Mom's voice again.

"Now leave it to sit quietly. It needs peace, time, and a warm place for the yeast to do its job."

I am the only one in the family who can bake babka as delicious as Mom. While I learned my mother's feel for the perfect dough—springy and alive—everyone else only has her recipe.

When I married, my husband and I moved to Israel. The lemon tree in our backyard gave us an endless supply of fruit. I made lemonade, lemon cream pie, lemon meringue pie, lemon soufflé, whiskey sours, chicken marinated in lemon juice and garlic, and I gave handfuls of lemons to neighbors. Now in my Seattle home, I have three lemon houseplants that are full of blossoms and only one lemon. Just like the song, "Lemon Tree"—the fruit is very pretty but impossible to eat.

The onset of the Yom Kippur War on October 6, 1973, took the country by surprise. After twenty-four hours of not eating and drinking, family and friends gathered in my Tel Aviv home to break the fast at the end of this holy day. Guests whispered a little too loudly that the roast chicken tasted bitter and the turkey sweetish. While we complained about the mundane, the air raid siren shrieked. A few minutes later there was a loud knock at the front door. Without waiting for an answer, a soldier strode in and announced the names of army reservists. They were ordered to report for immediate duty. Husbands, fathers, sons, and brothers packed underwear, razors, shaving cream, and toothbrushes. We had no idea that Egyptian troops had already crossed the Suez Canal. Tanks advanced toward Jerusalem. Only four hundred miles away, we women laughed when we realized that my friend Abby had left the gall inside the chicken, and I'd sugared instead of salted the turkey.

Three days later, while children played hopscotch in a deserted street, we learned that one of our friends, Udi, had been burned alive in a tank near the Suez Canal while trying to block the Egyptian invasion. There was nothing left of his body to bury except for his identification necklace.
    I baked a babka and took it with me as we sat shiva—a seven-day mourning period—with Udi's family. The room was silent. The only sounds were chunks of babka being ripped off the loaf and mourners swallowing. Eyes closed as if to shut out the bad news that trickled our way. No one spoke until we recited the Mourner's Kaddish, the prayer for the dead.

When my marriage dissolved, I moved to London where I met my second husband, John. I loved the smell of whiskey but only developed a taste for Scotch when John held a glass to my lips. I took a sip and my tongue tingled. Soon a glow filled my belly and I took another larger sip. We married soon after.

On vacation in Barcelona, John introduced me to Spain's famous salt cod dish. In a side street, in the shade of Gaudi's Crypt, he leaned in to smell the succulent fish resting on fragrant samfaina sauce, gleaming with green peppers, onions, tomatoes, courgettes, and aubergines. John took a mouthful of the delicacy, leaned back in his chair, kissed his fingertips, and chuckled.

To celebrate our first wedding anniversary, I prepared salt cod, hoping it would remind him of our weekend in Barcelona—the weekend he proposed. I followed the recipe in the *River Café Cookbook*, written by the chef of the one-star Michelin restaurant. After soaking the fish for twenty-four hours, I grilled it and placed it on top of the simmering sauce. The cod was tough, skin burned to ash, and it tasted like old shoe leather. I tossed it in the bin. Instead, we ate vegetable omelets filled with the sauce, along with a toasted baguette and French butter. We drank a jug of sangria made from a bottle of Spanish rioja, sugar, Calvados, slices of lime and lemon, and chopped peaches and apples. John's kiss tasted of tomatoes.

When John contracted mesothelioma, he took morphine to ease the pain. He lost his sense of taste. As asbestos fibers sucked and destroyed the pink linings of his lungs, it made no difference to him whether he was eating kedgeree, duck breast with cherry and port sauce, or day-old pizza.

John hardly ever complained. Not when he was in pain and not when the nurse bruised his arm, when she tried again, and again, to draw blood from his shriveled vein. But he did complain at his last supper.

The night before John died he asked me to prepare a special meal for him—grilled Dover sole with lemon butter, new season peas, and mashed potatoes with chives.

"The fish is dry," he said after the first bite. "And the peas are soggy."

He only ate a mouthful of his favorite dessert—mille-feuille from our local French patisserie—and pushed it away.

That night, I knew that he'd die soon. I died too.

For years I didn't bake a babka, not even when the kids begged and badgered. When I finally did, I was still overwrought and the kneading overthought. I hadn't realized I'd lost my sense of touch and smell.

A bruised Granny Smith apple, a moldy piece of cheddar, a can of Heinz ravioli, and a bottle of cheap Riesling became my evenings' staple diet. It didn't matter; it was hard to taste anything anyway. I struggled to search for a deeper meaning in my life, understand "what it was all for."

Unexpectedly, I was offered and accepted a job to work with a team to set up supermarkets in India. The local cuisine—chickpeas in tomato sauce, creamy black lentils, chapatti, curried vegetables served with grated fresh coconut, tandoori chicken, Alphonso mangoes, sugar sweet bananas, and salted lassi seduced me back to the pleasures of eating.

When I lived in Mumbai, I was invited to join Rabbi Gabi and his wife Rivka for the sabbath dinner at their home. On a warm September evening, we sat in the front courtyard and feasted on hummus, falafel, pita, finely chopped vegetable salad, and barbequed chicken seasoned with familiar Middle Eastern flavors: zaatar, sumac, garlic, and onions. Their two-year-old son, Moshe, clapped his hands and giggled as he ran around in circles. I felt at home—the language, the culture, the food. Under the light of a full moon, Moshe finally flopped asleep on his mother's lap.

The Mumbai Massacre began close to midnight on November 26, 2008. Earlier that evening I had dined at the Taj Mahal Palace hotel with my boss. Over a feast of potato samosas, lentil soup, curried vegetables, garlic naan, chili crab, saffron rice, and fresh coconut, we discussed the structure of the leadership team. While we savored creamy kulfi ice cream and drank spicy chai, a group of Pakistani terrorists edged their way on a dinghy through fishermen's boats and landed at a dock near Mumbai's commercial center. A few hours after we left the restaurant, the hotel's lush Persian carpets and ionic columns were burning. From my apartment, I could see yellow and crimson flames leaping up into the dark sky and a charred smell filled the air.
    What a difference a few hours could make.

Rabbi Gabi and Rivka Holtzberg, my new friends, were slaughtered by the terrorists. Moshe's Indian nanny, Sandra Samuel, lifted the baby boy off his dead mother's chest, ran down the stairs, and into the street. She saved his life. Moshe ate nothing for hours—no cookies, no ice cream, and even refused to sip chocolate milk through a straw.

Moshe's grandparents, Rabbi Shimon and Yehudit Rosenberg, came to Mumbai to collect their grandson and take his parents' remains back to Israel. The city was in lockdown, and the Israeli consul's apartment was filled with embassy folk sorting out visas, flights, and counseling support. I made cup after cup of Nescafé with UHT milk and an endless number of kosher canned tuna mayonnaise sandwiches on white bread. A fishy smell lingered in the hot, humid air.

Although I hated oatmeal as a child, I've learned to enjoy eating plain oatmeal for breakfast. To keep my glucose levels down, I add no sugar, no butter, nor honey. Yet I scrape and sometimes lick the bowl to get the last scrap. No one nags me to hurry up, or tells me I have to eat it all.

How my tastes have changed.

Intoxicated by its earthy scent, everyone loves the smell of my babka browning in the oven—the crust embracing the soft, sweet belly. Now three generations later, my kids and grandchildren have fun kneading their own dough in my kitchen. When freshly baked babka appears on our brunch table, chatter ceases as cinnamon bursts on our tongues.

Hands, big and small, reach for second, and sometimes third, helpings. Mom is there with us in spirit. I imagine John's lips on my cheek as he hovers, and when he thinks no one is looking, he snatches a slice.

Forever Dream / Ping Wang

The Eternal Shine Room / Ping Wang

Discrete Infinity

Cassandra Moss

You wake up at 5:34am, rain dribbling down panes, the room shadowed by the dying of the night. *What am I?* is your first thought.

In the bathroom, the overhead bulb above, your face is caught in an elucidation of itself. You realize your features owe you nothing: your forehead, eyes, nose, cheeks, mouth and jaw are unwavering, but their wholeness is inadmissible in the examination of what the consistently reoccurring patterns of yourself are, or *if* they are at all.

Later, at work, in the midst of a complicated disciplinary hearing for an employee in the Distribution Department, you glimpse a look of mortification on a colleague, as if mere ontology appalls her. You don't know if it's intended for you or not, though you suspect it is. Why wouldn't it be? You feel that everyone susses you out eventually. It's your instinct to placate, to plead mutual humanity or, if not, leniency towards yourself for your lack of human qualifiers. At some point, you must have had the basics of a person, but over the years they dried up, calcified, and disintegrated. So, you smile at her now, thinking how you've heard she has a comatose brother who's been going on, hagiofied and inert, for nearly seven years. It has to be miserable for her. If you were her, you'd feel it's you, not him, who's been wronged for it's you, not him, who's aware of the pile of time stacking up behind you as the one in front declines. You picture her sitting by the fleshy slab reading out global events, commenting on the terrible turn of the world, pausing every so often to wonder how she and he came to be where they are, what precise alchemy was wrought to render these conditions of existence, at once astonishing and wholly explicable, only to be disturbed by the duty nurse on her rounds, inspecting for boils while stating *it's a shame there's not the budget for waterbeds for all, even the vegetables.* As you continue to smile, you hope the action is connecting to a quantifiably genuine feeling of sincerity inside yourself. But it's impossible to tell. *We're in the same boat*, you want the smile to say. *I may not have suffered a family tragedy and I may not have to waste the last days of my youth swallowing the instant coffee of the high-dependency ward, but there is a sameness to you and me. We are alike in that we, along with everyone else, are sinking and unsure we ever learned how to swim.*

It's a shitshow for sure: too many people, yet also too few. This makes you feel agitated by the entire idea of company and spending your hours in it. How is it you're to behave? What is it you're to say to demonstrate your authentic self? Your valid nature? Making matters worse is the fact that there's not a single clean, flat surface to be found in these toilets. You're in a cubicle sweating slugs because you ran as you were already late for the gig after being surrounded by men in religious garb on a Central Line carriage. Their white robes and square hats were an affront to your duplicity: abiding secularity swaddling a tiny squirming spirituality when what right have you to either if you aren't willing to commit to anything? As the men's chatter softly commandeered the particles between and in amongst you and them, a harrowing began in your skull, spreading down along your spine, awakening the squatters in your nervous system who began to, yet again, demand a greater standard of living. You think of the endless intoxication of belief as you shove your housekey into the powder: to live the life of an ecstatic, reason sacrificed to intuition, whereas your reasonableness has you resorting to several key bumps to raise your expectations like a cretin hoping to be accepted into the normal household of a normal family, bug eyes masked, balding scalp wigged: an ad hoc disguise pulled from an embedded sense of ordinariness, the façade always about to fall even as the man and wife of the house are setting you up with the blondest son of their richest friends.

A man-child is at the back of the pop-up bar emitting something slow somewhere between a song and a rap, an unattended keyboard to the left of him providing backing and a vulgar fashionableness troubling the stage. It is precisely when this evening is just going to get on and start that is most on your mind as you're pressed into the back of a strange body by the toing and froing of various friendships behind you.

You notice your crowd in a corner, unaware of being observed. For a minute or two you watch them and wonder who they are without you. Do they retain unmistakably unique, immutable traits for each and every interaction they're involved in? You know you yourself can be easily swayed by the moods and idioms of any given consortium. One person from this group could silently observe you with another group and not know if the person captured by their senses was the same as the one they'd conversed at length with, offered up secret thoughts and confessed terrible acts to, or if who they thought they'd known was an apparition with a similar face to the stranger they were currently staring at.

    Ordering a pint, you tap your card on the wood, some splashback hitting your handbag, a vintage hand-me-down from an aunty who is neither sister nor friend of either of your parents, rather an antipodean passing through the northern hemisphere who you met in the carpark of a club and then went on to a party in a squat with. An easy bond was formed with the older woman as she told you that night: *I thought I chose not to have kids but maybe it was the other way around. Thinking about it, I would've liked to have been an aunt, but I've just never had the connections.*

    A presence is felt to your right and your turn your head to see a guy you met once at a house party who was a friend of a friend of one of your flatmates. Neither of you were meant to be there. Your flatmate had no one else to go with and couldn't bear being seen alone so said if you had nothing else on you may as well come along. In the cramped kitchen, fixing yourself another vodka and soda, you were searching for a lime when he walked in with a bleeding finger due to a rogue shard of glass from the last get-together snuggled in the settee cushions. As blood ran out of the wound and onto the chrome sink, you imagined him liquidating in front of you. The blood could keep coming. He could faint, his life abandoning him. And all the while it would've been in your power to do something, but you chose inaction as you felt you were a spectator of a particular series of events that had to happen to maintain this version of the universe so that it was distinct from another one where you jumped in and saved his life.

    But, as it happened, in yet another version of the universe that is the one you are currently living in, you did nothing *and* he didn't die. After applying some pressure, the bleeding ceased. *My girlfriend thinks I'm on a stag in Dublin*, he said. You asked him why he wasn't. *Been a bit worried I was developing a stomach ulcer*, he replied. You waited for more detail. When none came, you didn't push but kept thinking you really should have as that would've been an intimacy that would've bound the two of you together forever. Instead, over the following couple of hours, your conversation stuck mainly to social generalizations, only now and then flirting with the intensely personal before giving way to glib carnality.

Now you don't know if he's seen you, and, if he has, if he's recognized you or not. That night was four years ago. To you it could've been last week due to your mental cognition seemingly being so out of sync with the officially documented passage of time: a year can take double or more to catch up with you in respect to your coming to terms with it, that is with its effects being fully integrated into your thoughts. That was a night which let you know you regret what doesn't happen, not what does. When you return to it now, it's the comforting buzz of the dimmed halogen lights as you undressed in a complete stranger's bedroom that you most clearly recall.

Ruminating on the idea of going over to the guy, who's definitely called Paul or Tom, to test your perception of the experience against his, you absently answer Jen and David, the friends standing next to you, that you think the music has so far been shite. Afterwards, when you're all out of the pop-up and on the way back to someone's rented accommodation, you question your choice of 'shite'. You could've used the generic 'shit'. It is perhaps because of these particular listeners' sensibilities that you went for the more regional option. As the night wears on in the form of another party, you fixate on if the words you say are in any way representative of who you feel you are at your core, if they could be argued to put forth the mulching of inner sensation, the coagulations that form what is taken for your unique entity, the one being, one body. Whilst you know 'shite', 'shit', 'wank', 'rubbish' and so on run along a continuum, you were urged to choose the more colloquial option to express a locality, an alignment with a specific tribe. You don't always do so. Yet with this group, it seems to matter. You don't want them to think of you as unspecific, nondescript. You want an identity that can exist in some minor way in the margins.

But if your word choices are somewhat calculated rather than automated, then what does that make you? A calculated being is a being after all as *I am myself* you say to yourself. But there's a division of one self into two: the acting and the directing. The subject 'I' is located in the director, whilst the reflexive 'myself,' the object, is an actor, well-studied, yet requiring constant reassurances from the director that the way her hands dangle by her sides accurately resemble real hands on a real person really dangling as said person goes about her existence unnoticed. The actor receives scripts from intermediaries, confers with the director and then sets about assessing their context and meaning, scrutinizing the dialogue, marking intonational rises and falls, writing out the subtext as text to ensure a thorough understanding of motivation, and then committing all to memory to give the sense of spontaneity, just as she was directed to do so, to hide the acting so that the performance is, ultimately, believable, which perhaps may prompt a critic to write 'X is unrecognizable as Y; every movement and gesture of X's as Y utterly convinces: X is Y,' which results in the actor being self-satisfied because audiences were persuaded that they were spending time with Y despite clearly looking at X's face and body. The actor, buoyed by her success, starts to feel like a pro, like she had it in her all along and hadn't ever needed the director's help. But the director observes more keenly than anyone on the outside and knows that X is not Y, that X is pretending, producing an imitation of Y as only Y is Y whilst X forever remains X. The director tells the actor she is complacent, warning her that one day she won't be so lucky: there will come a time when her techniques become visible and spectators will despise her for her failure to convince them that she really is a different person from the one she actually is. But all the director can do is watch as it happens. Consequently, as the savage notices mount up, the old actor will be replaced by another seemingly newer and more flexible one who is once more eager to take direction from the ever-same, irreplaceable director.

With the music accelerating, you abandon Laura and the conversation you were half-engaged in while perched on the arm of a multi-stained chair to get up and dance. Opposite you, David's zoned-out stare causes you to think of what your colleague's comatose brother's face must be like at this moment. Slack and infantile, you imagine. *Isn't life a pile of* . . . . You question if you've ever used 'shite' with your colleague. Has there been an occasion when you have had to dismiss something in her presence? Yes. What language would you have used? You would've wanted to sound professional. You would've wanted to sound like a person who has dialectical opinions rather than views copied straight from another source. You wouldn't have wanted your colleague to feel uncomfortable or embarrassed, so you'd have followed her lead and only sworn if she'd sworn. And you don't recall her doing so. Instead, then, in order to convey criticism, you would've applied words such as 'terrible', 'awful', 'dismal' and perhaps 'rotten.' The last one especially seems a thing you'd never utter as it carries no aspirational properties for you, no markers of a class that you'd want to claim as your own. At least, that's how it sounds in your accent, or rather, the accent you adopt for matters conducted within the higher echelons of your job. In another, more glottal, iteration of your speech, 'rotten' is stripped of its nobility and can slum it like a child of industry moving out from rural placement into urban internment. If you said 'rotten' now, it'd be the urban mill child. But if you said it with your colleague, who you suspect comes from the sort of soft money that prioritizes a private education over intercontinental holidays, it'd be the child of the mill owner.

As one song shuffles into the next (a tune you can all joyously sing every word of), it occurs to you that an authentic self executes thought with an essential vocabulary. And when you conceive of authenticity, you can picture everyone except yourself as you are a perennial outlier. Yet at the very same time, you disregard any such notion of authenticity as essentialist nonsense, something for only the most fragile minds. Though also, in yet another concurrent stream of consideration, you question what you can really mean if you suggest there is no faithfulness, no truthfulness, no continuity in all of anyone's experience ever. Do you mean that the atomic and subatomic levels are constantly up for grabs at every moment of every single person's time alive?

You feel a rush up your spine as you move your limbs. Your skull, such a manageable lump of bone, rocks back and forth to the pulses from the speakers and the image of your auntie from Australia on the toilet floor in a gastro pub too upscale for vomit comes to your mind. She is leaning back against the door, her legs spread, pink Docs peaking under the stall walls, and, though her makeup is smeared and some sick is loitering on her chin, her face is a picture of mature grace, of lessons well-learned. *I've seen that bloke behind the bar on Tinder. The fit one. How old do you think he is? We were a match, but he never got in touch and neither did I. But maybe I should've instead of going with all those bogens. Who knows what would've happened? We could've really hit it off. I could be staying here. I could have a whole life for myself here instead of moving on again. But, then, he's a fucking child, isn't he? Twenty-three, I reckon. That's my minimum age. My maximum's thirty-four because I'm just not going there with anyone older. Not to knock, but blokes my age and above are feisty as fuck.* From above, sitting on the toilet, you continued to listen to her calm explanation of her sexual preferences, and you watched her intensity, the focus and determination of her desires, and concluded that she was an absolutely fine human being. The image lingers, slowly fading into nothing as you dance, your heart pounding, a lukewarm can in your hand, drops of cheap, frothy beer falling sometimes onto your bare legs and sometimes onto the old camel lino.

Your head is a barely liftable weight when you step out of the basement flat and into the light of day. But it's also of zero mass and that contradiction equally delights and scares as you ogle the scum on the pavement by your foot. Both states cannot be true. Yet here you are experiencing the two of them at once. It is almost 11 a.m. You take one long, final drag on your vaporizer and begin the stumble to the bus stop. It's only thirty-five minutes at most and then a five-minute walk, but the thought of you managing the whole journey to eventually get back to your bed where you'll slip under the covers for the rest of the day and speak to no one makes you feel truly, truly heroic.

On the 393, several women are wearing bright floral patterns and matching hats. They are chatty and lively. You figure they're on their way back from worship at one of the small evangelical churches nestled in between chicken shops. You recall the men on the tube from last night. All these believers in transit. They have a destination and you don't. You want to ask these women what they prayed for this morning and to whom they prayed. However, you feel filthy. You're high. You're secreting all the dirt of the night out through your almost translucent pores. *They must despair at the sight of me*, you think. To observe your ungainly, dilated pupils and long, regulated, heavy breaths must be a sure sign to them that they've chosen the right path. *Yes, but when I rest my forehead against the cool porcelain of the toilet later, sighing in relief, I will have purged all of my impurities.*

Then there is a sequence of days and nights, weeks and months in which you continue.

One evening, you are talking to your mother on the phone about the Alaskan moose you're planning to adopt for your father's sixtieth when, midway through the conversation, you come to be hyperaware of your language again. But, this time, you feel you have no idea how actual people speak, offering up only a poor, lifeless imitation. The actor's struggling to turn exposition into emotion. Listening at the monitor, the director's racking up the number of hours to be spent in the edit trying to salvage something even semi-relatable to an audience. Your words feel unfit. They are a lead nib in an infant's mouth. You recall such a classmate, Liam McNamara in the infants, forever sucking on a pencil, labelling the circumference of a rectangle. The teacher corrected him to perimeter, but he kept saying *Miss Epstein, the circumference of a rectangle is two by four centimeters.* He had the concept, you think, but not the lexis, and without that he couldn't legitimize his thoughts and that would not do in the world he was going out into. The one you are now fully in.

Your conversation is proceeding as follows:

Mother:		How do you know which moose you're getting?
You:		You select one from a group. They have profiles with statistics.
Mother:		Profiles?
You:		There's a picture and then it tells you their name, how old they are, who their parents were, what breed they are, their weight and height.
Mother:		And how do you know the one you've picked is the one you get?
You:		Why would they lie about that?
Mother:		No, but you can't actually check, can you?
You:		You can go to Alaska.
Mother:		And would you be able to recognize the moose from the profile in person?
You:		I mean . . . do *you* have any other ideas of what to get him?
Mother:		Oh, he's a right so-and-so to buy for.
You:		It's better than a book. And he likes nature. And he's sixty. And he doesn't want anything. What is there he could really want anymore?

You sound machine-like. A smart machine, but a machine nonetheless as your speech has been stripped of idioms and therefore of familiarity, of regionality, of nationality, of humanity. Instead, you have a series of sophisticated algorithms that can mimic human speech perfectly so long as language is accepted as essentially literal and disembodied, as an autonomous system of information transfer in which a lexical item is either a function of grammar or neatly corresponds to the thing it denotes. Then, you suppose, you are a passable person. Of course, if you really tried, you could throw in something figurative, something embodied. 'Swings and roundabouts': that's a thing that people say. Your mother has just said *Why don't you get him a book about moose to see what he makes of them? Mind you, he might be a bit underwhelmed by another book.* You could reply: *Swings and roundabouts, innit?* The crux of the metaphor, you reason, is that the equal pros and cons in the experience of two different amusement rides are the equal advantages and disadvantages in outcomes produced by two different choices. It strikes you to apply an individualizing variant:

You:	Rollercoasters and . . . Ferris wheels, right?
Mother:	Yer what?

You sigh and say you may as well get the moose and the book on moose too, say goodbye, and hang up.

The possibility dawns on you that 'roundabouts' doesn't refer to amusement rides, but to the things on the road that are driven around, in which case the metaphor must be about driving. But what are swings? Sharp turns? A car can swing left or right. So maybe if you'd said *Reverses and intersections, right?* your mother would've understood you to be using vernacular to convey that whatever you choose for your father's birthday is of equally little consequence to him.

It sounds strange to you, it all sounds strange, and you think back to the playground of your primary school where there were swings and what everyone did actually call a roundabout which Liam McNamara used to push as hard as he could, the other children clinging to the rail in fear as it spun, until he stopped and let one foot drag against the ground to slow the wooden circle down.

The problem, you surmise, is with these scripts. The director can't direct and the actor, no matter which one it is, can't act without a decent set of lines. Where does this dialogue come from? Who is supplying it? How are you ever to know when to say what to whom?

You are in the middle of a dream about Paul or Tom in which the two of you are at a funeral. It's a humanitarian service. The turnout is decent, indicating a well-loved person, though you don't know who it is. Paul or Tom gets up to give a eulogy. He espouses all the virtues of the dead individual. You begin to feel anxious, like something's not right, a thing that is concealed, yet very, very important. Now you are at the reception afterwards. The atmosphere is convivial enough and Paul or Tom is sitting next to you at the back of the room. You put your hand on his thigh and lean into his face. His expression becomes darker, his features rougher. He is scared. You attach your mouth to his and feel his fear, so strong it has a sickly scent that turns your stomach, and you continue not in spite of, but because of it.

As you wake, the dream is vanishing and a melody is emerging. It is from one of the manchild's songs from that night at the pop-up bar. Over a 60-66 BPM, the refrain *the migration of our souls to home* plays over and over in your head. His nasal whine conquers like an undercover agent of the state raiding a house of illegals, with ultimate purpose and scant sense of decency. Accompanying this invasion is an internal atmosphere of unease as if you've done something wrong that everyone will eventually find out about.

On checking your phone, you see there are ten minutes before your alarm. Looking up at the spears of light the blinds have let slide onto the ceiling, you think back to after the pop-up when you were talking to Laura as you were sitting on the arm and she the seat of the same multi-stained chair. *I was just thinking that there are some people you mostly like, but there's a little bit you despise. And it's so rare that you're with people you totally like, you know? And that's you people*, she said. Yeah, you replied whilst feeling inadequate for probably liking the people and things you like the most about sixty percent tops, and even though you knew Laura's words were hyperbolic, you felt hollow for being unable to apply the same rhetoric to your response. You felt Laura feel your hollowness. You wanted to express yourself, to represent the, at times, overwhelming feelings you have for the company you were in, but your technique was all wrong. The director was screaming at the actor, whose woodenness didn't even bother her anymore as she'd got all she could from the industry and would've rather been relaxing by the pool than faking conviction for someone else's vision.

Whilst the drugs had laid waste to Laura's barricades, it seems they forced yours to contract, raising unassailable walls around your most vulnerable part, which would never find escape, so you disengaged from the process of trying to verbalize what you felt as there was no way to say what comforts nor distresses you about the experience of loving people and needing them to believe that you do. At this moment, it makes you resentful. *Why does Laura get to feel things and express them?* you think as you watch the sunlight ripple from a passing double-decker rattling your windowpanes.

Leaving the house five minutes later than you should, you look up and see a middle-aged man in white briefs and a bowler hat standing in the gateway, turned to the hedge, with a lighter in his hand. With incredible calm and deliberation, he shifts and fixes his fleshy white gaze on your face. You are at a loss. There's a meeting at 9. You ask if he needs any help. He is silent. Gently pushing past him, you say *Excuse me* and make your way to the bus stop.

During the meeting, as a voice intones obstacles to overcome and aims to achieve, you wonder if the man was intending to set fire to your hedge and if he's succeeded or not. Under the table you search for news of fires in your neighborhood and see nothing. You search for sightings of a man in his underwear and a bowler hat and find nothing. In the group chat with your flatmates you start a message about your encounter then decide against it, unsure if you really saw a person or if he was a phenomenally convincing hallucination.

Before you can tune back into the voice, a picture of a moose comes through. The caption underneath reads: 'Alfred deep in thought.' The enormous brown animal, with its ludicrous head protrusions, is standing in a green and orange field. There is something in its stature and gaze that suggests an intense seriousness about its state of being. Either that, or sheer gormlessness is easily mistaken for solemnity. Since receiving his birthday present, your father keeps you regularly updated on the progress of Alfred. As opposed to contributing to the nihilism of his increasing years, as you had thought it might, the adopted moose has, conversely, brought about deep investment in the miracle of life. You imagine yourself at sixty: you have no head, torso or limbs, rather you're an abstraction of accumulated time whose potential has shrunk from a planet to a ball-bearing. What would a moose mean to you? And, perhaps more importantly, there is the unnerving question of who exactly you will know then who'll think to acquire a large North American mammal to lift your spirits.

In the afternoon, you have to get your colleague with the comatose brother to sign off on a report. Her desk is empty. The man on reception says that she had to leave early due to a family emergency. You wonder if her brother has woken up or died. The latter option leads you to imagine a painful smile ripping her mouth open like the ring-pull on a silky aluminum can of cava, only then for her grief and mortification at herself to stifle it until, inevitably, a new, sharper vision of the future can no longer be suppressed.

On the way home it takes you a while to realize the bus has barely moved in ages. You've been drawn into the center of your phone: news of wildfires, earthquakes and floods; a new insomnia cure recommending sleep suppositories; politicians' threats; TV shows you have no idea how to watch; kittens; people without homes dying; recent definitions of longstanding sexualities; the latest tech; your friends' achievements; lists of anxiety symptoms devastating your life; outrage at a famous individual who expressed opinions even some serial killers would deride; more kittens; and a selection of men for you to scroll through, with you trying to remember as you swipe left and right that these appearances belong to people who are probably, much like yourself, stuck on their commute and distracting themselves from the twin terrors of not having a clue who they are and knowing exactly who they are.

Accidentally, you swipe right on a man posing with a tiger because your attention is taken by the glut of flashing blue lights up ahead. You assumed it was just traffic for traffic's sake, but there seems to have been an accident. The tiger guy was a match. You are disgusted. The next face staring back at you from your phone looks stricken. Even though there's a smile, it appears nervous, uncomfortable, apprehensive about the unstoppable thing that's just about to happen. You project a whole life with this man and play out the scene when, after many years, after your friends' kids have left their homes, he reproaches you for ruining him so you finally say that you've never trusted him, that when he smiles it's like he's acknowledging past collaboration with an alien evil that's coming back to terminate all life on Earth. To that he simply appraises you from head to toe, tuts disapprovingly, and walks out of the door.

Looking up again, you catch sight of figures in high-res vests huddled around the same spot. The passenger beside you coughs, hacking something up and snorting it back down. He's probably sixteen or seventeen. You doubt your existence will have registered for him as you're just someone older. It's thirteen years since you were his age. Thirteen years since you were at Helen Kerr's house party standing in the kitchen concocting a drink from gin, rum and brandy with Chris Jones, Mark Johnson and Sean Scanlon. There were brownies on offer. You ate a whole one, unaware of how strong it was. Right when it started to hit, Liam McNamara came into view in the hallway. He'd gone to a different secondary school and you hadn't seen him since the juniors.

Not recognizing you, he approached and started speaking to Mark Johnson. Their dialogue seemed to exist separately from your reality, which had its own clammy microclimate, creating a humid haze, landmarks obscured. *Spoons was shite mate, no one there* you heard him say before he realized who you were, surprised at what had become of the child he'd known, stunned even. You weren't really sure if the sounds you made were words that fit into sentences that could be understood, but it appeared the both of you had become engaged in conversation. *Back in the day* he kept saying, implying your childhood had taken place in another era when everything was different. *It was only five years ago* you said and he replied *yeah, fucking years ago.* And maybe he was right: that was then.

Concentrating on that/then on the bus, you try to see your past self as someone else entirely. You try to picture your layers of experience as shed skins hanging up in the wardrobe as you're off galivanting in a brand-new epidermal sheath, flitting from scene to scene as a changed being, a different creature from the ones who've come before. But you don't feel changed. What you feel, as far as can be discerned, is like the skins aren't shed, rather they keep accumulating on the same set of bones, getting heavier and heavier yet further and further away from your skeleton so that although you're constantly carrying around their weight, they're also at a remove from the mainframe of you now. Because as much as the stoned person talking to Liam McNamara and the impressed person listening to your Australian auntie and the detached person watching Paul or Tom bleed into the kitchen sink and the unimpressed person in a pop-up bar are united as one by a lack of progress towards any point of life, to that thing that drives others to mold their desires to it, causing them to let go of the attitudes and activities they used to have and do, to move on to their legacies, surrendering to an urge to pass themselves on in genes and values, as much as this is the case, it is also true that when you revisit a memory of yourself you fail to conjure anything more than a one-dimensional avatar who's incapable of complex emotional states: you know that as you were talking to Liam McNamara you were freaking out due to the brownie, wanting him to like you but super anxious about all the eyes on you, about speaking at an inappropriate volume on some delicate matter like Helen Kerr's dad's academic papers on sterilization, but, other than that, of your quotidian inner-life from that period you have absolutely no insight now, so that it can be stated that you're the proverbial goldfish, swimming round and round its bowl, whose basic integrity never alters despite being caught in a continuous act of forgetting.

    Going back to your phone, you search for Liam McNamara. He's remained in a ten-mile radius of your primary school. In his profile picture he's clutching two small children, their cone-like heads a familial identifier. On his face, a beard and three deep lines above his brow make him appear like you never knew him, as this is an adult and not a child nor an adolescent. The boy next to you hacks up and swallows again. The noise emitting from his headphones is as though a group of captive particles is manically scratching through its container in a futile bid for freedom. You focus on his youth: there are mild acne patches and a developing jaw line, but, mainly, there's a total unawareness of what awaits him all over his nonchalant confidence. Knowing that he will age, just like Liam McNamara, and most probably succumb to the forces of change elusive to you, feels utterly devastating.

Notification of a series of messages from Jen slides down from the top bar. You open them and read:
- Not gonna make it tonight
- My job is the worst!
- Sorry!
- Claudia's insisting everyone stay late even though she's gone home
- Fracking knot
- *fucking knob
- Still on for Friday tho
- Gonna get fucked up
- CANNOT WAIT

Following the last message is an emoji of a round yellow face with lopsided eyebrows, the left eye significantly narrower than the right, its mouth an oscillating squiggle turned up into a crescent-like hook poking the patch of red on its right cheek. To reply you use a round yellow face in the throes of laughter with tears coming out of both eyes. After that, you send a GIF from Eisenstein's *Strike* of Tsarist police shooting workers, to which Jen responds with three laughing faces rolling on the floor.

The bus lurches forward, providing a fuller view of the accident. Behind the crouched high-res vests there's a mangled bicycle halfway under the front wheel of another bus. In front of them, an ambulance. Your movement is halted again. At this moment, the melody of the manchild's song comes back into your head, though his words have been replaced with *the circumference of a rectangle*, which, as you don't know the rest of the song, has no alternative but to continuously loop, its minor to major shift irritating and inescapable.

You look back down to the round yellow faces on your phone and consider if they represent one individual experiencing a range of emotions or if they're separate individuals defined by the one emotion. The regularity of their face shape and color suggests a consistent wholeness, the same person's features transformed in correspondence with their inner state. But how do you know there is internal consistency between each one? You don't have any evidence proving a base set of reoccurrences ensuring that the inebriated emoji is essentially the same self as the one rolling on the floor laughing. Except for color and shape, there might be no unifying factor between them. In a way, you think it's more manageable if they are separate beings with one feeling each as the alternative has a kind of seediness to it like a raw, naked creature has been laid out for you to drool over, devouring all of their moods, attitudes and reactions, any notion of privacy robbed from them, a savage violation of subjective solitude.

Movement within your peripheral vision causes you to turn your head to see a woman lying on the road, her neck twisted to the right, her blonde hair bloodied. Within no more than three or four seconds she is covered with a blue blanket. Those eyes that were staring directly into yours, you realize, were a dead body's.

Towards the end of Helen Kerr's house party, you and Liam McNamara locked yourselves in one of the bathrooms for twenty-five minutes. Before you left, he told you that his next-door neighbor, a childminder, had just been convicted for the manslaughter of a three-year-old. It hadn't surprised him because when he was little and looked after there a baby had died from cot death. He remembered his neighbor carrying the tiny body down the stairs, panicking, and then the mother arriving and beginning to wail, the sonic resonance of which lodging itself in his four-year-old psyche in such a strident manner that, in times of stress, he could still hear it now. You very clearly recall thinking of this moment in the toilet stall with your Australian auntie as behind her was a mosaic of graffiti, within which was written *What is existence if you're not desired?*, and you were taken back to exiting the bathroom with Liam McNamara and the contrast between the weight of what he'd just said and the weight of being seen by Claire Walsh and Susan Evans and this feeling of being desired and having others know it. These two weights seemed perfectly, if precariously, balanced, in that as horrifying as knowledge of death and its certainty was, the pleasure of reciprocal passion observed turned living into resistance.

An image of the fleshy, white man in his underwear and bowler hat comes back to you, his facial features of eyes and mouth forming an isosceles triangle. There was nothing readable about him, no clue as to the why, what and how of him and his situation. You wonder if he has any other expressions or if he is defined by one state: blankness. He has perhaps gone from one event to the next in the same unthinking, unfeeling fugue, unable to do or be anything different. You try to see multitudes in him, all the possible permutations of a lived life on the various contortions of his face. *There is a person throughout, a constant singularity* you tell yourself, yet remain unconvinced as every instance of the man as anything other than blankness plays like a contrivance, a fake.

The bus pushes through the last blockage and moves forwards to complete its journey as normal. Locked deep in the interior of the dead woman's eyes it seems to you there was one last enduring thought. After her heart had stopped beating, as her brain's electrical activity was ceasing and as the awareness of no return was fading, she was left with the final, unanswerable, horrifying question: *What am I?*

You push the button for your stop and get up, staggering as the bus judders and stumble down the top steps into the young man in front. Before you can remove your hands from his shoulders and apologize, he says sorry, so you have to repeat the words twice for it to have effect. He blinks and turns away. On your palms there remains the phantom sensation of possession, the spectral pressure of contact with another physical object. Stepping out into the early spring evening, you succumb and sing along: *the circumference of a rectangle, the circumference of a rectangle . . . .*

In Defense of My Stories

Roeethyll Lunn

Because of some of my works' subject matter and strong adult language, at first, I was reluctant to even submit some of my writings. I do not readily desire to "cuss" or include "nasty talk," as my family members say, in any of my work in order to attract attention to myself. I fear that this would have repercussions that would not be favorable to me. My desire is that my accounts will travel well beyond the realm of just a juicy or colorful story and that they will also capsulate a time, a people, a milieu and a cultural experience. I want to transgress the petition that stood between the black and white races of people during a time preceding that period which our federal government labeled as "Desegregation of the Southern Portion of the United States." I want to expose how days were spent and how lives were lived by a group of people that was "Jim Crowed" into living in areas that were sequestered on the far end of towns and on the back sides of rural roads in areas such as Grove Street, Black Street, The Bottom, Black Bottom, Sugar Hill, The Hill and Shanty Town.

 A story to a writer is like a Tithe. It is a gift from God. But it is not for you alone. You are merely a steward. Therefore, you must cough it up! Put it away from you! Get that hallowed thing out of your house! If you ignore it or try to withhold it within you, it will curse you and your life.

 My redemptive force came when I thought of a big, red woman from Johnsonville, South Carolina, named Mabel (pronounced "May Belle") Melvin. She told me that as she was driving home from work one day, she saw her husband riding a strange young girl in his car. She tried to catch them, but he outran her. Mabel said that she went home, got his pistol, and then drove straight to her husband's best friend's house. She placed the nose of the weapon to his friend's temple, cocked it and said, "Tell the story!—cause I know you know every word."

Sometimes I feel as if a gun, held by all of the "colored women" who had to endure, is cocked to my temple and all of them are saying to me, "Tell the story."

They were the colored women who: baked biscuits and sweet potatoes for their children when there was no meat; who fished all morning in a pond that they had walked miles to get to, and then sometimes had to fry fatback and make grits to go with it when they couldn't get a bite; who went into woods, wet with dew, in the spring, to pick huckleberries to sell by the quart to rich white ladies who lived in Southern small towns in houses that had sat for over a century on well-kept lawns or to the other white people who were the only ones selected to work in factories downtown; girls who gleaned field peas from between corn or cotton stalks in the fall because the crop "didn't do good" that year; the girl who cut her own umbilical cord when her twins aborted because there was no money to go to a doctor and because there was no one else around to help; the woman who, for the sake of all of her other children, said nothing all afternoon to the other field hands that she worked with, because she'd left her kitchen during noon hour (where she had been hurriedly preparing their meals) to go through the house to look for the knife that she liked to cook with, only to discover her husband, in his and her bed, molesting her oldest daughter, who was not his.

So with the encouragement of those girls, Langston Hughes, who left word to all aspiring black writers to write about the black man "and don't prettify it" in order to pacify a black or white reading audience, essayist/columnist Roger Rosenblatt, who told me that I was "a natural storyteller," and Poet William "Kit" Hathaway, who gave me a letter of encouragement on one of my worst days at Southampton College and told me to "try to have this story published" because that particular writing, in his opinion, can be compared to that of Zora Neal Hurston's. I will tell my stories. I will tell them in the voice of my youth and in the volume of my experiences.

Looking for Love:
To-Do List of a Lake Monster

Marilee Dahlman

    1. First things first, brush my matted hair. Braid a tadpole necklace and pin a frog behind one ear.
    2. Float in marshy shallows and forget cold crash and white bite spray, drowned descent and forced rebirth from skin to scales, all in turbid shades of gray and green and waxen blue.
    3. Scour lakebed for fossils. The diplodocus is almost complete! That missing rib, I'll find it yet, buried in sands from ages past. A beast's need for union is such a timeless quest.
    4. Search sunken tin pan freighter for ruffled shirt with button cuffs. Lie in shoal and watch the cove, where a dirt path winds and soft-skinned stroll. Drift away, but sense the shore vibrations still: dancing violin, coupled laughter, clinks of glass.
    5. Afternoon nap in western bog.
    6. Find a mate. Cast a line or throw a net?
    7. Twilight cruise near the beach, smell the flesh with every breath.
    8. Lure a lady from the path . . . wail a siren call and spew a lentic scent! Spy her in starlight, moonlight, gaslight glow; she'll sense my soul, my other half. Listen now, it's safe to step! Tread through muddy cattails and spreading ferns, slip-slide slick lichen stones, and wade into wavy warmth . . . .
    9. Hooked you! Seaweed bound, lasso round. Grind your heels, kick up sand, through clouds of silt and salty tears I see you yet! Don't hide beneath an algae bloom or I'll drag you to a deeper gloom. We'll build a bed of snails and burn it bright. Be my slimy bride, in veil of rotted sail and clanking rusted anchor chains behind. Webbed feet, pointed teeth, cool blood reborn, another spiny savage with red heart pumping deep.

10. We'll tumble through splendid years, embraced in wet blissful paradise, until rough green gods with seismic squeeze mold our home to mountain. Perched on peak, caged by icy crystal ocean, we'll bet on bobbing arks while glaciers creep.

11. I'll spot an emerald spec as the floods recede, follow me, we'll flop on down. Finned creatures crawling, pine needles pricking, we'll find a pond and dive again, forever to swim a murky heaven and ride this world's smooth blue-green spin. Together.

Villainy 04 / Nicole Foran

VILLAINY 09 / NICOLE FORAN

HEAT

Rayne Debski

You are thirty-five years old and you know better than to open the envelope that feels like a strip of hot metal in your hand. The return address is from the federal prison in Pensacola. You don't have to open it to know it's from Inmate 607439. You do know that if you read it, the letter will sear your heart. Just holding the envelope, you remember the cleft in his chin, the feel of his breath against your neck. If you read it, you will long for something you shouldn't, and you may risk everything you've achieved in the last eight years —career success, a fiancé who adores you, an upstanding reputation in the community.

Your fiancé Marc doesn't object to the nights and weekends your career requires, makes excellent paella, and sends roses to your mother on her birthday. You nod your head at the litany of his virtues. Yes, yes, he is a good man. But his love wraps around you like a shroud. You check your phone. Marc will be home any minute.

Words sit like sparks on your tongue. You crave talking to someone about 607439, the same way you used to jones for his fingers snaking down your stomach. Maybe you should call Joy, your best friend, and tell her you've received this letter. She'll tell you to burn it and flush the ashes in the toilet. She'll remind you of the years of therapy, the money you spent on lawyers to clear your conscience and get a divorce. You won't remind her that she arranged the blind date with the man who became 607439, that she was the maid of honor at your wedding, and that she never told you about the deception that simmered behind his sea blue eyes.

You sneeze from the lemon polish your cleaning lady uses. You don't recall asking Alexa to play Bob Marley, but his voice fills your living space. Your hips sway slowly, and you're on your honeymoon in Jamaica, making love on the beach, so in love—or was it in heat—that you ignored the sand fleas and land crabs making their way along the shore. You swallow the longing for his arm around your waist, for trips to rain forests and mountain peaks. You remember how he sent you to shop in island bazaars with a wallet full of cash. A sweet and generous gesture! And then you discovered he did this to keep you busy while he arranged drug drops on remote islands in the Keys. You laugh bitterly at your naivete.

Your phone dings. Marc will be late; the gym is crowded, and he wants to finish his routine. He says don't cook dinner, he'll bring home Thai. You tell Alexa to shut up.

You sit on the sunporch and hold the letter to your nose the same way you held 607439's shirts when he was in Columbia on business and, worried that he would meet a violent death, tried to breathe him into you. If you call your mother, she'll tell you to shred the letter. Whatever you do, she'll say, don't tell anyone about him, especially Marc. This has been her mantra since 607439 was imprisoned. She refuses to believe that you knew what 607439's import business entailed, and after a while you willingly participated in it. In an escalating voice she'll recite the sins of 607439: how he used you to transport cocaine; how he spent his nights away from you; how he blackened your eye when you flushed away his stash. She'll bring up her cousin, the state senator who arranged for a plea deal if you turned state's witness, and whose influence kept you out of the newspapers. She never hesitates to tell you any of this should the past inadvertently come up.

You've told Marc you were married to a man who was a deadbeat and disappeared after the divorce. Marc promises not to disappoint you. He listens to your opinions, introduces you to interesting people, and shares your love of foreign films. He is a competent, considerate lover. He believes the body is a temple that should never be tainted with anything stronger than alcohol. He says people who do drugs are idiotic for damaging their brains. You nod as if you agree with him. He works out, runs, drinks kale smoothies, and avoids desserts. You don't tell him that for several months the smoothies you drank were made with psilocybin mushrooms; the brownies you baked were seasoned with hash. Your mother is right. Don't tell anyone in your new life about your old one. What happened was years ago and has little bearing on who you are today. You repeat this to yourself whenever the hankering for excitement and adventure make you want to take a plane to South America and explore the Amazon.

Your phone dings again. Marc is almost home. You know the letter from 607439 is telling you he'll be released next month. For years you've listened to his voicemails about the things he made in woodshop, the books he's read, the stories he's written, the fights he's won. You've treated them like messages from the dead and never responded. But you know he's being released because you've kept a calendar and marked off the days of time served. You hold the letter tightly. No matter what happens in your new life, something inside you resists letting go of the old one.

The front door opens. Marc juggles the bags of food in one arm, and with the other pulls you to him. His muscles are taut, strong. The letter is folded in your pocket, a piece of lit charcoal pressed between you. You spoon the red curry duck into bowls. While Marc pours glasses of pinot gris, he talks about his day, his ebullience unshakable.

The heady scent of ginger and garlic unsettles your stomach. He tilts his head, his eyes soft. "Are you okay?" His concern rattles your heart. You want to tell him about the heat against your hip.

"You haven't tried the curry." He trails a finger down your back, igniting an unexpected shiver of desire.

You take a spoonful of food, inhale its tomatoey aroma, then let it sit on your tongue. His fingers travel along the waistband of your pants. The sweet and spicy flavors of the curry unfold. You swallow, surprised at how delicious it tastes.

The Heated Mission

Laurence Williams

Before Alexa Plowden threw the covers off, she knew the heat had stopped pumping. Her six-year-old Jonathan stood at her bedroom door shivering and her baby Isabella whimpered in her crib. Son of a bitch landlord, she muttered. She seized her son's hand, scooped the baby up, brought them to the kitchen, handed Jonathan his coat, hat and gloves, and wrapped Isabella in a blanket. She pressed her hand to the radiator and yanked it away. The boy coughed, the baby cried. The heat had been off all night, third time this winter, and that bastard was gonna pay.

She made hot chocolate, plopped Jonathan down in front of the TV, threw on her sweats and her hoodie, stuck her feet in her boots, hoisted Isabella onto her shoulder, stuck a pacifier in her mouth and down the steps she went.

The super, Ivan Milovic, had an apartment on the first floor and he stood in the hallway with some of the other tenants, his arms splayed apart in a hapless gesture, his woolen hat pulled tight over his head, his shared predicament evident from the way he kept blowing into his hands. He mumbled that he called the landlord who said he would take care of it.

Yeah, right, just like he did the last two times, Alexa said.

She hiked back up to her apartment and dialed 311. They placed her on hold for fifteen minutes. She registered her complaint and they promised to follow up. But unless they sent an oil truck over to make a delivery, the heat would stay off. Bastards, all of them, her deadbeat ex, the landlord, the mayor, the city, they didn't give a shit about anybody.

She ran up the stairs to check on her neighbor. Mrs. Simpson had just turned ninety last week, and was homebound in a deteriorating condition. What a way to start a decade. If someone didn't do something soon, she would freeze to death. Alexa knocked and let herself in with the key Mrs. Simpson had given her. The old lady had turned on the oven and all the burners and sat in her wheelchair by the stove warming her hands, and invited Alexa to join her. Alexa blew cold steam into the air. She'll blow the whole damn building up, and there's probably twenty other tenants doing the same thing. They'd all be toasty then.

Alexa turned the oven off, bundled Mrs. Simpson up in a coat and some blankets, ran back downstairs, checked on her son, and with the baby still on her shoulder ran back into the hall and banged on doors, raising hell, urging everyone to call 311.

Thirty-six families resided in the six-story building and most of them on some sort of public assistance, in a section of the Bronx everyone liked to forget about, which meant they were at the ass end of the priority scale. Didn't mean the landlord and the biggest city in the world could treat them like this, and Alexa would be damned if she let them. If the super couldn't get the oil here, then she wanted the number to call.

One of the tenants informed her Milovic sought refuge at the corner bodega. Back up to her apartment, zipped the baby up in a coat and hood, grabbed her son and still in her sweats and hoodie, the fire in her belly keeping her warm, Alexa marched down to the bodega with her kids in tow where Milovic cowered behind some boxes of Captain Crunch in the back of the store, a cup of steaming, hot coffee in his hand.

She demanded the name and number of the oil company, and he stammered in his broken English, which broke more and more as he spoke, that tomorrow was a scheduled delivery. What the hell were thirty-six families supposed to do tonight, light bonfires in their apartments, Alexa screamed? If Milovic could have climbed into one of the cereal boxes, he would have. He sputtered something unintelligible, and Alexa assured him that she didn't blame him. It wasn't his fault; it was the scumbag who sat by his fireplace somewhere out east on Long Island that wouldn't pay for the oil and dozens of other repairs that needed to be done. She wanted that number. She stepped toward him and he fished in his overstuffed wallet and handed her a card.

Back in her apartment, she dialed the emergency number and told the dispatcher that she was the landlord's representative and he had authorized an emergency delivery today. The dispatcher got hold of a manager on duty who informed her that not only would there not be a delivery today, but there would not be one tomorrow because the scumbag landlord, (Alexa's words) had not paid the bill for the previous delivery. Alexa demanded the oil and said she was the new super and had a check from the landlord for payment. She hung up, doubting that an oil truck would rumble onto their block any time soon.

Once again, she strode through the hallways, banged on doors, her hair matted to her head, her hood flying out like a superhero's cape, dragging her boy, and toting the baby. She gathered the tenants in the lobby. She inquired who in the building had cars, or knew a neighbor who had a car. About fifteen tenants raised their hands. She also told them that what she had in mind would most certainly get them arrested but it would get these bastards' attention.

A young couple, Robert and Precious, who shared an apartment and each other, stood there with their hands at their sides. Alexa knew they had a car because they had given her a lift a couple of times. She glared at them. Robert glared right back and told her she was loco and that her hair needed brushing. Precious held out her keys and Robert snatched them out of her hand. Alexa let go of her son's hand, grabbed hold of Robert's arm and escorted him down the hallway and whispered in his ear, asking if Precious knew anything about Robert's little visits to Apartment 5F.

The baby whimpered and Robert cursed her, creating a disharmonious chorus. Precious, in a trembling voice, informed Alexa she was scaring the baby. She shook her head, continuing her hold on Robert's arm while the rest of the tenants stood there stamping their feet, too cold to worry about one of their neighbors losing her shit. Alexa told Precious it was her hair that freaked the baby out. Robert handed the keys to Precious. Alexa ordered everybody that had a car to get ready.

By this time, the news of the building with no heat had spread through the neighborhood, and like the old game of telephone, by the time it reached the Laundromat two blocks away, the story was the landlord had evicted people into the freezing cold. That got everybody seeing red. Alexa ran up and down the block, her hood flapping against the wind, asking anyone with a car to help her get the heat back on, warning them of the likely consequences. When she had another ten rebellious volunteers, she told everybody to meet in front of the building.

Alexa made the first call to 911. Fire on the sixth floor. Seven other tenants followed at one-minute intervals. Alexa ordered her co-conspirators with a car to assume their positions. The fire chief's SUV followed by an engine and ladder roared onto the block, their tires screeching and sirens and horns blaring. Another fire truck stopped at the top of the street blocking traffic. The firemen jumped from the truck, got their equipment and hustled toward the building. Alexa stood in their path, baby squirming on her shoulder, her boy twisting in her hand, her hair stuck in her mouth, and her hoodie zippered up against it all.

She told them there was no fire. She didn't know if they were shocked more at her statement or her appearance. The chief spoke into his radio and the truck up the street pulled away. The men got out of their gear and the chief turned to Alexa and demanded to know what the hell was going on. Alexa told him the building had no heat and that's why she called the fire in. His face turned red, and then purple as he radioed for the police, and informed her she wouldn't have to worry about heat where she was going. At this time, ten or so cars rolled into place on each end of the block, four and five deep, blocking both ends of the street. One of the firefighters on the rig called out to the chief, and his face turned all kinds of colors now. Alexa told him again, we need oil and you're going to help us get it.

The first patrol car showed up and the officers were none too happy they had to get out of their car at the end of the block in this frigid weather. They screamed at the drivers blocking the street, banging on their windows with their sticks. Everybody on the sidewalks had their phones out recording the scene, and the cops stepped away and called for backup.

That's when the news crews showed up, trudging down the street with their cameras and microphones. The chief screamed at Alexa pointing his crooked finger in her face, when one of the firefighters came over and draped his coat around her shoulders. The chief approached seizure status now and wanted to know what the hell this firefighter was doing. He walked the chief back to his truck, as the news reporters held microphones in front of Alexa's face. She cocked her head to the side, told them how nice of them to come down, and the building needed oil. Alexa repeated the address three times nice and slow.

Then the news people ran up and down the block filming the police and firemen and doing sound bites for the six o'clock news. The firefighter who had given Alexa his coat came over, took off his helmet, wiped the sweat from his brow and his nice eyes, and smiled at her. What's your name, he asked.

Alexa Plowden.

He told her his was John Driscoll, told her they needed to leave so they can save lives. Alexa smiled at him, told him that's exactly what he was doing right now.

The street teemed with reporters from all the major stations, and the minor ones too, sticking microphones in the faces of Alexa and the fire chief, but walking right by the nobodies with plenty of stories that nobody wanted to hear. A man in a shabby gray overcoat, a rumpled blue suit, with a lavender shirt, and a pink tie flicked a card from his hand into Alexa's like a conjurer pulling a rabbit out of his hat.

We can sue, he said.

We need oil, she said.

You need a defense attorney, the chief said.

There were other lawyers now mingled among the crowd, distributing cards to prospective clients.

Driscoll, let's go, the chief ordered, and then turned to Alexa. See what you've done, lady. You're so concerned about these people, they're all going to be arrested.

A reporter stood behind him and asked for a comment, and the chief scurried away. Driscoll pleaded with Alexa to end the madness before another call came in, otherwise she'd be in serious trouble, and he told her the chief would ram those cars like they were tissue paper anyway. The reporter begged for a statement. Alexa told her there was a ninety-year old ailing woman in Apartment 6F freezing to death, while the Interstate Development Company, a/k/a Devlin Brown, sat in his palatial estate on Long Island. He knew how to collect the rent but he forgot how to pay for the oil and the broken pipes and the exterminator and the roof repairs. Why don't you run out there and ask him about it. The reporter moved away, having gotten her thirty second blip for tonight's news.

Driscoll offered to let Jonathan sit in the rig to keep warm, and then Driscoll and the chief got into an animated discussion; Driscoll with his kind eyes, the chief with his colorful face, and then the police captain trudged down the block and brought his red face into the conversation. The brass got on their phones while two police officers ordered Alexa to follow them.

Don't you see I have a freezing baby in my arms, she said while cameras and cell phones captured the moment.

The cops looked at each other. Maybe it wasn't a good idea to drag a woman in a firefighter's coat and sweat pants, with matted hair, and a baby on her shoulder away in cuffs, one whispered to the other.

Driscoll asked the officers to give him a sec. Alexa said she had to go check on Mrs. Simpson, make sure she didn't blow up the building. Driscoll told her no worries, that he sent some men up with some hot soup and blankets to look after her. We're working on getting an oil truck here. Can you ask them to move the cars now?

She blew the hair from her eyes. You giving me your word, she asked.

He nodded. I am, he said.

She had told the drivers when she gave the signal to drive away and keep driving. The cars pulled off and the police drove down the street.

Anything you can do for those people, Alexa asked. I scared the shit out of all of them. Driscoll laughed. I bet you did. I have some connections. I'll see what I can do.

There were now dozens of people running back and forth, and a helicopter hovered overhead. A loud honking drew everyone's attention to the corner, as an oil truck made the turn and thundered down the block The street grew quiet and everybody watched with their mouths hung open as it pulled up behind the fire truck. The people parted like the red sea for the oil man who approached Alexa, her hood fluttering out from the huge fireman's coat draped over her shoulders. Even the chief gaped at the scene, Alexa standing over the oil man, like Emperor Augustus greeting one of his generals after a great victory.

You the lady who needs the oil, the delivery man said.

No, the whole damn building needs the oil, she said.

The oil man nodded, and he unleashed the hose from his truck like a giant snake, and the flow of black gold poured into the building. A cheer went up from the crowd.

A limousine flanked front and back by cop cars paraded down the street and pulled up behind the oil truck. The driver ran around and opened the door, and the mayor stepped out. All the media people ran to him, as he pontificated on how he came to the rescue of his constituents, and would hold the landlord accountable, and send a message to anyone that would dare do harm to his great city.

What a guy, Driscoll said.

Alexa tilted her head and smirked. Really? and they both laughed.

Driscoll shuffled his feet, looked around and down and then up into Alexa's eyes.

Do you have someone to take care of the children for a little while, he asked.

Yeah, I already asked my neighbor, Carmen. Time for me to go, I guess, she said.

You should be out in a couple of hours. Like I said, I have connections. Here's my number. He handed her a card and she handed him back his coat.

The police allowed her to go upstairs and get dressed, and then put her into the back of the patrol car. It pulled away and she turned to look out the rear window at Driscoll tipping his helmet to her, at the mayor shaking hands, at Robert flipping her the finger, at the chief screaming at no one in particular, at the people dispersing, their lives not important to the news outlets, at the oil man, the lone player with no allegiance to anything but his hose, at her children, who at least tonight would be warm.

Color Burn / Hayley Patterson

QUILTED LANDSCAPE / CHRISTINA KLEIN

The Tower Bells

Alli Parrett

Doctor Cate comes into my room to sit with me like she does every night before she goes home. She tells me not to use her last name—too formal for friends, she says. I'm delighted that she calls me her friend though she's only known me a few months.

Awful business being stuck in a bed all day. Not long ago I used to have these talks with Doctor Cat while she walked me around the church next to the hospital. Same one I got married in forty-six years ago, then buried my husband in forty-two years after that. He wore blue both times. Dying isn't a pretty business, no matter how hard we try. I miss him but am thankful he can't see me this way.

The tower bells ring calling the end of Doctor Cate's shift. She squeezes my hand gently between her own and says she'll see me tomorrow. Though I'd never tell her, it hope it's the last time I hear those church bells.

The tower bells go off at the church. An end of the day for some. For me, another reminder that I've missed the visiting hours at my mother's hospital. I steal a look out the window evading notice from my boss and wonder how she's doing. She is hearing the same chimes. It won't be like this forever, I tell myself. My heart twinges.

I am still at my desk staring at the same report carrying out new tasks at my boss's request. My mother is still in her bed with nothing new on television, still complaining to the nurses. At least she has Doctor Cate. She says she likes her. Sometimes, when there weren't a lot of people, Doctor Cate took her inside. It was where she and my father got married, where they baptized me, where they went to church every Sunday even after I stopped going with them. Where she buried my father three years ago. She stopped going after that.

Tomorrow I will have time.

The morning is still dark. The hospital's number displays itself across my phone. Doctor Cate gives me news I both hoped and dreaded for months. My chest twists like a dish rag being rung.

The Jellyfish

River Elizabeth Hall

On top of what had been the last President's desk lay a dead jellyfish. Gravity had pulled it into a widening, gelatinous puddle. Visible on the desk beneath its transparent body was a blurred and torn briefing. The only visible words remaining were "Martial Law."

Eve looked around to see where the lonesome sea creature had come from and spotted a broken window that overlooked the overgrown lawn. Bonfires burned at intervals along Pennsylvania Avenue, and smoke hung over the quieted city. A single snowflake flicked down from the heavy clouds and then another. When she turned back to the jellyfish, she thought that it looked curiously larger than before.

She walked the perimeter of the Oval Office and found a broken, framed picture of the last First Family. Someone had driven their heel through the glass, obscuring the last President's face, but his smile peeked out below. His bleached teeth hung suspended in a flaccid grin. She hoped he had glass in his eyes wherever he was, and tossed the photo back into the pile of broken objects.

She turned back to the jellyfish and it was suddenly as big as the desk. Across the room, the plaster had been torn from the wall, revealing the old nails, boards, and supports. She considered the ancestors that built the older portions of this white house. How their bodies had been forced to assemble its skeleton, plaster it, paint it— knowing one day, inevitably it would be razed. How joyful, how perfect it was that their offspring should tear it down to the studs together. She hoped wherever they were that the satisfaction of this moment could find them.

She approached the jellyfish for a better look. Startled, she could see that it was very much alive. Within it, a beating red heart was visible deep in its center. She put her hand on her own heart and noticed it was beating in unison with the heart of this being.

The snow began to spit harder out on the lawn. Someone coughed loudly and Eve jumped, realizing she was no longer alone. A very disheveled-looking white woman stumbled over a curtain that had been ripped from the rods as she entered the room. The woman startled as she took in the scene. She stood still, eyes wide for quite some time. They looked at one another. Neither one said a word. There was nothing left to say. Only work to be done.

The jellyfish had grown even larger. The smell of salt and seawater filled the room. They stared together, hands over their hearts as though pledging allegiance, as though singing the former national anthem, even though they had both forgotten the words.

With wonder, they watched as inside this swelling, jelly-like womb, the tiniest new life form curled around its own steadily beating heart, floating peacefully in its own little sea. Then, in silence, they continued gathering anything that would burn.

Is This the Ritz?

Doley Henderson

Viv always said I was never the same after the crash. It was snowing like billy-o when we left the dinner party, we couldn't see a damn thing through the windshield. Wipers scraping back and forth, the old station wagon poking its way out onto the autoroute.

Big fat truck came out of nowhere, right at us. I sailed straight through the windshield—no seatbelts of course, it was the '50s—and came to, lying on the highway. Stockings in shreds but still had my shoes on so, thought I was fine. Jack was trapped under the steering wheel. Hours later, there I sat in the ER, holding my head with twenty-three stitches, while they rushed him to surgery. The great doctor needed all their attention. I don't know who I was supposed to be.

Now here I sit, parked with the old-and-sick-and-tired-and-stupid, waiting for I don't know what, the next bus, maybe. It's called Sunrise. Sunset, more like. The end of the road. I've been around the world. There's nowhere left. Jack's gone, Viv's gone, friends all gone. No more martini lunches, just the odd splash of wine. I think it's dealcoholized, no zizz. And they keep bringing new people to my table. The other day, it was someone from Winnipeg. "You two will have so much in common," said Matron. I took one look at the polyester leisure suit and got very busy buttering my roll. Winnipeg tried valiantly anyway. "How long have you been a resident?" Bla-bla. It's dullsville, where's the glamour?

Viv and I thought we were royals, handed to the wrong parents at birth. Meant to be leading a much fancier life. Twins we were, born twenty minutes apart. Spent our lives finishing each other's sentences. Had our own language, punished Mum for not returning us to our proper family. Poured milk on her newly waxed floor, then flour on her Oriental rug. Poor woman, couldn't keep up, four kids in three years, out there on the prairie, in a boxcar, while Father ran the railway. We were just as clever as the boys, older too but only girls, so they got the degrees and we dabbled in art and music. That's how it was. None of this women's lib business.

Those smelly, noisy brothers, always busy with their little science projects. We ignored them most of the time. One day, we found them burying the poor old cat behind the shed. Turns out, he'd been hit by a car, so Bob crossed some wires, started up the Ford, and euthanized him with the gas fumes. Then Tim practiced his dissection and suturing skills. He was set on being a surgeon but Father insisted on engineering. They both married beneath them, in the end. Bob got the butcher's daughter pregnant, just by looking at her, apparently, so that was him then, done like dinner. And Tim was snared by some dietician, who cooked his goose, I guess. Spent all that time measuring instead of tasting. Couldn't, for the life of her, produce a proper meal or kids. Said it wasn't her fault. Nonsense, it wasn't Brother's.

And poor old Viv had that nearsighted fellow all hot and bothered. He gave her a string of pearls and proposed. Mother put an end to that—not an RC, it wouldn't do. Never had another serious beau after that. Sad, really but then she had more time for my girls. "You spoil them with those sloppy kisses," I'd lob. "You mock them with those arched eyebrows," she'd return. Fifteen love, neither of us ready to concede. So, we shared them, just like everything else. I gave them life and color and she gave them love and cookies.

All those years, Viv did the running monologue, yackety-yack, life of the party, while I sprinkled the conversation with bon mots. Madly gay over cigarettes and cocktails. Players, in the blue tins. The girls used the empty ones for crayons. Crown Royal, in purple velvet sacks, with gold string. Made tidy ballet-slipper bags. The other dancers frowned behind their patent leather. Not their fault, their mothers had no imagination or style.

Formal ball season, those were the days. I was a vision in cerise satin, off-the-shoulder, cap sleeves, evening gloves, kid leather with pearl buttons. I'd scan the horizon for the smoothest dance partner. Jack had that boyish charm but two left feet, so that was a total loss. He was busy anyway, fending off the women who slid by, batting their eyelashes and wiggling their derrieres. I'd raise my cigarette for a light or wave my glass for another rye-and-water and see which handsome fellow would spring forward. The PM swept into St. Andrew's one year and asked me to waltz. Told him my card was full and he laughed. A lot shorter than I thought he'd be but quite light on his feet. Devilish smile under that little Nero haircut. Smoked Gauloises.

Paris was our theme for the oyster party one year. I painted a Moulin Rouge mural. Everyone wore berets and the latest French styles. I was a broken-down ballet dancer in a black leotard and tulle illusion, Jack a bartender with fake moustache. Viv came as an artist's model, in a fur coat and bare legs. The girls sneaked downstairs, lured by the laughter and tinkling glasses, hid under the coats in the front hall. Their little secret, they thought. We pretended not to notice, then later Jack found them asleep and carried them back to bed.

Don't be shy, I'd say to the girls, always make a statement. With AY and the Group of Seven, we'd talk about having an eye, knowing when to add just a touch of color. Splash of orange in a sea of green, like a dash of curry on a bed of peas. "Stop before it's too late," I'd say to Mum, as she overworked her sad, little landscapes of Lake Winnipeg. Her only pleasure I guess, after years of nursing the Cree, finally saying yes to Father, and raising her own little hellions. We were cute though.

My eldest brought me this hideous blanket the other day. I loved the soft fleece but hated the shade, so I said, "Whatever possessed you?" She was all hurt. "But you loved that orange pillow at home. It's the same." "A hint of color, dear, don't overdo it." She quietly tucked it under the green one at the end of the bed, and slipped back out the door. She's gone all funny, living with that old coot. What was she thinking, shacking up with someone her father's age? He can be charming and funny, then suddenly, he's all depressed and angry. It was the war. PTS they call it. XYZ, for all I know. Wasting her life, could have been anything she wanted, I told her. She replied, "I am who I want." Like a Dorothy Parker line but not as clever. A wilting lily, that one. What's the matter with those girls anyway? Not a shred of me in any of them. One's with Methuselah, the next with another woman, and the last with no one at all, just her kids. Not a proper marriage among them.

I had strings of suitors, U of T and McGill, busy playing the field but Jack won me over, with his big grin and rugged profile. I slaved over his oil portrait in intern whites. Quite a good one, actually. Mum loved watching him gobble up her pies. His own *maman* was a terrible cook and a hypochondriac but his papa was pleasant enough, a GP. It was wartime, so a simple wedding, then off to Quebec City, waiting for the call. Suddenly, there I was, pregnant and alone, himself shipped overseas.

We studied the newspapers for months and months, found the odd photo: trim nurses with wounded servicemen, everyone smiling bravely. How desperately far away it all seemed, as I spooned more pablum into Baby. Years later, I'd tell the girls, if they were ever worried, I'd say, "Stop your nonsense, it's not life or death, put on some lipstick, and press on regardless." People don't know how to cope anymore. No sense of perspective.

Jack was a medical officer, safe in England, I thought. Turns out, he was up to his waist in the Atlantic on D-Day, flagging down transport for the wounded on Juno Beach. Had to leave the rows of dead soldiers on the sand where they'd been mown down, fresh off the ships. Lost his tin hat and his LST, what with the tides and wind and chaos. Spent days crossing the channel back and forth, collecting the rest of the wounded. Seems to me, that's how he spent his life, taking care of other people's families, while I held the fort, easing the girls' pains with Midol and crushed ice. "The shoemaker's children," I'd say to no one in particular. His patients loved him, especially the little old ladies. A million friends all over the world. Never missed a reunion, medical, fraternity or D-Day. Chatted up the Queen Mum over there one year. Lovely smile, he said. Well of course I was jealous. The road not taken, so sure I was meant to be royal.

Jack's bedtime story about LST-541 crossing the English Channel, "up-and-down and up-and-down" was the girls' favorite. He would grab the mattress and roll it from side to side. They'd squeal in delight, afraid but excited, with no idea what he was really talking about. It sounded fun, a big adventure, not the living hell it must have been. His friend Bud was in *The Great Escape* camp. Wasn't chosen to tunnel in the end, but they consulted him on the screenplay.

The drama queen, my middle one, arrived for my birthday, alone, thank God. The staff sailed in with a big, fat, gooey cake. When I looked suspicious, she announced to the room that I was ninety-six. Well, I had to shush her that fast, before anyone turned up a hearing aid. "One never reveals one's age, my dear."

No manners. My pearls of wisdom, fallen on deaf ears, all those years. Must be that American's influence, the so-called "wife," she knows that grates on my nerves. No sense of restraint, those people, living their lives out loud. In my day, they were discreet. That hair! Looks like a mistake, shaven down the sides and floppy in the middle. "What's that supposed to be?" I asked her one day. She snapped right back, "At least I don't need a man to define myself." Viv said her sharp tongue was my fault. "You never picked her up when she cried." "Nonsense," I'd say. "Crying develops the lungs."

That all-girls high school maybe was a mistake. We thought it was the solution after that business with the math teacher when she was twelve. Grabbed her bottom, she said, so I raced down to the school. He denied it, of course. They say he was in the Navy. All those men in tight quarters. She did have an active imagination, though. Always so physical. Couldn't sit still for five minutes, constant motion from day one. Little legs, going like sixty on her tricycle, racing down the sidewalk. When she was really on my nerves, jiggling and rattling, I'd tell her to run around the block a few times. Jack would take her to the park and they'd smack a few softballs across the field or slap some pucks around the rink. Never had any trouble with the other two. Happy as Larry, they were parked at the kitchen table, squishing little sculptures from flour-and-water paste, with a dash of food coloring.

When I looked up, the inmates were all singing "Happy Birthday." A sea of white-haired widows, hardly a man in sight. We outlive them, of course. The one at the next table suddenly lurched to his feet, saluted me, then slid back down, muttering. Poor old soul, in his own little world, not a single visitor. They tried pet therapy on him, a black Labrador. Well, he shed and panted and drooled. Sniffed around my lap too, until I shooed him away. Revolting thing.

Jack could be a little unglued too, from time to time. He'd get all sad and serious when anything was broken or needed fixing. Neat and tidy to a fault, ever the dedicated surgeon in his OR. One day, I found him quietly sticking together chips from an old teacup. "Oh, take a small loss, why don't you?" I said. "But it was Mother's," he moaned. "Part of the Crown Derby." "Well, its little gold swirls don't line up anymore," I zinged and thought to myself, I'd be happy if the rest of the set broke, too.

Suppose I was hard on him but someone had to be practical. Too close to his mother, no siblings to share the load. She let me know I was never good enough for her one-and-only. A real piece of work, she was. Drifted around, all Sarah Bernhardt, hand to forehead, no focus. At least I did volunteer work. Years of running the Red Feather campaign and the women's auxiliary at two hospitals. In charge of the Christmas parties, up to my eyes in glitter and glue. Got high on the fumes, just like those hippies, I suppose, felt all queer. The Age of Aquarius, whatever that was. One day, I said to the girls, "I'd like to try some of those funny cigarettes, that marijuana stuff. Just to see what would happen." They looked alarmed and disappeared into the woodwork.

Mahogany it was. "Just sell the damn thing," I waved over at Jack's pride and joy, the Chris-Craft that never worked. He shook his head, hands at ten and two, turning the steering wheel back and forth, and grinned up at me. "She's a beauty, sleek and smooth, rides the waves so proudly. Just needs the right touch. Reminds me of you." Then he patted the red leather seat beside him and his big hazel eyes went all moony. There I was, left with a mouth full of teeth. It took me back, I must say. Quebec City, the final farewell, after so many false starts. Same sad eyes but the brave smile that said, "this is it." Donned his officer's hat, straightened his tie and jacket, and stepped out into the war.

Loved his boats the way he loved his girls. Didn't mind that I couldn't produce a boy, just three girls, after six attempts. When the son-and-heir died, seven months in utero, I was lying in a Catholic hospital bed, on Christmas Eve. Crosses on the walls, everyone tiptoeing, clutching their rosaries, praying to Saint this-and-that. I thought I'd never make it. Then, in marched Jack's best man, the six-foot heart surgeon, straight across the room, just like that.

He put his foot up on the windowsill and stared out at the snow, twinkling in the moonlight. "Oh, Holy Night," indeed. "Poor little bugger never had a chance. But you've got three healthy girls. That's more than most." He turned, and patted my blanket on the way out. Well, that was all the bedside manner I needed. Pulled myself together and never looked back. Besides, most sons of doctors never amount to much. He might have been an artist, though, and that would have been something.

We could have painted together at the lake. It was Grand Hotel most of the time down there. Never a dull moment. Friends would come from the city for the weekend. Everyone dressed in old plaid shirts, let themselves go. Steaks on the barbeque, lots of clever drinks. Late one night, there was a huge racket in the hallway. The girls jumped out of bed. "It's all right," I called, "It's just Mr. Price falling down the stairs. Probably needed the bathroom and turned left instead of right." His wife hauled him back into bed and silence reigned once again. Next day, there he was, sleeping it off in the hammock, never the worse for wear. His *avoir du poids* must have cushioned the blow.

Well, those sailing races were something. Dotty, old Leslie was the Commodore, not quite up to Tuesday but he got the job done. We'd tow the Enterprise down the lake at half speed, the girls all nervous in the back seat. Who would win this week? That handsome fellow in the Y Flyer or one of the Brody family, as usual. The daughter was pretty swift at the helm. Everyone jockeying for position at the start. My hands would be all stiff and cramped, clutching the sheet. Those were the days before jam cleats. Jack would jibe neatly, just as the cannon fired and we'd slide out, ahead of the fleet. Our finest hour, his grin ear to ear, as we flew along the course, shrouds singing in the wind. "Always keep them guessing," he'd laugh, his tanned face and crisp, white collar profiled against the blue sail.

    Nobody dresses anymore. The girls flew me to Toronto that time for Swan Lake, Karen Kain's farewell. It was gorgeous. There we were, front-row-center, tears streaming down, flinging roses onto the stage. I could have died right then, it was heaven. But we stumbled out into the lobby and the scruffiest people were standing around. Army boots and crinolines, jeans with holes, tacky little outfits. What's happened to a sense of occasion, basic black and a string of pearls? It's all gone downhill.

    Viv would fit right in, with her funny little ankle socks and rubber soles. Lost her marbles, most of them, crazy as a loon, after that cyclist knocked her down. It was her own fault, jaywalking like that. Couldn't get her to smarten up. She gained all that weight, eating nothing but ketchup. They gave her those psych tests, asked her to draw a clock. So, she drew a fancy Swiss one, said that was her flying over the cuckoo's nest. *Touche!* I tried to get her interested in walking again but she said she didn't like the wind in her ears. Made her nervous. "Well, you're not going to fly away," I told her, "besides, I've given away your broomstick." She looked at me all queer. Finally, she had her own head injury.

    Well, my youngest came to see me, with this cloudy looking drink. I took one sip and almost gagged. "It's a London Fog, Mum," she said, "Earl Grey, like the olden days, in Nana's good cups. Remember, after school?" She's always so cheerful, that one, despite the sad divorce, a real Pollyanna. Everything's a nursery rhyme. And that hugging business with her kids, far too clingy. Surprised she could tear herself away from them long enough to visit. "Nonsense," I clucked, "milk and sugar ruin it." "I love you too, Mum." She smiled and squeezed my hand. "Not so hard, dear. Brittle bones." I'm forced to remind her that I'm not one of her workout pals. Looks like a racehorse, all sinewy and strained. "What happened to that nice round face?" I asked. "I finally lost my baby fat," she laughed.

    I wasn't always so frail. All those years skiing in Switzerland. Then, suddenly, my bindings wouldn't release and I was sliding down the Jungfrau. They hauled me to the hotel in a toboggan, wrapped like a mummy, in some rough old canvas, couldn't understand a word they said, all in *Schweizerdeutsch*. Well, Chevrolet coupé was all I could manage. A shot of cortisone and back in the game, we used to say. Thank God, it finally kicked in when they taped my ankles. Jack insisted we fly home for x-rays and casting but I didn't want to ruin the party. Besides, every night, I was carried into the bar, in the arms of a big, strong lederhosen. Swiss fondue indeed.

Best time of my life. Feet were never the same but who needs rotation? It's forward motion that counts.

Always walk into a store as if you owned it, I'd tell the girls. Holt's is the worst. Those little salesclerks, with their nothing salaries, sneering at me, in my Aquascutum and Liberty scarf. Just because I'm not wearing my mink today. I have a purse full of credit cards. can take taxis everywhere, and stay in a hotel, if I want, any night of the week. It's all those years travelling the world, one has a certain *savoir-faire*. Ne Plus Ultra—that was Jack's beloved whiskey—from the Highlands. Humble beginnings, though, he'd remind me. Born in a small town, buried in a simple pine box. "No one is any better than anyone else," he'd say, "It's not right to put on airs."

Even so, you must always show you're a lady. What's this dropping into a chair that you girls do? Letting go, as if you were cut off at the knees. Would it kill you to ease yourself down gracefully? You may well laugh but one day, you'll remember, especially with girls of your own. Let's see if you can do better. Don't tell them how gorgeous and smart they are. You don't want them all full of themselves.

They say I'm seventy-eight pounds. That doesn't sound right. I was always one hundred twelve and five-foot-two. What do they mean four-foot-eight? Maybe it's metric. I just don't seem to have the energy for meals. But I wouldn't say no to a dry martini. Tanqueray of course or Bombay Sapphire. Is this the Ritz? Well then, yes, very dry. Can you just pull up the blanket a bit? Not that awful orange one, the green. Where are those girls when I need them? Never visit, never phone, never write. They grow up and have their own kids and then they're no good to you anymore. That's it, right up over my ears. Hmmm. Yes, with a twist, on the rocks, lots of rocks.

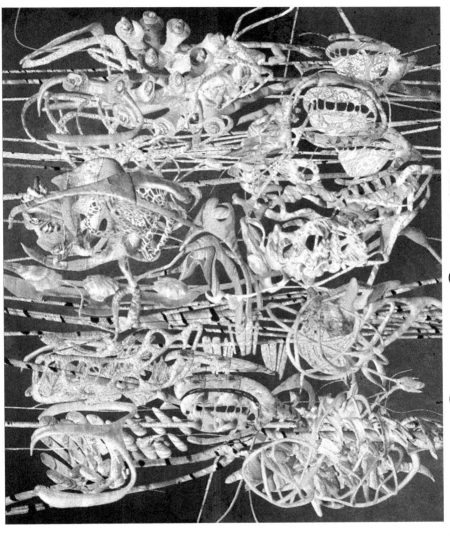

CHEBYSHEV SPECTRAL OVERCAST / RYOTA MATSUMOTO

Recursive Topography of Uncertainty / Ryota Matsumoto

Swimming Lessons

Virginia Watts

Of course, it was a privilege to take swimming lessons at the community center. I never had to swim alone there. Never a private lesson. Always a group lesson. Sixteen of us middle schoolers doing the same drills, attempting the same skills. I could never breathe right for him. That rotary breathing required for freestyle. I cheated. I had to. And he always caught me, even when he turned his back on my body slicing through the rippling, chlorinated waves churned by the moving arms and kicking legs. Even as he retraced his steps to the other side of the pool, something he did constantly throughout every thirty-minute session, he knew how I would react when he caught me again. Pacing the pool deck, pacing the pool deck, he kept catching me and catching me and catching me.

She was young, my daughter. An undergraduate. Inexperienced, yes, but so smart. I knew and I know how brilliant she is, how clever and funny, and how much does the average woman of nineteen, as she was at the time, how much does the average woman of such a new age possess in the column of life experience and how much self-determination can any person truthfully claim without more life experience than that?

I didn't like anything about the windowless women's locker room in the basement of the community center until I disliked the basement pool even more. Then I dreamed of climbing the ladder, grabbing my towel and scurrying back there, pool water dripped onto floors always colder than it feels inside the pool. The locker room, at first, made me gag. It reeked of bleach. Long, dark hair coiled in the shower drain. Coppery growth along the shower curtain hem like an old man who has dipped his white beard in beef stew unaware. A bright menstrual pad tossed carelessly into an open trashcan, no coat for her shoulders. Band aids reproducing, multiplying. One fleshy circle wiggling up between my toes.

Something made me think of my old swimming teacher as I soon as I saw that guy's bare chest, smooth and muscled, blood cascading over a mountain of a shoulder. Adonis swathed in ebony ooze chiseled against a blurry backdrop. A black-and-white photograph from social media. He looked too good to be good. It was fake, the blood. A play or something. It doesn't matter at all. What matters is she met him in a class. It doesn't matter that this guy from my daughter's class had a name I had often used when writing fiction stories, but it was a tad creepy and I never use that name now. There were things he said to her in class before what happened, happened, that were dismantling and demeaning and as accurate as guided missiles launched to belittle her, to set her up, but that's all hindsight now.

The swimming pool was startlingly opulent for something erected underground beside the furnace room and janitorial supply closet. High ceilings. Pillars worthy of a Grecian temple, inlaid mosaic tiles and two enormous stained-glass windows high above the pool that delivered light to people jogging around a balcony track. Pounding steps and squeaking sneakers mostly drowned by the baritone boom of his voice, his shrill, silver whistle. The echoes that deafened and deafened and deafened. *Take your mark! Pull! Pull! Pull! Kick! You aren't kicking! KICK!*

There had been no previous lunches for my daughter with this guy from her class, no preliminary walks, cups of coffee, dinners out or movies. There had been nothing before and there would be nothing after that one time she was with him alone.

In rotary breathing, when you turn your head to the side, you are supposed to open your mouth and take in the air of the world. Then you close your mouth and put your whole face, and here I mean your whole face, back down in the water and blow your guts out. In a pool crowded with bodies that's a lot of carbon dioxide to ask a stagnant ditch to handle. Don't you think? And don't you think it's very logical to wonder whether when you roll your head to the side and open your mouth, you might miss the air completely and drag only water into your alveoli? I did try to master rotary breathing. I tried very hard. The harder I tried, the faster my heart beat. Vice grips descended and clamped around my ribs. His voice the dark charm that spun the crank tighter and tighter. Eventually, my lungs didn't want anything to do with air anymore. *Find some other way to oxygenate the blood you need.* I sputtered and spit. Gulped and choked. Halfway across I had to stop swimming, tread and float. *LANE THREE! WATTS! MOVE! MOVE! MOVE! EVERY TIME!* Gasping, I'd start in again for the other side.

That guy tore my daughter. Ripped her. Multiple tears. Made her hurt and bleed for three days. I worried her heart would be unable to work the same way it had before that night. *Find some other way to oxygenate the blood you need.* But thankfully, there is goodness along with evil and that never came true. A promised car ride to a restaurant swapped last minute by him for an excursion to his apartment. Probably the moment right there she could have refused. Hindsight. In some ways, I wish she had been drunk so details would be blurry, but that's not how it went. The access to his apartment a narrow corridor, the inside modern, clear-surfaced, impersonal, as if the space had been leased furnished and decorated, and he never changed or added a thing. One abstract painting hung centered on the wall above the living room sofa. His bedsheets were black. And let me be clear. She let him, even though it wasn't what she wanted. She didn't know what would happen. She didn't know what to expect. She didn't know what to do. He was the size of a grizzly. When she didn't want to kiss him at first, she felt the shape of his fingers come up around her throat. What was he was capable of? Frozen in a slow-motion moment in time, she let it play out as he repeated this phrase in her ear: *I could do this all night.*

WATTS! STOP SPUTTERING! WATTS! NO FULL BREATHS! NO BREATHING OUT! ONLY BREATHE IN! STOP! WATTS! WATTS! NO FULL BREATHS! ONLY IN! ONLY IN! WATTS! STOP!

But I didn't stop. I kept coming back, trying to do what he wanted me to do as he yelled louder and louder, paced faster and faster. I skipped breakfasts and lunches, unable to chew, lost sleep the nights before, trembled in the back seats of station-wagon carpools. Mothers of friends asked, *Do you have a fever?* Never opened my mouth. Never told parents how terrified I was of / him / his echoing voice / his shocking whistle / his massive chest. Never told them I was terrified of swallowing so much water I'd die trying to do something I didn't want to do in the least. If I had told them, I am sure they would have allowed me to quit, but I felt too silly and irrational and smaller than a little pink circle band aid, so I kept going back, the stained glass in the balcony like church windows with no choir of allies peering benevolently down. Those gemstones of color, sapphire blue, ruby red, emerald, and topaz waiting for me to launch myself back into the water. Brilliant birds perched on dark tree branches with green and yellow leaves, some of them just spreading their wings, ready to take flight.

My daughter sought medical treatment the following morning. Upon examining the ravaged condition of her vagina, the doctor in Montreal asked repeatedly if the incident had been consensual, urged her to have a discussion with the police "anyway," tried to persuade her to see a therapist at the very least. My daughter refused. The doctor scheduled subsequent appointments to see her again, repeated these pleas, resorted to scheduling more and more appointments not entirely medically necessary. My daughter stopped going to see her, began ignoring her calls and her messages, desperate to gather distance from the incident and move on. She will always remember this fellow woman with eternal gratitude, her face, the sound of her voice, her kindness and compassion, how she tried everything she could think of to help her. Of course she should have listened to the advice. Hindsight.

    I know what you are thinking now. These stories are starkly different. They are. My swimming coach wasn't really trying to drown me. My daughter's story is the opposite. But there is something excruciatingly the same about the young girl and the young woman. Both of them holding off too long, not believing enough in their own instincts, their own power. My daughter is the daughter I dreamed of and hoped for. I have been steadfastly proud of her in all the moments of her life. After that night, she grew stronger than before, as the life behind us does for all of us, and then, she went further. She is triumphant. She soars. Of course, she is the clear victor transcending the depth and dark sheets. She's not looking back. She has no reason to. Nor do I.

BURNING

Robin Bissett

She was always burning, especially in the evening, when the sun began to set and her thoughts refused to slow.

We walked down to the lake, sat on the edge of the dock, and dipped our feet into the still water. I wrapped my arm around her shoulders and pulled her close to me. She shivered, goosebumps sprouting along the edges of her round arms. This time was, at least, more peaceful than the others.

Once, she had held me at gunpoint and demanded I take off my mask. At first, I had laughed along with her, then cried, then screamed, saying over and over. *Baby, I'm not wearing a mask.* After language failed us, I finally grabbed my blue pocket knife and sliced open the right side of my forehead. *Do you see now?*

Later, facing the mirror, I applied Neosporin and dabbed at my thin wound with a damp paper towel. She came up behind me and wrapped her arms around my stomach. Head wounds may bleed profusely, and those of the heart seldom heal without leaving behind a scar.

Another time, she had come into my office, demanding I stop working on my laptop and listen to her interpretation of her most recent dream. I had nodded, eyes flickering between my computer screen and her violet-tinted face. She threw her bottle of water at me. It splashed all over my keyboard and the artificial life that sat atop my lap sparked one last time and died.

Now, I see her, running head on into the flames that threaten to swallow her whole. If I could take the pain away from her, absorb it into my own body, swallow the harvested toxins and clog up my bloodstream, believe me, I would. But, I cannot, so instead I let her rest her head against my right shoulder as we watch the light, a warm egg yolk, fall into the lake.
For now, me and the setting crimson sun, we stay beside her, thankful for the breaths of fresh air we catch in the midst of the brightest burns.

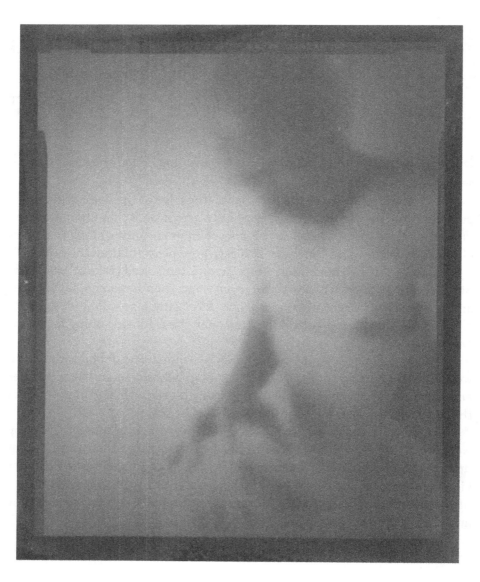

Untitled Zone Plate Photograph 1
/ Robert Oehl

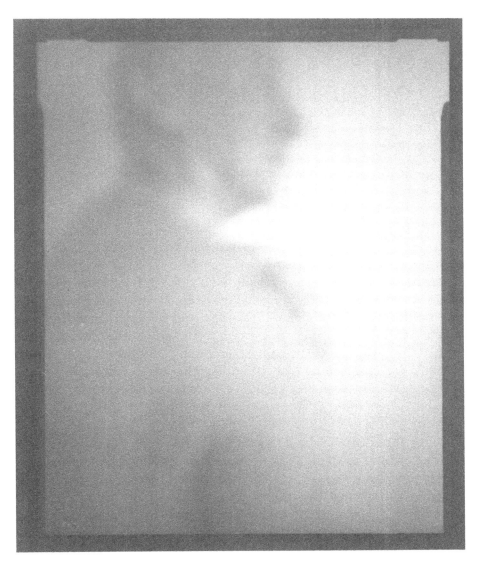

Untitled Zone Plate Photograph 2
/ Robert Oehl

The Other Margot at the End of the World

Zach Sheneman

On one particularly unbearable night in The Still, the other Margot admitted that the only reason she got clean was because it's impossible to find smack in the multipocalypse. We burned rubbish in an adjacent tenement, tried our damnedest to keep warm as a frozen tempest enveloped the streets. We shivered against the woolen fabric of the former occupant's Afghan. As the physics of the universe broke down—as reality morphed into impossibility before our glassy eyes—heat evaporated immediately into coldness, the shivering lick of warmth dying but a kiss away from my chapped lips. Untold months had passed since I'd felt anything more than cold; and yet, that same night, the other Margot peeled away, removed Chad's old UCLA sweatshirt, let the chill grace her bare shoulders.

"You're a fucking furnace," she said. "What is biologically wrong with you?"

In the feeble firelight, I saw the needle burns for the first time running up both arms. I didn't need to see the ones I knew ran down her legs to etch them with electric clarity in my mind. She spied me gawking, instinctively scratched the insides of her elbows. She ground her teeth, glared into our makeshift hearth, sniffed so hard the lone remaining stud threatened to dislodge from her flared nostril. She never took her hand from her arms.

I didn't know what to say. I settled on, "I'm pretty sure I ruptured my hymen when I was barrel racing at the Madison County Fair." It was an equivalent revelation in my mind. The other Margot stayed silent, lost in thought as she stared into the embers. I worried over how to bring her back from the wound I'd opened, but she wrapped back into the blanket, clasped my arm, curled into me.

"When you're dying long enough," she finally said against the crackling of the flames, "the strangest things start feeling like living." I didn't know what she meant and I didn't pretend like I did.

Later that night, she spoke about her addiction for the first time. She'd never had any illusions about what she was doing to herself Before. She'd started with the intention of never stopping. She thought she'd die high and only came up short when every drug dealer in the entire city had succumbed to the Great Quake, the tsunamis, the Illuminati bombings, the Second Coming of the Multitudinous Christs. She thought she'd die, too, sweating out poison in her apartment all alone. She never explained why. I suppose she didn't have to. There was a darkness there, just beneath her punctured skin, slithering around her organs like a tapeworm. She was unnaturally experienced with endings. She knew more about death than I ever understood about life.

My mom was the first person I actually knew that became a victim of the multipocalypse. She didn't die; at least, not in the conventional sense. She was in the middle of a lesson on valence electrons—on volatile elements and inert gases and everything in between—when she, the janitor, and two dozen students disappeared in anticlimactic silence from their respective outfits. I was halfway through a shift at Kozlowski's Collections when my paternal grandma finally overcame the overburdened communications satellites. "Your mother has been Raptured," she said, an absolute accusation. She was, like my dad had been before he died, devoutly Christian Reformed, and had always viewed my mom's atheism as a calculated affront on the entire Christian religion. I pulled off my headset with my grandma still on the line, choking back sobs as I ran to the fourth-floor women's bathroom and wept openly on a tampon-clogged toilet. I stepped out an hour later, but only after I'd attempted to reapply my eyeliner with my hand shaking so violently that I came back to my cubicle looking like Marilyn Manson after a grand mal.

Back then, before shit *really* hit the fan, every loss was fresh, every death unparalleled. The Rapture took more lives than the coastal flooding before it, which killed more people than the sudden sinkhole pandemic had in the weeks before. After the Rapture, everyone lost somebody close enough to them that the calamity that followed felt almost tedious to endure.

All to say, then, that my mom would have loved and hated the absurdity that followed. It stuck to the script of any genre show I'd seen on Netflix—the armageddons both natural and manmade: innumerable comets on a crash course for Earth; the bees and the frogs and the coral reefs and the Amazon all fucking off into the sun; Kashmir and North Korea and, quite inexplicably, Luxembourg, all disintegrated in a thermonuclear hailstorm. I remember one particularly bad strain of infectious disease that ran down the entire West Coast from Vancouver.

"What happened to Angela in HR?" I asked a coworker. "She was just here Friday. I borrowed her hair tie."

"She's gone," he shrugged. "Whole family came down with Ebola. Heard it was pretty gruesome."

I tried my damnedest to think about my fallen comrade, to focus on my ill-fated sister-in-arms, but all I could worry about was the prior Friday's hair tie. My skin itched the same way it did whenever someone talked about head lice. That was back when there were still jobs, still coworkers, still the thinning expectation that things were going to turn around. That was the moment I started becoming numb to all of it—to shock, to empathy, to every stab of grief.

With as strange as things became, I could only laugh that my mom, the lifelong atheist, rotted in someone's Heaven somewhere, apparently bare-ass naked. Not long after she started crashing on my futon, I asked the other Margot about where she thought her parents might be. "Court-mandated marriage counseling," she said reflexively, lashing black paint onto the easel she'd stolen from the long-abandoned art studio four blocks down on Lakeside Boulevard. The paint hit the canvas in razor-thin lines and spread out a smidgen, the paint bleeding out from each stroke as if she'd cut the canvas with a bullwhip. I thought about my scientist mom, long removed from this abused and lifeless lump of clay, and then I watched the other Margot make Jackson Pollack goth art with forty shades of darkness in my cluttered apartment. Mostly, I thought about valence electrons—about unstable elements—about colliding in the chaos and never coming apart.

The night we met, the moon exploded. It shattered in the way a Faberge egg might if dropped from a sufficient height—detonated into a trillion glistening shards of stale rock and 1970s moon rover parts. The nebulous cloud of lunar dust scattered a few rays of red light from the dying sun across all of creation, drenching my corner of the apocalypse in ruby glitter like some sort of demonic disco ball. I faced the night sky a few moments into the mayhem and watched it fracture in silence. It should have been tragic, maybe even beautiful. I found it a bit underwhelming.

She stood at the foot of a weathered fountain at the center of Monument Park, the neighborhood hangout Before for drug dealers, hookers, and the homeless. For a moment, I saw her as a hobbit's shadow in the crosshairs of my flashlight, but as my eyes adjusted, I beheld her as she truly was: a four-foot-nothing Joan Jett wannabe comprised of an amalgam of punk haircuts, a face full of cheap metal, and absolutely no capacity to choose a single color with which to accentuate her black hair.

"Hey," I called across the way, wincing at the warbled sound of a voice I hadn't heard in weeks. "You going to kill me? I'm not necessarily against it, but I have a few ground rules about facial disfigurement and cannibalism we'll need to hammer out first."

Her gaze snapped from the murdered moon to my gangly Slenderman silhouette in the distance. She said nothing. As I shuffled closer, I watched as she held herself and shivered. I considered walking away, seeking heat in my bed under the fourteen blankets I managed to accumulate in my looting. Twelve months into the various ends of the world, it was both easier and safer to leave everything to die at its own speed.

"Hold on," I muttered, fishing out a strike-anywhere matchbook from my back pocket. "There's bound to be something to burn in this apocalyptic shithole."

I shone my flashlight around the park until I found an overturned trash bin still surrounded by a smattering of its previous contents. "Come help me with this," I grunted, struggling to lift the steel receptacle from the frozen dirt. "It's heavy. All five of my meals today consisted of Town House crackers, so, you know. Not a lot of 'go' power right now."

Tiny Joan Jett hesitated, sized me up as I cursed and kicked at the rubbish strewn about.

"Look, I'm pretty sure like, one hundred and five percent of serial killers are men, so I think the statistics are in your favor here."

I doubt what I said actually made any difference, but the child-sized woman shuffled over, extended her tiny hands, helped me to right the trash can. We tossed Five Guys bags and Styrofoam cups back into it, and I wasted fourteen matches as I futilely attempted to start the fire. I went to strike a fifteenth match, but the Monument Park vagrant held out an outstretched finger. Within seconds, she produced a Zippo, which she used to ignite an *L.A. Times* from eight months ago and dropped it into the fire. Through the sickly moonlight, flakes of snow started to fall, and I groaned.

"I told my parents I was moving out of Nebraska to get away from this nonsense." I shrugged as I blew hot breath into my hands. "To be fair, I'm pretty sure Nebraska is just the real-life *Hunger Games* at this point."

The stranger nodded, her shivering wracking her entire body. After a few minutes of thawing out, she peered across the fire and in my general direction. She said, "I'm Margot."

I sighed. "Me too." Somehow, even after a year of suffocating in absurdity, this implausibility irritated me more than anything. "What a crock of shit."

We huddled close to the fire, passing the time with awkward small talk and craning our heads to the heavens to watch the moon as it fell to literal pieces. Once the feeling returned to my exposed nose and cheeks, we left for my apartment together. In the world Before, I might have found it unsafe to bring a stranger home to sleep on my futon and eat my gas station candy bars and drink my hoarded Dasani. In the multipocalypse, though, we were likely amongst the select living few in a city that only months ago teemed with millions. *The world Before*, I mused as I waved the other Margot forward down the snow-kissed avenue. The wind whistled as we navigated the stairwells of my abandoned apartment building, the broken moon obscured by billowing snow. We didn't speak a word as we trudged across the newly minted tundra. The fire still burned when we left it to die.

It became apparent to me and any semi-rational human being in a short manner of time that the end of the world was not singular or anything less than positively ludicrous. It started with the Rapture, which most people in America at least saw as absolute proof in the existence of the Christian God. Their self-assured spiritual swagger was short lived; by the end of the next day, every major news outlet projected live feed of the Norse God Odin in a brutal fistfight with Kalki, the tenth avatar of Vishnu, onto every television on the planet. This wasn't the two Monument Park Jesuses getting into fisticuffs over a pair of thong sandals, either. The two warring gods leveled city blocks with conjured magic. Civilians screamed as they shielded their babies with their bodies and then liquefied in their holy light. The desolation was shocking and appalling and absolutely total.

What had started as a sobering but natural reminder of the finite nature of life devolved quickly into a demonstration in supernatural absurdity as a groundswell of gods and goddesses materialized and terrorized the planet. Every god brought his diabolical and über-powerful foil to Earth with him, flooding the planet with countless demons and devils and trickster gods and titans. The mighty Ahura Mazda could level the entire Persian empire with a flick of his finger. Instead, he preoccupied himself with mud-wrestling his nemesis Ahriman, the Zoroastrian god of darkness.

I didn't know Sekhmet from Imhotep before I met the other Margot. When she began her occupation of my living room in my apartment, she brought with her the *Jeopardy!*-level trivia lodged in her brain from her community college World Mythology class. On the rare occasions we caught word from passing refugees about the most recent holy heavyweight to blight the region, the other Margot filled me in over a can of cold Chef Boyardee mini ravioli. She lamented that we never seemed to get lucky with a party god like Bacchus, that we were constantly showered in brimstone and sulfur and not wine coolers and dynamite sex.

I sometimes wondered what my heathen mom would have thought about this whole mess back Before, in the time preceding her abduction by my dad's God. I alternated on any given day between the hope of my making it into my own personal heaven and the despair of wondering if I could have gotten into a better one. In The Still, I asked the other Margot which god she was backing, what eternal life she most desired to achieve. "If everyone was right," she shrugged, black paint dry at her fingertips, "then everyone was wrong." I rolled my eyes and left her to paint alone. She had a knack for ruining everything. I was also afraid her cynicism wasn't entirely off the mark.

She was the one who first called it The Still. After nearly two years of air inundated with screams and wails and smog-induced gagging, the pandemonium quite literally died out. Once the sandstorms stopped raging and the acid rain cleared up, the tumult ceased. At first, the silence was unendurable. In every moment, we anticipated something more sinister lurking around each corner, so we camped out in my apartment for a week straight, taking turns peering through binoculars from the balcony and surveying the desolate hellscape below. Once I finally found the stones to leave the apartment, I stalked the city armed with a Cutco knife, a piece of lead piping, and some brass knuckles I'd looted from a pawn shop. Not a mouse nor maggot had survived the total desecration of the world.

That first night out alone in the city we sat on the five, feet dangling over the edge of the concrete barriers on the overpass, eating spoonfuls of crunchy peanut butter and marveling at the other Margot's ability to see the gold flecks of the Milky Way for the first time in her life. The next morning, using old tube socks for mittens and wrapping ourselves in some of Chad's old Bruins sweatshirts, the other Margot and I sojourned out into the tundra of Southern California and laid waste to each other in a snowball fight square in the middle of Seventh Street. When the sun would set, we would watch the light glimmer off the powdered down, a crimson glaze shining off of the snowfields that stretched from the city to the horizon. We tore insulation from empty buildings and superglued the cellulose to our walls. Some nights we'd build a fire on the balcony and huddle together for warmth; on others, we would lie under a dozen comforters and tell stories about the women we were Before.

    It was in The Still that I caught the candid whole of her in the wavering sunlight. I would wake to find her wrapped in blankets in her nest on my living room futon and reading de Beauvoir or Vonnegut, overgrown eyebrows furrowed as she squinted through the smudges of her glasses. The buzzed portions of her hair had grown out, the blue streaks faded to a twilight sheen over her sable locks. Tangles of dirty hair framed her slight face, curled toward cushioned lips. In the preceding weeks, her paleness had dissipated as the drugs left her system. She'd also gained some weight, an inevitable result of a Hostess Donettes diet that fortified her frailness with substance. There was a fullness to her that wasn't present when we first spiraled into each other, a dimension gained from losing everything. The other Margot was unbathed, disheveled, wild—and, quite suddenly, the kind of beautiful that transmogrified me into an anxious idiot.

    I resisted my growing attraction to the other Margot because I feared it to be a case of interest by proximity. It had been a fairly sexless multipocalypse across the board, and I longed to be caressed by hands and kissed by lips and desired by someone as desperate for attention as I was. I could sense the tension from her when we passed each other in the kitchen, when our glances collided from across looted convenient stores, when we huddled together for warmth under Princess Moana comforters. Eventually, I spent my time finding awkward excuses to stay as physically far away from her as possible without simply throwing myself off the balcony.

    Perhaps sensing my trepidation, she leaned in one night during a game of Uno, her breath hot in my ear. "You look like you might need a little help," she whispered, inching her delicate fingers under my blanket and up the seam of my cotton sweatpants. I shivered at her touch, bowed my head, shifted on the futon as every muscle in my lower body seized involuntarily. My breath quickened as she leaned in carefully.

"This is," I managed, "new for me."

She pulled back, cupped an icy hand against my hot-blooded cheek, softened her gaze as she looked up at my face. In that moment, behind those endlessly dark eyes, she might have thought about it, too: about the lovely convenience of our closeness, about whether our chemistry was simply a product of supremest loneliness. She hesitated, started to pull away, and instinctively I pulled her face to mine—kissed it—caressed its contours in all of its glorious coldness—pressed against her so aggressively that I nearly knocked her incisors clear out of her mouth. That night, the other Margot pulled me under a half dozen blankets and would not come up for air until the whole of it was no longer new for me. I suppose that, even Before, love's always been more than a little about proximity.

Before the other Margot, there was Chad. Truth be told, there was a string of Chads preceding her, a line of utterly milquetoast and smarmy young suitors, each Chad in the progression slightly Chadder than the last. The final specimen, the ultimate Chad, was pleasant enough, someone I didn't have to be embarrassed about when I brought him around my girlfriends and inoffensive-looking enough to include in my social media pictures. We'd seen each other in some capacity on and off for two years but only knew each other in strangely superficial ways. He knew I could burp the entire alphabet, that my left boob was smaller than my right; I knew he was afraid of the dentist and had no concept of how to navigate a vagina. I dragged him on occasion to work parties and he coerced me into paying for us to see every unnecessary *Transformers* sequel. We settled for each other in blissful compromise, never demanding much of each other, orbiting each other in periphery and possessing each other so we each could have something to possess.

Somewhere between GMO-induced brain death and super-SARS, Chad wound up moving into my apartment. Initially, I didn't mind; as the looting and rioting proliferated, it felt like a good thing to have backup in an increasingly dangerous world. I quickly realized that our obligatory cohabitation was the greatest threat to our survival. No one had prepared me for the grotesqueness of living with a man—the pissed-upon bathroom floors, the body hair choking my sink, the inability to rinse a dish after eating from it—and yet we were trapped together in an apocalyptic Roach Motel. Chad appeared equally horrified to live with me, the audacious candor of my mere existence as an actual woman annihilating his shallow construct of the feminine mystique. His revulsion at my natural state—at my freedom from having to impress him for any reason at all—satisfied me in ways his dick never managed to.

We lived in discord until Jesus came. He landed a dozen time zones away in Jerusalem, but the infrastructure of the world still held on like the last tenuous stretch of skin clinging to a nearly peeled scab, so we still had internet. We watched the video postings every morning of whatever new lunatic had arrived in cataclysmic fashion while we slept. Up to that point, our newfound awareness of the existence of lesser spirits and demigods had no effect on Chad, but the Lord Jesus got to him. As Chad watched the sandaled Son of God descend upon Golgotha to a cosmic light show that would make Pink Floyd blush, I watched something change behind his eyes.

The first few nights after the Second Coming, Chad simply didn't speak. It was enough of a relief that I didn't question the blessing. The dynamic shifted dramatically from bliss to discomfort when I walked in on him praying before dinner, which felt somehow more invasive than the time I opened his old apartment door to find him in a compromised position involving *Swordfish*, a gym sock, and a bottle of baby oil. After one night of scavenging, he brought back a copy of the NIV nestled between a carton of cigarettes and an entire dorm's worth of Ramen. Soon after, he stopped going out altogether. In short order, he started packing his bags for his last crusade.

"A few of the guys from the Y downtown heard that there's a flight heading out from Vegas in a week and they're taking everyone they can to Jerusalem," he informed me, stuffing a duffel bag full of hair paste and Listerine. "Please come, Margot. I mean, this Jesus thing is the real deal."

I scoffed. "We haven't seen or heard a plane around here for the last two months. You think I'm going to strap myself in for a mystery flight with poor man's Captain Sully and the cast of *Fury Road*?"

Against every one of my better instincts, I tried to get him to stay with me, but his mind was made up. I promised him that his "Jesus" was a false prophet, some standard-issue fraud taking advantage of circumstance, but I was wrong. He *was* the real deal, the actual son of actual God, and he performed miracles beyond the scope of my imagination. Unfortunately, Jesus was Catholic Jesus, and Chad grew up Baptist. Catholic Jesus was not kind to his Protestant followers, calling pillars of fire down upon the poseurs amongst his worshippers and turning an awful lot of people into salt. To further complicate matters, Baptist Jesus *did* descend from heaven to Earth, although he arrived some time between Eastern Orthodox Jesus and

Presbyterian Jesus. I doubt Chad ever made it to Israel and, if he did, was surely destroyed with all the rest of those gathered in the supernatural carnage that ensued. By the time the videos stopped pouring in and my internet sputtered out, a thousand Jesuses had been at war with each other for weeks, fighting over whom so loved the world the most.

I tried to hate him for leaving me alone, but I couldn't blame the man for acting in his own interest. Everyone placed bets when the screws came flying loose. Chad put all of his chips on the most familiar horse and rode it straight into oblivion. My theory was that the reckoning came for everyone but those that shared our name, that strewn across the husk of the world were a few thousand Margots resisting the march of time. When I told the other Margot my hypothesis, she just laughed. She believed our perceived invincibility had less to do with supernatural circumstances than it did with what those circumstances forged us into. We were nothing at all before we were poured together into the crucible.

In every end-of-the-world movie I'd seen Before, society went to shit within days of whatever disaster befell it. In reality, the cogs in the wheel kept turning long after the car had died. Some hardnosed blue-collar unknowns kept the generators running even through super-volcanic eruptions, through fracking-induced earthquakes, through Jörmungandr and Thor tearing each other into pink meat. For me, however, grinding on past the world's expiration date became psychically exhausting. I continued working at Kozlowski's even as the cubicles emptied around me and HR stopped trying to fill them.

Working for a collection agency was already the occupational equivalent of a botched spinal tap, but trying to collect on whackadoodles at the various ends of the world proved to be the epitome of fruitless. The fact that we still had cable at the office was my sole motivation for going to work after the assorted divine started climbing out of the woodwork. It was my window into the multipocalypse: the reports on the fissures and power plant meltdowns; the havoc wreaked by magnetic pole reversal; the sudden emergence of AI in Japan and the resulting conquest of Kyushu. The Large Hadron Collider begat a tiny black hole that swallowed all of Sweden. Millions succumbed to brain cancer developed over years of cell phone use.

The night the New York Financial District succumbed to the epidemic of the undead brought on by fluoridated city water, the power finally cut and the flat screen in the break room *fwip*-ped off. I thought about ending it then. There appeared no point in protracting the misery of loneliness any longer. I knew some horrifying and absurd death lurked around one corner or the next. I thought about raiding the nearest pharmacy and washing down the remaining pills with a fifth of vodka far above my paygrade before falling asleep. I studied the texture of the primer on the ceiling in my bedroom, stored it in the part of my mind that used to remember the face of everyone I used to know. By the time the red morning light shone through my frosty window, I was determined to see the cosmic freak show to its illogical conclusion. The multipocalypse was going to devour all of existence before it was over. I wanted to be there when it did. I wanted to perch at its maw and quiver at the darkness.

Underneath the surface tranquility of The Still, existence still careened toward the end of its tracks. Time itself grew sick. Moments repeated, skipped in place like a scratched CD, leaving the two of us stuck on the same line of a joke or the same snark in an argument or the same orgasm for what would normally register as seconds, minutes, hours. I woke up once with a tragus piercing and a bottom-shelf tequila hangover with no recollection of how I'd earned either. It was a day the other Margot couldn't recall either, despite the fact that she managed to paint a twisted homage to Edvard Munch's *The Scream*, using my gangly likeness as inspiration. Entire swaths of our lives went missing from time to time as if someone had hit the skip button on a literal universal remote.

While gathering supplies one frigid afternoon, we found the trash can fire we'd lit months before in Monument Park still burning. We crouched behind a dead palm tree, craning our heads to see who might have started it, but after finding the fuel comprised of the same carry-out bags and Styrofoam cups I threw in the night we met, it became apparent that our initial bonfire simply never died. It flickered in slow motion, tendrils of flame swaying in a wind that did not blow. I moved close to the rusted can, took off my makeshift sock-mittens, held my hand up to the blaze—but felt nothing save the chill of the flurries falling from the sky above. The fire burned out of time with the rest of the world, and I could not feel its heat.

In the subsequent weeks, we noticed the desynchronization of time in all things. Tides waxed and waned on the hour; distant mountains ground to dust overnight; constellations burned out of the sky as we traced them with frostbitten fingertips. Scavenging became increasingly difficult as everything from food to tools dissolved in our hands. We awoke to find our clothes threadbare but the previous day's Cokes still carbonated. Life creaked on like that for some time, the two of us weaving in and out of time for seconds full of minutes, minutes full of days, days full of years. I fell asleep with her miniature body curled into mine and woke up with her a decade later. We stopped keeping track of time altogether as the laws of physics were purged in the great dumpster fire at the end of the cosmos; all the while, the other Margot and I made a home for ourselves, spending the prolonged days exploring what was left of the world and the endless nights exploring each other.

On one particularly tender evening in The Still—interlaced together in our bed, the other Margot's lashes fluttering against my neck, I murmured, "But really, how long have you loved me?"

"For at least a day," she said finally after a pause, "which is to say, in this place, maybe forever."

I knew something was wrong when I woke one morning to a painting hitherto unseen. With stunning luster and arresting beauty, the other Margot had painted my old farmhouse in Norfolk, a hand-me-down two-story gathering dust at the edge of the cornfield my grandfather had sold to the Murdochs decades before my father was a tax credit. I recognized the vantage point from a picture I kept on my bookshelf in the living room, a photograph faded almost beyond recognition from rapidly increasing age. Even with the source material diminished, the other Margot managed to capture the ripple of the cornstalks as a breeze raced through it. Her version of my childhood summers shot phantom sears of sunburn up my back.

"When did you paint this?" I asked when she entered the room with two fists of perfectly preserved rice cakes. "It's incredible."

"This last week," she said. "While you slept."

As time frayed, choice days ran slower for me than it did for the other Margot, only to snap back to the same pace further down the line. On unison days, time ran more or less equally for the two of us. Sometimes we lived in synchronicity for days, weeks even, reading books and scavenging the ruins and watching the moon grind to fine red powder. I suspected she hid many of the early days she spent alone to spare me the guilt. On shorter divergences, I caught her with a new cut on her hand or a freshly patched pair of jeans; on the longer jaunts, her hair was two or three inches longer than it was the day prior. When she sped forward, it was always while I slept. In The Still, I never lived a day without her by my side. The other Margot, however, lived an entire life away from me while I remained suspended in our bed, biding daunting swaths of time alone until I woke my very next day to see her.

In the space between my awakenings, the other Margot painted prolifically. Miraculously—perhaps mercifully—time left her paints and canvases untouched even as most of the world atomized erratically around us. On any given night, we kissed and clasped each other tightly and I would wake to find another painting, three paintings, twenty paintings of the world Before, each one exponentially more skilled and more staggeringly picturesque than the last. When she ran out of canvas, the other Margot crafted murals encompassing our apartment, the adjacent hallways, the face of the old brick building across the street. Her command of color shocked me, enthralled me, reminded me of both a world that once existed and a world that I'm sure never did. Time treated our slice of Armageddon more kindly than it did the rest of the world, save the other Margot—my Margot—who woke next to me with each passing morning more acutely grey and weary than the day before.

"How long were you awake without me?" I asked her one of my years into this exercise—at least fifty of hers—as I stroked the white hair away from her craggy worry lines.

"Three years," she whispered, voice hoarse, squeezing me as tight as she could with her feeble hands.

I stockpiled as many resources as I could when I was with her, knowing full well that I could not stock enough food for years at a time and that she could no longer brave the frozen desolation of the world outside alone. I fell apart one night stacking cans of pinto beans in the linen closet, slumped to the ground as tears crept onto my cheeks and immediately started to freeze.

"It's okay," she said, pressing my blearing eyes into her gaunt thigh. Her voice was tender. "I mean it. You've done everything you could. We've lived longer than we had any right to."

Maybe if I'd grown old, too, I would have attained her level of serenity or achieved her sense of acceptance. Instead, I sobbed against her diminished body and could not find the strength within me to stop. "You can't just stop painting," I finally choked. "You're just starting to get good."

For the first time in what may have been years for her, the other Margot smiled. We huddled on the remains of our futon, tag-teamed a Twinkie, dreamt of where we might have traveled together Before. She said Nepal, or Bhutan, or some other place I could never locate on a map. I wasn't paying attention. I stared at her, searing her existence into every fold of my brain. We shivered against each other like that for one, two, ten nights. Eventually, I woke up and she simply wasn't there. Any note or trace of where she'd gone had blown to dust some unknowable amount of time before. I lied in bed for hours and listened to the wind whip across the barrens, to the waves of ice crush against themselves on the shoreline. Outside my apartment, the world died at a thousand different speeds, equally hurtling and crawling toward oblivion. Inside of it, I died at the same pedestrian constant I'd managed my entire life before.

While the rest of us dodged the wrath of Ishtar or extraterrestrial invasions, the other Margot spent most of the early days of the multipocalypse hallucinating on the sheets in her old apartment. It took two full weeks, she once claimed, for her to realize that the screams and the sirens and shelling of the world outside her bedroom window were more than a side effect of the heroin occluding her mind. Amidst the fever dreams of withdrawal, the other Margot occasionally experienced moments of blinding lucidity. She would wake in the cooling night, stagger between the abandoned rooms of her building, force down a spoonful of peanut butter, fight the sensation of it creeping back up. She said she'd wander to the courtyard on the roof, stumble into the empty community pool, lie on her back and shiver under the starlight. Above the clamor of the world cannibalizing itself below her, she would stretch out a delicate, trembling finger and trace the stars, whispering the names of those she remembered as the poison licked at the edges of her consciousness.

On cloudless nights in The Still, she would point a steadier digit at the heavens from our favorite perch on the freeway overpass. She announced the constellations as she drew them, dreamily describing the princess Andromeda and her vainglorious mother, Cassiopeia, her hand deftly swaying against the deepest blue of the night as if the sky were her personal canvas. She spoke of the Pleiades and the goddess Demeter as if she knew them personally in a lifetime where she very well may have. All the while, I absorbed her in her fervent glory.

"Chaos to cosmos," she murmured, galaxies inside her eyes.

In her absence, for a time, I traced the stars too, many of them still obscured by remnants of the broken moon. I invented names for them, connected the surviving stellar dots in the ever-darkening sky. I drew the lines deliberately, taking great care to sketch the other Margot as sprawling and megalithic and gorgeous to behold. In the twilight of existence—in my final act of worship—I painted the last goddess to grace the Earth.

On her longest stint alone in The Still, the other Margot took up a grease pencil and drew the two of us together in front of a new moon menacing at the horizon, her head nestled against my breasts and my face buried in her dark hair. The strokes were black and heavy—some smudged lovingly, others etched with violent precision. Last night, I pried the canvas from our bedroom wall, rolled it up, trudged the four miles up the road to Monument Park. The towering high-rises of before were mostly ash and dust, either pulverized into some misbegotten shape or standing hauntingly unmolested against the new skyline of decay. The avenues had disappeared, replaced only with fused layers of ice and snow. Comet and meteors cut vermillion gashes into the void above me, the heavens always one fracture of time away from erasing the Earth from the cosmic record. As I approached my destination, an anemic light appeared ahead in the obsidian darkness. The trash can fire flickered on at the heart of the park, consuming the same debris I'd thrown in perhaps a thousand years before. Shivers wracked my body as I stood before its uniform, heatless light. I slid the drawing into the impossible flame. I imagined the canvas catching fire in another thousand years, the wind picking up its ashes and carrying it across the fields of the dead. When it became apparent that the sun was long past rising, I faced what I once knew as west and headed for the wintry coast. The fire still burned when I left it to die.

The Bridge / Hediana Utarti

Trevor in Tenby

Penny Jackson

He could only get one job, and that was calling the Bingo every Friday night. That Welsh winter in Trenby was so cold that the air cracked with rebellion every time he tried to breathe. The memory of Jamaica drifted warmly over his skin like a ray of sun. The Bingo Hall was a roller rink during the day, the scent of teenage sweat still sour it was only women at the Bingo, smoking unfiltered cigarettes, leaving ashy smudges on his cards. They treated Trevor like a celebrity – no one colored had ever been in their town. The women told him if you touched a "wog" it brought good luck. Their fingers felt like fat rolls of pastry. Some even pinched his arm so hard that it left a blue bruise. A few even touched his ass. One old woman, no teeth, spit spraying from her lips: "Come on love, let me grab you again." They winked at Trevor, rolled their eyes, and wriggled hips forever ruined by children. He could never remember the numbers called. If someone called BINGO he wouldn't bother to check. He remembered their words: *If you touched a wog the night was magic.*

In his bedsit Trevor could not scrub hard enough. The water was cold. The soap left a think white veil over his skin. To feel all the women's fingers all over again. As if his blackness would turn silver into their palms.

Come Live with Me and Be My Love

Michele E. Reisinger

Somehow, I acquired a dead man's interrupted life.

His grey stone cottage, mid-forest. Books, a barn, blank stationery veined with mold. Curled edge photographs stacked like kindling in a dusty hope chest. They claim me.

A rusted horseshoe slumbered in the cook stove. I burnish it with wire, secure its resurrected luck with a trinity of nails above the threshold. His ashes, scattered within the orchard, coalesce. Wonder.

The locals say he lived sad and died fierce.

Me, too.

I lower onto our front porch stoop and caress its sun-warmed face. Yes love, I say, as he approaches. Welcome home.

On No Account Should You Shout "Fire!"

Mary Byrne

> *And some rin up hill and down dale, knapping the chucky stanes to pieces wi'hammers, like sae many road makers run daft. They say it is to see how the warld was made.*
>
> Sir Walter Scott, *St. Ronan's Well*

Clinamen

You'd cooked the dinner: a big fresh fish on a bed of tomatoes (doctors would be pleased) in an earthenware pot on an outdoor fire.

Old friends and new (of whom I was one) cheered by wine and newness and dusk, I didn't know who lived where or with whom.

A muezzin sang out hoarsely from a minaret exotic against a rich sunset.

Storks settled to sleep in their huge nest.

When you offered me more fish, I swerved from predicted course, and things were never the same again.

History Recorded in Rock

After dinner everyone relaxed over cake and champagne. There was talk of a son, freshly graduated in geology, now hunting for gold in northern Canada. Outdoors on a warm July night, the candlelit company was enthralled by memories. You had barely left us. Someone asked if I could sense your presence still.

Each of us had a tale of yours: of the canoe that capsized, losing radio and food a week before the seaplane was due back, of the intense damp that made you light a stove in the tent at night so you could fill your notebooks, of a hat with a net against flies, of Native American cemeteries but no people as they'd moved south for the summer, of how pre-sliced white bread was flown in regularly – until one day the seaplane couldn't make the drop and it turned out the cook could make wonderful bread; and of how you all had pedometers because the land was so flat and wooded it was the only way to mark it out.

You laughed at the idea of such a summer, mocking yourself who had up to then imagined all summers Mediterranean. You never blinded us with science, you just smiled at our idea of old: "Old is billions of years," you said patiently.

Your green metal trunk was bumped and rusted, the paint missing in many places. For field missions you filled it with things like the rock hammer, the handheld loupe, compass, special pens for marking and the bags for carrying stones, knife, ziplock bags, plastic bottles, and the all-important notebooks with the squared pages in which notes were made by firelight in smoke-filled tents. You'd given up bringing medical gear and salves. All other bags were soft so they fit easily around things and you could use them for pillows. The trunk also contained tinned sardines, beans, toothpaste tubes a Russian colleague had cleaned out and filled with jam. You could make a fire anywhere, and once did so in a river bed just before a flash flood, then told the story against yourself. Once, you forgot the barbecue grill and made one by crisscrossing green twigs. When driving, you rarely spoke, too busy reading the landscape. It spoke to you in voices we couldn't hear.

The young people at the table that night were happy. I found their voices loud. I remembered that geology had only come into its own a century or so ago. Each generation has to find out for itself, and this will go on until there are no generations left.

The Lead-in

The cardiologist resembled W. C. Fields, shuffling amid a chaos of machines as elderly as himself. He asked you to describe how you felt. You shrugged. The doctor looked at me: "He's worse than the Normans."

The radiologist was only slightly younger, his office pristine, his secretaries noisy and efficient. He looked at your head, sat back in his chair and studied you. "Nothing unusual for someone your age who once smoked sixty a day."

The ENT man was young, decisive. When he put his camera-scope down your throat and saw the way you trembled, he said, "Not another millimeter without seeing a neurologist."

Your Man Charcot

In the latter half of the 19th century, French neurologist Jean-Martin Charcot transformed neurology and prepared the way for psychoanalysis. Among the things he discovered was a neurodegenerative illness that attacks the motor neurons of the brain and spinal cord, causing the brain to lose contact with muscles and leaving patients unable to swallow, talk or breathe. In another version of the disease, trouble walking is often the first problem noticed. In France it is called *Maladie de Charcot* (Charcot's disease). In English it is called a motor neuron disease (MND), specifically amyotrophic lateral sclerosis (ALS,) which Americans call Lou Gehrig's disease after the legendary baseball player who died of it in 1941. Because it is an "orphan," or rare disease, diagnosis can take time, in your case over a year. The disease attacks both young and old, all ethnic groups, more often men over fifty. Average prognosis at first symptoms is usually three to five years. Scientist Stephen Hawking went way beyond that, but some, like you, only get a matter of months. In all cases, the mind of the patient is unaffected, so they can watch and understand exactly what is happening to them. The end is usually caused by respiratory failure. The cause of the disease is unknown. There is no cure and no truly effective treatment.

Attic Insulation

It seemed a simple enough affair, to insulate the attic. It would make the house warmer. The dormice wouldn't be able to get in any more.

Sometimes a dormouse sat on top of our open bedroom door, studying us, as if to say, "You people really disturb us, you know." They'd already wreaked havoc with the previous insulation – we didn't know if they'd eaten it or taken it away: first we heard them gambol in it, then it disappeared.

You said, "If they managed to eat it, they'll survive the next big global mess, like cockroaches."

So I said, "Right, go ahead with the insulation."

But first we had to redo the roof.

I get vertigo, so all I saw of the roof work was the guys in my kitchen. The older roofer complained about having cold feet. The middle roofer just drank the coffee, a judgmental air about the set of his shoulders. He disapproved of chitchat but needed the coffee. The youngest of the three had a cherub's face and ears that pointed upwards like an elf. He smiled all the time. The older man said he'd seen self-heating boots advertised. He wondered how long the batteries would last. The middle man wondered if they worked on solar energy. The youngest looked like twelve years old although he was obviously old enough to be a roofer's apprentice. He said nothing and only spoke if asked a direct question. The others told us that he was doing extremely well at school where he attended one week in two, learning how to measure and calculate for estimates, how to mix lime even on a cold day, how to arrive at a shade of pointing the client would agree to. His smile wasn't a social thing: I later saw him smile to himself as he labored alone on some aspect of our roof on the coldest day of the year.

After the roof, we got down to the insulation. Dismayed by the sheer volume of the material and the weight of the various things that weren't the actual insulation itself, I was utterly at a loss to imagine how they would tack all these various layers onto our poor rafters.

"Might stop the roof blowing away during the next storm," you said.

It took huge amounts of brute force to manhandle all the stuff off the trucks and up the stairs before sawing and hammering and installing. And I felt, in a very little way, the strength and determination it takes to make war, to fight beyond one's own energy, beyond tiredness and pain, to the death. It dawned on me that, in spite of having a fair amount of brute strength myself, I didn't have the kind that some are made to, expected to, possess. This was why I would always seek compromise and conciliation, would always hang back from the bigger things, stick to being evacuated, godhelpus as my mother would say.

I felt very sorry for our dormice. In my very foxed copy of *Alice in Wonderland*, the dormouse was always nodding off, being bullied by the Mad Hatter and the March Hare who pushed his head into a teapot, and by the Queen who told him to shut up. I wondered if, once the insulation was over, it would be too late to get back to that original me, the one who read Lewis Carroll, was gentle and kind and dreamy and who, like the dormouse, would tell stories about girls who lived in a treacle well and ate treacle and drew pictures of objects beginning with M, and quite unlike the dormouse in the new film version.

On No Account Should You Shout "Fire!"

Day is just discernible through heavy fog. Across from us a row of little houses, one a cheery yellow with a light in the kitchen: how warm the coffee must be! How wonderful to ignore our grey side of the road with its over-cheerful nurses, its porters waiting in the night, its fire instructions (*On no account should you shout "Fire!"*), its empty sitting room, its notice announcing that someone hangs around to listen to our grief, its bookcase of disparate books clearly abandoned in the little rooms and bathrooms littered with notices (*Don't grab the grab-bar, it's not steady; Water 60 degrees – risk of burns*), and its table of magazines considering the misery of others: just how *is* Vanessa Paradis getting on without Johnny Depp?

In the hall, an ambulance man's jacket reads *Ambulances Malnuit'* (Badnight Ambulances). I wonder if he does the job because of his name, like the one who trims our hedges severely after a few scoops of homemade apple-brandy and whose name translates as *Bad Drinker*. Once, in Germany, I knew a doctor called Friedhof (cemetery) and an insurance man called Leich (corpse).

We are here to see the neurologist. He has already guessed what is wrong with you but has to examine you twice before pronouncing, his computer converting your twitches into graphs and screeches.

Finally both of you come back to his desk and the neurologist announces some of the disease's colorful names. He watches us carefully to see if we realize just how bad this is. Your version will see you lose your ability to speak, breathe, swallow (you will walk to the loo and play Scrabble till the end).

You ask no questions, so neither can I. You're relieved to put a name on it. You smile as you tell friends on the way home.

Before and After Photos

We took a narrow winding road down to the river bed. You sat on a rock watching the water's green reflection on the cliff on the other side. Electricity company warnings showed dramatic photos of the water level before and after the dam released water. This might take only a minute or two. We were exhorted to flee as soon as the alert sirens sounded.

You did one of your Gallic shrugs and we got out the kind of rough picnic you loved: garlic sausage, local fat cucumber with thick skin, flavorsome tomatoes. Where once you would have torn at the crusty bread and drunk your rosé with gusto, you ate little and stared at the water. Sometimes you dabbled your hand in it, as if amazed.

I took photos that day that I don't need to look at ever again: you so handsome in a black T-shirt with a work of art on the back, looking at me over your shoulder, the reflection of the water moving over the rock in the background.

The Parallel Universe of Country Life

Robert Frost could take his time over a poem. He didn't have distractions like emails and internet – let alone Twitter – maybe a few leisurely letters, and he could go about his country business meditating on a phrase or a theme he might tackle: a dividing wall, a tree at his window. But life in the country has changed. Now I run between universes – preparing classes, driving to classes, teaching classes, feeding the cat, checking the stew on the stove, pulling ivy off the garage roof, tying up the wisteria detached by a big wind – sending an email confirming a review, confirming receipt of book for review, starting review of book that is about nothing in my present. Feed the stoves, bring in more wood, brush cluster flies out of the attic, peel apples for stewed apples, prepare fruit for jam. I do a lot of things while stuck between two universes: headset on, I listen to news of other places, to books being read. You make bread, call the roofer, the plumber, the electrician, the carpenter, the internet provider about glitches since the last storm. I click on an article that looks interesting. At the very same moment, the phone rings, someone knocks at the door, a tractor drives through the gate tearing a big branch off the pine which suffered during winter snow, my chair rolls two feet to the left, following the slope of the floor. I give up trying and go to sort things out downstairs. Better than pretending one can write anything, even in the country.

Search for a Lost Paradise

We talked about and planned the outing: *Search for a lost paradise: best of Austrian baroque,* the brochures said.

We flew. North of Rome, villages snuggled against soft hills in the sun. A dusting of snow over the Alps surprised us, darkening Vienna by four. Bussed to town without looking around, we jumped a bright warm train that dropped commuters all over a twinkling valley.

Late and cold we came to the Goldener Stern – reasonably priced and very old.

Above us it loomed in river fog, monstrous, yellow, unthreatened: Melk Abbey. We'd made it.

Frau X served beer to us, her husband and several of his peers. A giant spaniel slept at our feet (it was cold out, but here we could hardly stand the heat). Men like uncles of ours talked of cracks in vaults, cement and plaster, and how much time it would take to pay the bank back, after.

In time Herr X straightened himself and his apron to serve us soup, then sauerkraut with *knödeln*.

On the landing later we passed another dog, porcelain and grey, it watched over us all night.

Next day we climbed the steps through the great doors, wandered from room to room, heads thrown back, nonplussed by church walls dripping gold, then on its great terrace we tried for panoramic photos of the bend on the Danube. We pored over models of paradise (none of which was the one lost), watched videos of monasteries elsewhere – places to visit in other years – were disappointed with the cellars, linked arms through gardens in fog, listened to Mozart's *Apollo and Hyacinth* again and again, on special earphones.

In the staterooms a jeweled monstrance in the shape of a tree housed the jawbone of St Colman – an Irish prince – and miniatures of the instruments used to try and make him speak. On his way to Jerusalem, his strange tongue and clothes had forced a halt: Was he a Moravian spy? A Danube pirate smuggling salt from Traunsee to Bohemia? His Irish language and lack of German rendered him steadfast under torture. Once hanged, his scaffold came alive, sprouted leaves, his body incorrupt. The about-turn was abrupt: the Austrians made him patron saint, his day October 12th.

At day's end we reached the library of caged books, in room after cosy room they lay, in ornate cases beneath baroque ceilings: books about everything, going back centuries, collected by and for monks. Books.

Near the door the post, momentarily abandoned, of the library guardian, her own book open on a simple green table: the Austrian equivalent of *Hello* magazine.

Back down the town, the lights were lit. A lone Romanian, the only beggar we'd see, played accordion for the last of the stragglers in the fancy boutiques.

You and I had 'done' Melk, and Paradise was still nowhere to be found.

Hindsight

That time we ate in a five-star place in a tiny village in deepest Normandy: we were exploring. You liked to drive and walk and explore. Gourmet dining wasn't really your style, but there was nothing else within a huge radius. Deep France villages didn't do fast-food. The place was empty, even on a Saturday night, the owner-waiter smiling but distant, the food all right but nothing special, you'd have produced a feast at home with less. I wondered if they were on the way out, about to close, perhaps reheating yesterday's leftovers. You said nothing. I think now perhaps your illness had already begun, making you more patient, less critical. The pall of silence in the high-ceilinged room, empty of all but us, and we quiet too in spite of the wine, the stillness of a green Norman evening, the lack of music in reverence to food – Norman dining rooms sacred and somber as churches – the décor old-fashioned, smacking of the 19th rather than the 21st century. Looking back, all the silence and seriousness seems to me now a presage of the thing that was hiding within, waiting to activate and eat your life (mercifully fast, but too fast for me, for us), prevent you making better meals than this, cut short our plans for years of traveling, exploring, querying, puzzling, of enjoying simpler meals in places with no glass in the windows, a cold desert outdoors, a television high on a wall shelf replaying the moon landing in black and white to a room full of men.

Your Man Freud

It was you who introduced me to Freud, really, although I'd studied him a bit, at college. Only later would I discover his connection to Charcot. Freud had already been a medical doctor for five years, and was still far from inventing psychoanalysis, when, in 1885, he came to Paris to study with Charcot who was director of La Salpetrière, a large women's asylum on the left bank of the river Seine south of the Jardin des Plantes, a city within the city.

Freud found Paris "magically attractive" but also "repulsive." It was Charcot's work on hysteria and hypnotism, rather than his work on ALS, that interested Freud. Freud seems to have felt an outsider, his initial enthusiasm for Charcot waning until he got invited to Charcot's house. On that first visit he wore a white tie and white gloves and had a little cocaine "to loosen my tongue," as he wrote to his fiancée Martha Bernays. Freud was at La Salpetrière the same time as Gilles de la Tourette and also met Alphonse Daudet who was a visitor to Charcot's house. Freud was nevertheless very ambivalent about the whole Paris episode and swore Martha Bernays to secrecy about his boredom during such outings, and about the lie that Charcot kissed him on the forehead "à la Liszt."

You Were:

French and Italian cinema; doing the tango to a scratchy vinyl of Carlos Gardel; Leo Ferré singing Louis Aragon's *"Est-ce ainsi que les hommes vivent?"*; Jacques Brel's "Amsterdam;" Boris Vian's *"Le Déserteur;"* Paris cinemas where you forgot everything but the film and never needed to smoke, although you chain-smoked everywhere else; mover of mountains: on paper, tectonic plates and continents pushed into each other, on field trips you hammered slivers of rock, licked then viewed them under a loupe while a gang of kids imitated your movements in every detail, fascinated as I was by the magic of the gestures; rationalism and scientific attitude, frowning at anything silly or unproved or impossible or emotional; readings in psychoanalysis: Freud and Groddeck particular favorites, you couldn't get hooked on my interest in Jung; the garrigue: walking the Larzac plateau, stirring up perfumes of wild thyme and fennel and rosemary, we slept outdoors and studied the stars (if it was a test of me, I must have passed, although I complained bitterly about having to carry water); Collioure, where as a child you'd summer-camped for years in the old buildings on the port that have now become a military training center; Morocco, where you felt at home from the minute you arrived; Béziers stories about a saint who walked off with his head under his arm, and a man who made soup of stones; words and phrases in Occitan which you understood because your grandparents spoke it when they didn't want the grandkids to understand them; France Culture's *Les Chemins de la Connaissance* when you would decide what to do with your day or what to prepare for lunch; France Inter's afternoon scientific program when you picked a spot for a siesta, head in the shade, feet in the sun. Near the end, you were like a happy child in front of a DVD of funnies put together by your children and grandchildren, our entertainment was watching you.

It Begins

A crossroads near the hospital in A, driving through the late-night desert looking for food, a bag of chips, a kebab, anything, before heading back to you lying with the hitherto-unheard-of PEG installed in your side, maybe gasping for breath, and the gastro man confiding, "If I'd known how thin he was I'd never have operated."

Even talking to him in a dilapidated corridor was better than the outdoors emptiness of the sleeping provincial town.

I Thought I Was Strong

I hated words like feisty and gutsy (I liked gung-ho right enough), I thought I'd do better than others in my position, expected I'd be loved by you and yours, admired by neighbors and friends, so tough I'd refuse all offers of help, find time for my own work – headphones pumping Patti Smith in the darkest hours "Because the Night"..., thought I'd look after food, laundry, rising in the night, setting up your feeding tubes, wheedling you into accepting more liquid, taking your meds, finding lights and heaters to replace electric points that mysteriously stopped working (you'd've fixed them, *ni vu ni connu*, now the electrician didn't return calls – I hated the artisans too), tending stoves to keep you warm, hauling wood before dawn when you were stable and dozing, rushing to shops while other women held the fort, forgetting essentials because I pored over shelves and fridges in the hunt for tempting morsels – "Just a little, not to lose the habit, the pleasure," they told me – for you who used to feed the hordes so well, your glass-in-hand-French-chef antics in the kitchen.

I still pour your glass of rosé each time you agree to eat, you pretend to take a sip each time, I throw the rest down the sink, we hide our sorrow from each other. At the local *8 à 8* they know cases like ours so well they sell half bottles of champagne at Christmas. You drink a glass – after I threaten to syringe it down your tube – and I polish off the rest. I'm surprised next morning to find lights burning in odd places, marveling at what a mere sip can do for someone in distress.

Hysteria, Hashish and Orientalism

Effectively, it turns out that the most interesting aspect of Charcot is more his interest in hysteria than his discovery of your disease. His fascination for bizarre and exotic behavior began as a student, when he would smoke hashish and sketch weird and wonderful scenes. You might say this partly explains why it took him nine years to qualify (in all your years in Morocco you took no interest in hashish). I would reply that medicine was a slow business then and anyway there were only 400 medical graduates countrywide the year he did qualify. His greatest strength was observation. He called himself a *"visuel."* Freud considered him an artist.

Charcot had patients from all over the world, including the Grand Duke of Russia and the novelist Ivan Turgenev (whose mysterious pains Charcot diagnosed as *angina pectoris*). Crowds flocked to watch him hypnotize famous hysteric Blanche (Marie) Wittmann. She was dubbed the Queen of Hysterics, but then it was an epoch for such monikers: Charcot was known as the Napoleon of Neuroses. I feel guilty using the term hysteric. Asti Hustvedt (*Medical Muses,* 2011) sees 19th century hysteria reincarnated in today's eating disorders and self-mutilation, CFS, MPD, and reads all of these as a metaphor for women's repressed position in society and woman's image in the history of scientific discourse: "Hysteria, that bizarre rupture between symptom and source played out on the female body has resurfaced in our post-Freudian era in new but oddly familiar forms." Charcot worked with two other renowned hysterics, but Wittmann was made famous by the young Pierre Aristide André Brouillet who painted *Leçon Clinique à la Salpetrière 1887*: the scene from one of Charcot's Tuesday clinical demonstrations in which a fainting (?) and scantily-dressed Wittmann is supported by a man, while two nurses hover expectantly. A crowd of fascinated men watch, many well-known and identified (one is Charcot's son who will abandon medicine for polar exploration), many have moustaches and beards like you, although Charcot, who will be dead in six years, is cleanshaven.

Apparently Freud had a lithograph of this painting, which hung in his Vienna rooms until he moved to London, where it was installed over his famous couch. Today the original hangs unframed on a wall of the Université Paris V René Descartes which is just up from the statue of Danton at métro Odéon where you and I used to meet to go to the cinema, and just down from the Café de la Sorbonne where we'd meet when you were moving mountains and tectonic plates on paper.

Wittmann stopped having convulsions when Charcot died. A fictional account of her life after Charcot has her working with Marie Curie (whose notebooks will remain radioactive for another 1500 years, according to nonfictional reports). The real Wittmann did have both legs and one forearm amputated due to radiation, which may have happened when she was assistant to a photographer who experimented with radiation. She died at fifty-three from hemorrhaging. It is said that twenty years after her death Wittmann's notebooks were discovered, but I can find no trace of them. I picture her writing about love with her remaining arm.

I follow Brouillet down the rabbit-hole of the internet. He stares at me intently from a self-portrait with a handlebar moustache and beard. Your beard and moustache were modest affairs based on your unwillingness to shave every morning and the impracticality of shaving on field trips. Another of Brouillet's paintings, *The Exorcism*, hangs in Reims and shows Arab musicians chasing a djinn from the body of a child. Brouillet, a fervent orientalist, often traveled in North Africa, and married a woman from the Jewish elite of Constantine. He would die on the front, bringing help to Belgian refugees, on a freezing night in December 1914.

Dead Horses and Things

It is said that artists' supply shops in Paris run out of shades of grey in winter, for grey is everywhere: sky, buildings, pavements, river, faces.

One such Sunday we slip into the Musée Delacroix on a deserted Place de Furstenberg. In the entrance hall two English-speaking ladies hover, crestfallen, clearly mother and daughter.

The mother: "De-la-croix all one word? Nothing to do with religion? No crosses?"

The daughter (shifting from one foot to the other): "Apparently it's not the 'Musée. De. La. Croix,' it's Delacroix all-one-word – the painter."

The mother hesitates. "What kind of painting?"

The daughter eyes a reproduction on the wall, shrugs: "Dead horses and things."

They pass through the door into the greyness, abandoning enough color to brighten any Parisian winter.

Later, you and I repair to a café in Barbès, full of men in winter djellabahs, their hoods up, hands warming up wool sleeves. In mismatching jacket and trousers – like a bachelor farmer in the city for the day – the boss by the stove, the only source of heat, keeps endless mint tea on the go while studying some far horizon beyond the windows. You and his assistant exchange pleasantries in Arabic. Over mint tea and fresh doughnuts doused in sugar we discuss our surroundings, the people, the cool outdoors, Delacroix's visit to Morocco and his amazing notebooks, anything to help us forget the low winter sun creeping towards the grey horizon.

The Little Man in the Big Coat

"Your" disease "progressed." All shame gone, I ranted, bawled, harassed the doctors to a man – they were mostly men – who, asleep at the helm, were awakened from time to time by an army of women nurses, secretaries, carers, dieticians who kept them informed.

"Like clerks in Dickens' England," I bawled at you. "They sit behind their desks and write scripts!"

You said little, sunken into your pillows, twenty kilos down and counting, your voice already hoarse, hesitant.

The only woman doctor we saw had arrived from Eastern Europe to help make up for the shortage of doctors in rural areas. My abiding memory is of her wringing her hands in a hospital corridor, eight months into a foreign world. ("They're a referral service in Bulgaria," a local practitioner said. I hadn't the repartee to ask, "And what, pray, are you?")

In reply to my tirade, you looked at me from under your eyebrows and growled, with great effort, "Keep ridin' 'em like this, you'll be pickin' iron outta yo' liver."

Amazed that you remembered my movie quotes from decades earlier, I was more impressed that you managed a whole sentence. The little man in the big coat in *The Maltese Falcon* took on new meaning, and I knew that I was weak and you were strong, the old you buried inside that tired bony hulk.

Somehow you communicated with carers and nurses, although by then your voice was almost gone. I left you all to it so am not sure how you managed. They asked about your career, your travels. They were delighted to find you on the internet: "He has loads of publications!" they said when they came down for tea. You smiled at the thought of the fat roll of maps in the attic, not to mention the thesis that moved mountains.

I wasn't jealous, I thought I was strong.

I complained to the nurses, "I thought medicine was a vocation," I said, remembering family doctors in old movies. I referred to a local practitioner.

"Should've become a butcher," the nurse replied, "He could stand behind his counter, chop up meat and ring his till!"

We laughed till I nearly cried.

But I saved my keening for the day you left that bony hulk, and went, at peace from MND, and me.

Edith Wharton is Alive and Well

I stopped reading. Edith Wharton's *Morocco* hurt – so much *indolence*, so many *Lazaruses* in *grave-clothes*. I got out of the car.

I could see no sign of you. "You stay and read, I'll deal with this," you'd said, pocketing the car keys out of habit and heading off with my passport and yours.

It was almost midday, Saturday, first day of Ramadan, already hot. There wasn't yet the razor-wire climbing the hills around Ceuta to hold the *harragas* back from Spain and Europe. The only sign of a border was a line of little booths where passports were stamped.

I approached the place I'd last seen you and inquired.

"Oh he's here all right," the official replied. His voice indicated trouble, possibly hatred.

"Is there a problem?" I asked.

"He's being taken away." They wouldn't say where or why, told me to wait.

The sun climbed hotter. No fresh cars arrived. No one was visible, in grave clothes or any other kind.

After what seemed ages a small official in mismatching jacket and pants appeared, you following. You indicated our car and you both came towards me. "We have to go back to Tetouan," you muttered. The man indicated we shouldn't talk and got in the passenger seat, with you at the wheel. I got in the back.

As you drove, I tried to read over the man's shoulder the documents he was perusing. It appeared that a Frenchman, with a similar first name and the same surname as you, had kidnapped his children from his Moroccan wife. This wasn't uncommon, there'd been a famous case involving a Scandinavian sportsman.

At Tetouan I was turfed out of the car, again without keys or passport, and you were swept into the Commissariat.

I contemplated setting fire to petrol from a pump at the filling station next door to draw attention to my predicament. I wasn't sure I could carry it off – or even if that old cinema trick worked at all.

Luckily I had some loose change. I took a taxi to family friends of yours. One of the young men of the family accompanied me to the post office. We stood in line for a booth after giving the number at the desk. I listened to a message saying the embassy was closed for the weekend. There didn't seem to be a contingency arrangement.

Your friends advised me to be patient.

I went back to the Commissariat and begged that they at least return my passport. They refused. They were waiting for the Commissaire to arrive. He would make a decision.

Given the heat and Ramadan, I guessed he was in bed.

I remember little of the rest of the day. There was a lot of mint tea. I had time to recall other trips to Ceuta, your amusement at my delight with some very salty bacon and cabbage in a Galician restaurant.

As the sun dropped towards the horizon, the Commissaire arrived. He immediately spotted the error. You were brought out, mild as ever, smiling a bit now. The Commissaire apologized to us both – "A minor official hoping for promotion," he said – and invited us to dinner. We instantly refused.

As we drove across the border at last, into Ceuta, I asked you to slow the car. I opened the window and spat on the ground, as I'd seen Moroccans do, completely forgetting my earlier dislike of Edith Wharton.

Rational and Irrational

By December even your spam emails are drying up. In an irrational attempt to keep you close for a while longer, I research ALS. I become adept at skimming through medical abstracts. I fill notebooks.

You always used the word *go* when playing French Scrabble, for the Chinese game using black and white pieces called stones. This often led to argument but *go* always emerged as a valid, an allowed, Scrabble word. Only now do I see that a board game in which the pieces are called stones was an obvious notion for a geologist.

Can't Hurt You Now

Late one Friday coming up to the shortest day of the year – when primitive peoples in northern climes must have thought: *Dude, this thing is over* – I have an appointment with the notary. Country roads are busier than usual with what I imagine are happy people rushing home to happy arrangements. The light is fading rapidly, it is that time the French call *between dog and wolf.* If a deer were to cross the road now, it might be mistaken for something else, or not seen at all. A murder of crows explodes into the air, cawing loudly.

Here is the very spot where your trouble started, not so long ago: one late afternoon, two big deer burst out of the forest and ran straight into your car on the driver's side, denting it unmercifully, blocking the door, exploding the window next to your ear. The deer ran off, big enough to be unscathed. You continued to your destination – an important and successful interview. Arriving home that evening you climbed out by the passenger side of the car and made light of the whole episode. Yet you were never the same again, more silent, I might have said mystified. Your hair grew whiter and stood up as if in shock. It took almost a year to find out what was wrong.

In reply to a question posed by the professor of neurology, I told him about the deer. He looked at me as if I were one of Charcot's hysterics. He repeated my words back at me: "The. Car. Was. Hit. By. Two. Big. Deer." By then you were unable to join the conversation – you had all of ten days left – but you didn't indicate agreement either. You were still you, more on his – scientific, rational – side than mine. These were our roles.

I still think a trauma like the deer might have triggered and accelerated a quietly sleeping disease.

I arrive in the town. It is clogged. I am angry with Christmas lighting, plastic snowmen, idiotic Father Christmases climbing walls and chimneys.

The notary is no longer tanned and gung-ho. Now winter-pale and distant, he favors a modish quiff at the top of his head, some statement related to the many car magazines in his waiting room. His office is dilapidated, dusty, its ancient moldings in sharp contrast to his glass desk, another statement. I sign another piece of paper affirming your death, as if they are trying to make me admit it.

As I return to the busy street, a lone secretary leans over her work in the only pool of light in the penumbra of the reception-area.

On the way home through the forest, I open all the car windows, to give those deer the benefit of my mood. I scream along with Patti Smith. *Can't hurt you now.*

Always Inevitable

I was jealous of your radio, of you wrapped into another culture and language, immensely smug and sure of itself. (A colleague once bent my ear about France having the best education system in the world – I and other adjuncts delivering it against all odds without tenure, bitterness our state of being, our *être* with no *bien*.)

You may have felt the same when I wandered house and garden sporting earphones, listening to BBC or Russian novels, chuckling at American standups, applying the secateurs as Raskolnikov planned his murder and Mark Twain mocked "the awful German language."

Now it is I who listens to France Culture on every radio in the house. It echoes through the garden, slightly out of sync with my headphones.

I pretend that you are here too – somewhere – listening – planning the next meal – working on your laptop – fixing a plug – puzzling over big things, like pain and suffering which, as Raskolnikov said, are always inevitable for deep hearts and large intelligences, causing them great sadness on earth.

Eating Artichokes

It is April, the year advances quickly. I am a large still rock in the middle of a fast river.

Each year I miss you not less, but more.

An appointment has been cancelled, I am eating lunch early. I didn't sleep much after the burning of Notre Dame.

As the artichokes cooked, I read David Foster Wallace's "Consider the Lobster." The artichokes on their plate now have a strange association with lobsters and a summer festival in Maine. DFW discusses whether or not lobsters feel pain, describes how they shrink backwards when you try to empty them into the boiling water and how, when you manage it and cover the pot, they rattle the lid. Some cooks flee the kitchen at this point.

I will probably never eat lobster again. The last time I did was with you, in Al Jadidah, in a dining room open to the sea where birds flew in and out. The patronne, in a striped djellabah more like a man's, sat beside the cash desk. She had a little *kanoun* for tea, and called the town by its old Portuguese name, Mazagan, now the name of a nearby resort and golf course.

Then I made mayonnaise for the artichokes. I don't often do this, because you did it so well, adding the oil to the spoon before dropping it into the bowl, because the secret of mayonnaise, you said, is having everything at the same temperature. You added more and more oil until the mayonnaise was pale and thick. I joked that it was geological. In the kitchen there was often discussion about why mayonnaise might refuse to take, and French rumors that it couldn't work if a woman having her period was making it or nearby. This often branched into discussion of the patriarchy. Madame Saint-Ange – your cooking bible – has four whole pages on mayonnaise, in French: the bane of my life as I tried to cope with Arabic in the street and French at home, with memories of Sister Philippine and Kennedy's French Grammar, and the excruciating subjunctive (*"Elle s'est brulée la main,"* said Sister Philippine). I still can't remember the rule. One night on a book program, George Steiner used a past subjunctive and the audience went "Oooooh!" because the French just dodge it.

You forbade a blender for the mayonnaise, and showed all my friends how to make it. They still think of you when they do.

I peel off the outer leaves of the artichoke, select a fat one and dip it in my mayonnaise.

And I've got it right, finally, after all these years: plenty of lemon but not too much to drown the taste of the egg, the oil, pleasantly tart with just enough seasoning. You liked lots of pepper.

I don't remember when I first ate artichokes with you. I recall you making mayonnaise in a kitchen in Morocco, blinding sunlight outdoors, a hibiscus-lined alley, a lemon tree where the chameleon hunted, stepping and gripping cautiously, giving himself time to change color, and his long toffee tongue when his stereo eyes spotted an insect.

The pomegranates were small, unlike shop-bought ones. You prepared them for us, adding rosé to yours. Pomegranates appear in the Bible and in Greek mythology. You said Adam and Eve probably ate a pomegranate, not an apple. Normandy made more sense for apples.

There was a tree with red flowers resembling bottle brushes. No one knew its name, but everyone with access to the internet now knows it is Callistemon.

All these things had been planted lovingly by an elderly Frenchman who thought he was in Morocco forever, believing that colonial privilege could protect against age and fortune and change.

The avocados all ripened at the same time. You can only give away so many avocadoes or eat so many dips (although I know now we could have added pomegranate to the dip). Giving things away was easy in Morocco: you put things neatly near the dustbin and within minutes they disappeared. Nothing went to loss. Shepherds grazed their sheep in the green sward along the outside wall of houses like ours, with watered lawns. I suppose shepherds still do that.

So there we were, in a past life, eating your mayonnaise. We were young and handsome but we didn't know it. We were funny and hard and cruel and nice. We had visceral likes and dislikes. Later we would drop the harder bits, when it was too late to make any difference.

OUT TO SEE / Valyntina Grenier

UPRISING / VALYNTINA GRENIER

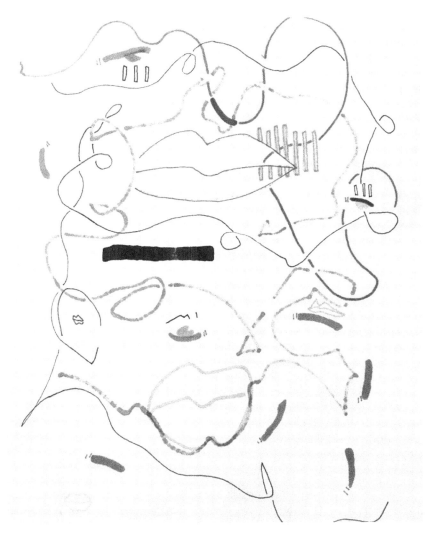

We Make This Wind It's Wrath
/ Valyntina Grenier

Alternate History

T.B. Grennan

Here's how it finally happens.

At thirty-two, you're working at a tech startup after years with nonprofits and publishers. Getting used to wearing t-shirts to the office instead of button-downs, to being among the oldest employees instead of the youngest. And then one day, you're asked to take somebody's picture.

Your boss likes profiling new hires for the company blog, but this one is just a year out of school and doesn't have a headshot. (On LinkedIn, he's using a photo from a college costume party.) You arrange to meet him by the elevators. The light's good there; the wall has your company's name written in foot-high letters.

He's waiting when you arrive, sunlight hitting him at an angle, hot and bright. Shirt open to the third button; chest hair peeking out. And suddenly you feel it. In your chest. At the top of your head and the back of your testicles. A shudder, an electric charge. Your hormones flickering like neon.

You take a dozen pictures. His eyes half-closed in the first few, like he's sleepy or drunk. The fifth photo comes out perfect—it's the one you end up using—but you just keep snapping away. The two of you chatting now, joking about startup life and the company's kickball team as you move him in front of the window, his white shirt blurring into the gauzy curtains.

His gaze grows softer with each picture, his smile brighter. And when it's over, you sit down at your desk, waiting for the monitor to warm back up, and wonder what just happened, what it meant.

At first, the attraction feels like a fluke. But it's still there when you see him again, see him week after week for a year, for two years. In meetings and happy hours. At company parties and a season's worth of kickball games. Until there's no way to pretend that the sparks in your chest are any different than the ones sent up by the girls you pined for in high school.

So you mull things over. Let your eyes linger on men the way they always have on women. Accept the erotic flashes you get, the confused yearning. Trying to give yourself permission to be whatever it is you are. And when a different coworker casually mentions she's bi during a coffee run, you find yourself wanting to say, "Yeah? Me, too."

You start seeing a therapist and eventually the topic bubbles up. She's surprised you haven't told anybody; you're surprised how easy it was to tell someone. A few weeks later, your girlfriend brings you to the Bowie exhibit at the Brooklyn Museum and as the two of you take in the kimonos and knee-high boots, you decide that this is the time. Back home, you close the bedroom door and, after an agonizing prelude, you say it. She laughs with relief: "Oh, thank god! I thought something was wrong!"

You tell your male best friend over beers and your female best friend over breakfast sandwiches. You tell coworkers one after another after another. The process easier each time, though always a little hard.

Until here you are. Still figuring things out, but comfortable, finally, with yourself. Appreciating your lack of guilt or shame or angst—which could be luck, or chance, or maybe just what coming out in your thirties feels like. Thinking back, now and again, to all the other times you could have figured things out. All the other lives you might have lived.

PETWORTH — 2012

You're twenty-nine and in Washington, DC for the week, helping out at your nonprofit's profoundly dull annual conference. Forcing smile after smile. Answering endless questions about where, exactly, the bathrooms are. And when it's all over, you crash for the weekend with a college friend who works on Capitol Hill.

Your first short story has just been published and your friend takes you out for a celebratory drink—then drags you along to a full day of Oktoberfest happenings. A German-themed brunch. A temporary Bavarian biergarten on a blocked-off street. A combination canine parade and pageant dubbed "Dogtoberfest." And finally, as the light wanes, you descend into the DC metro and emerge three minutes later in Petworth.

The house party is in a newly gentrifying section of the neighborhood. And as it winds down, you find yourself on the front porch, drinking a Märzen and chatting with a bright-eyed government administrator who's been watching you all night.

He went to grad school in West Virginia, and because it's the only thing you know about Morgantown, you bring up the experimental transit system that the Nixon administration built there. He nods, says he loves the PRT. Raves about the convenience, the speed, as his free hand flits between the railing and your forearm. Then starts talking about his boyfriend, implying that they have an open thing. And asks about yours.

"Girlfriend," you say.

He purses his lips. Like he's been there. Like you'll get through it, too.

BLASPHEMY — 2011

You're twenty-seven and walk into your favorite bar in Brooklyn (formerly a lesbian dance club, formerly an autobody shop) wearing a faded Scott Pilgrim tee. Alone for the night, because your girlfriend decided—as she often does—that she didn't feel like coming out. Surprised, as you push your way to the bar, how packed the place is on a winter Monday.

You drink one of the best double IPAs you've ever had and chat with two graying men who are sipping wine at the table next to you. It takes a minute for you to register that they're a couple, and another minute to realize you've accidentally crashed the bar's queer night. CONFESSION, it's called, the iconography all crosses and sexy lesbian nuns. Both men are lapsed Catholics—one's Irish—and feel somewhat leery about the theme, but the electropop and disco eventually loosens them up.

They buy you a drink, buy you two, and talk about gay marriage and their ex-wives and Ancient Greece until midnight. They excuse themselves, joke that they're getting old. Squeezing your hand as you shake goodbye.

You're waiting in line for the bathroom when a guy in an incongruous tank top tries to strike up a conversation. "Love your shirt," he says, running a finger slowly down your chest, tracing the outlines of the illustrations. "You're so, like, artistic." And you think both how handsome he is and what stupid shit he's saying; wondering suddenly if this is what it feels like to be a girl getting chatted up in a nightclub.

Across the bar, the promoter—a chubby woman with a half-shaved head—fawns over the DJ, who's tall and blonde and incredibly cute. The DJ's obviously queer, but she's just as obviously not interested. Watching them reminds you of yourself, of the way you were in high school.

Then it's the last song of the night, and that song is "Dancing on My Own." You close your eyes, the synths drilling into your head, making your body move. And then you're dancing with your arms above your head, feeling drunk and happy and free, the song's beautiful melancholy filling you up. When you open your eyes, you're surrounded by a knot of queer men and women, all of you swooning there, moved almost to tears by the music and the crowd and the feeling.

And as the little bells finally stop chiming at the end of the song, the promoter hugs you, thanks you for being there. Says, "I love it when my gays come out." And instead of correcting her, you just hug her back.

CASTLETON — 2000

You're seventeen, spending two weeks of your summer vacation in a cinderblock dorm room. It's July and you're attending a government-run arts program located at a state college best known for being mocked in an episode of *Mystery Science Theater 3000*.

Every high school in Vermont gets to send one student here—except yours, which sent a half-dozen. Which means that you've got friends here, but also that you're surrounded by bright-eyed kids from nowhere towns breathlessly proclaiming that, wow, they never knew that anybody else cared about music/painting/writing/sculpture/ whatever. "I never knew anybody else liked french fries!" your classmate deadpans at the dining hall, dipping one in ketchup. "This place is opening my eyes!"

You're an aspiring fiction writer stuck taking classes with a gaggle of wannabe slam poets. They're writing confessional lyrics about their angsty relationships and difficult fathers; you're working on a dark comic epic where someone hijacks a medical transport flight. In your free time, you're corresponding by letter and payphone with an adorable girl from home who you're beginning to suspect just doesn't like you like that.

All that means you're spending a lot of time in your dorm room, typing and deleting and typing some more. In the mornings before breakfast, in the free periods after lunch. Before bed, while your roommate—who's here to be an actor—strips down to shorts and nothing else to practice his lines.

"People think I'm gay," he tells you practically the minute you arrive, "but I'm really not." You nod. Okay. Good to know.

He's a pretty decent actor, and there's a matinee idol vibe to him—the floppy hair, the slender, muscular chest, the smile that seems to explode out of him with the curl of a lip. A little slow on the uptake, a little dull. But handsome and friendly and perfectly nice, as long as nobody mentions the G-A-Y thing. The two of you aren't close, and though you talk before bed and do the nod of acknowledgement when you see each other in the dining hall, most of your time is spent apart. You've got hijackings to plan and a girl to pine after; he's got lines to memorize.

Which is why you're surprised how you react when a friend from high school tells you that she thinks your roommate is cute. She's quiet and shy—except when she's on stage—and this is the first time you've ever heard her express interest in a boy. But instead of teasing her, or asking follow-up questions, you startle yourself by saying, "Yeah, I think so, too."

WILLISTON — 1998

You're fifteen, and it's summer in Vermont. You've never had a girlfriend. Never kissed a girl. Never done anything more than accept a pity slow dance from a friend of a friend. But you're getting paid $50 to carry boxes in and out of a couple office buildings, so you've got that going for you.

The day begins in a hidden office above Evergreen Eddy's Wildlife Grill, a three-room setup where the walls are stained a sickly gray with grease from the burners downstairs. You make a half-dozen trips, carrying empty filing cabinets and desk drawers and computer monitors so big that you can barely fit them in your arms. Trying not to trip on the carpeted stairs. Trying not to brush up against the rancid wallpaper.

Then you're in the passenger seat of your father's massive new SUV, a company car from his new job. The kind of vehicle where you practically need a stepladder to get in. Classic rock on the radio. A hot, humid wind blowing in through the open window, sunlight painfully bright as you come around curves. Your dad is talking about the company, a tech startup building a device that lets you check your email on the TV. "They've got the device down to a pack of cigarettes," he says, "and it just keeps getting smaller." Smiling now, like he can't quite believe it.

The new building is down the road in a Williston office park. And when you arrive, it's just an empty shell: exposed pipes, exposed wires, drywall still being installed. You're introduced to the other employees, most of whom are in their twenties—one's a former Olympic snowboarder. You meet the CEO, who's gruff and friendly and drinks a half-dozen gold cans of Caffeine-Free Diet Coke over the course of the morning; he'll later leave the company under ambiguous circumstances.

The foreman of the construction crew has brought his son along, too, and the two of you are put to work together. He's sixteen or so, taller and skinnier than you. Blond and serious, dressed in a preppy style you know only from movies. The two of you carry old pipes and debris out of the office, making room for new desks and cubicles. He chats happily about sports and other things you don't care about. But even though he's not much of a conversationalist, you look for reasons to keep talking.

But eventually the back-and-forth fizzles out.

The last time you see him, he's standing near the door to the outside, the afternoon sun streaming in, lighting him up. You don't remember his name, or where he's from. But you remember what he looked like just then, remember it to this day.

Miscellaneous

Samantha Schlemm

Every Monday, she wrote the list of spelling words, looping white cursive on the board as we spilled into the room, scrawling powdery white chalk across a sea of green as we copied them down cockeyed and tilting on ruled lines. By then, the Word of the Week—the extra credit word that made my grandma whistle and say, "That's a doozie," the five-dollar word that Miss Tighe posted the definition beneath to unlock its full power—was already pinned to the yellow paper-covered corkboard.

This is the room where I must have learned words like pedantic, ostentatious, or connotative. Miscellaneous. That's the one I remember. The way it rolled off the tongue, each syllable dancing to the next. Mis-cell-an-e-ous. A word to describe the random, the indescribable which now could be named, to cover an entire category which had never been open to me before. Even though it was the longest word our fifth-grade class had come across, studying how each letter came together, memorizing how each sound kissed the next was easy. It tugged at me. It curled up in my lap, a nuzzling kitten that purred its syllables, single notes in a melodic song, and it hummed, a stir fry that sizzled on the stove, a harp that plucked a chorus of notes together in one miscellaneous jumble, a jumble that opened my childish eyes. A jumble that scared me because I wasn't ready to grow up.

Lately, my days feel miscellaneous. Before the coronavirus shooed us all into quarantine, there was always wake up, go to work, come home, make dinner, go to bed. Now, there's wake up, work at home, head to the kitchen to make tea, notice the dishes are still in the sink from the night before, unload the dishwasher, fill it back up, pour hot water through herbal tea leaves that smell like someone squeezed an orange into my mug, sit and work, resist looking at social media, more tea, work, give in and check Instagram, spread Nutella on toast for lunch, notice the laundry needs folding, answer the door for a package, get back to work, call and reschedule an upcoming wedding-related appointment, work, work, realize it's after seven, make dinner, watch TV, sleep. I think about how we're lucky, my fiancé and I, we're lucky to have jobs we can do from home, we're lucky to be healthy, we're lucky to have this time together before we get married—if we can get married this summer. I feel at ease. I feel stressed. I feel something I can't quite name. As the weeks at home drag on into the double digits, I think about Miss Tighe and how she knew the world wouldn't always be a place you could categorize, a place where every thought, every feeling, every experience had a name. Sometimes, things are just miscellaneous.

A Certain Perspective

Marjorie Tesser

Annie steps inside the studio, a light-filled barn behind the Arts Center, and a familiar aroma hits—like bread baking with a lower, rough note, the tang of turpentine and solvents. She recalls the aromas of the paints themselves, each color different, with an unaccustomed lift, a stirring. Not one familiar face, although the Arts Center is just the next town over from Annie's; she'd half-thought she'd run into another mom from the PTA or someone she'd met through work. But no. Her classmates look like college kids.

Annie takes an easel in the back. A girl dressed in a white strapless sundress (not very practical for painting) gallops in on coltish bare legs. "You're new," she says to Annie. "You haven't studied with Tim, have you? We all have. I'm Phoebe."

The night before, and then again that morning, Annie had reminded Celia that Madison's mom would drive her to and from ballet. She'd warned Skyler not to attempt any new skateboard tricks, and asked Jake to check in on his siblings, from his part-time job at the music store. She packed her new expensive art supplies and thought about what to wear for class. She'd be going straight from work, in what Matt calls her "girl reporter" outfit (his little joke; Annie takes photographs and write brief profiles of local businesses—bakeries, hair salons, real estate offices—for a glossy promo magazine). She no longer had her old college painting clothes, faded overalls worn over a stretchy tube top; anyway, those days were long gone, so she stuffed jeans and an old shirt of Matt's into a tote. He'd encouraged her to take the class when she'd been accepted. "It's just eight weeks, you should be able to work it out. You've been saying for ages you want to get back to your art."

The teacher appears in the doorway, and the students, who'd been setting up, or chatting, or checking their phones, look up, pocket their devices, and watch him cross to the front. Tim Caine is in his mid-forties or so. He's dressed like the male students, in worn jeans and a V-neck t-shirt.

Hair spiked jauntily in front but thinning at the temples, bit of a Dad bod (though she's no one to judge). Annie's only seen a couple of his paintings "in person" but she's checked him out on the internet. Tim is a wonderful artist. His works are representational with a twist, the narratives hard to pin down. He's represented by two galleries, one in Chelsea and one upstate in Hudson, and has had a respectable number of solo shows. Annie feels lucky to have gotten into to the class, on the strength of an old group of sketches she'd worked on the first year Celia was in school.

Tim Caine waits while everyone quiets down. "So," he says, "we gather here to make art. Your art, whatever that is, and we will help each other make it better." The girl Phoebe waves her hand; Caine frowns and gives a quick shake of his head and continues. "I will help you make it better. We will engage in an investigation, an inquiry, a honing. Hopefully each of you will end up with a few pieces that have stretched your capabilities, whether or not they prove marketable." He'll provide a focal point for each session, a still life set-up—as he talks he arranges some fruit in a bowl and places it, along with a metal watering can, a vintage man's wingtip, and the skull of a small animal, upon a drape of iridescent greenish cloth—or once in a while a model, but students are under no constraint to paint it, and should follow their own inclinations.

It's been twenty years since college and Annie's barely picked up a brush. She sticks to painting the still life Tim Caine had set-up. The other students all seem to be doing something different. Chatting during a break, Annie learns that they're actually not college kids, but are all post-grads; a contingent had studied under Tim in the Bard MFA program and followed him here; Maria and Niles, the guy with the huge Afro and striped suspenders, had gone to, respectively, Cooper Union and RISD before studying with Caine. Annie waits after class to talk to Caine. After each of the other students has had a lengthy chat, she gets to say, "I'm so glad to be in the class. I saw your work at my town library exhibit. It was wonderful." Tim shrugs. "Just a favor for a friend," he says, turning away. "I usually don't bother with those things."

Just a couple of weeks into the class, Annie already can see that each of Tim's students has developed a signature style. Quinn Reynolds, the boy with the dark hair who reminds Annie of a young version of Matt, does stick-figure people and shiny robots on fields of mottled white. The one called Jinx paints big rocks. Phoebe Klein's work, mythical winged creatures in nursery hues, reminds Annie of Chagall and also of Lisa Frank (Annie recalls a notebook she'd loved in middle school). Maria Vega paints abstracts with super-saturated color; a smoky blue, a deep, ferrous Rothko red. The rest, three voluble young guys Annie secretly dubs "The Art Squad," produce socially-aware, hard-edged propaganda pieces, indistinguishable save that two of them work big, the third, Niles, only in miniature. This is an Advanced Class; the students are expected to know what they're doing. These kids consider themselves serious artists, the ones to be famous in a few years' time. Annie had thought that herself, back when she was their age.

Now, she's just happy to be back in the studio again. Tim puts on music (last time, vintage jazz, this week, cowboy songs) and Annie sketches and mixes and paints. Her body remembers the old gestures, and her mind, usually a running litany of worries, reminders, and concerns—work, the kids, Matt—becomes a neutral contemplative blank. She notices how painting differs from photography, the only thing close to art she'd been doing lately, not just in the execution, but in the way you see. Taking a photo, you're aware of the interplay of light and dark, and the arrangement within a frame. With painting, it's more about depth, breadth, and choice, what to omit and what to show, and how; the opportunity for the symbolic. The once-a-week class is her own creative time, which she realizes she's not had in any structured way for the past seventeen years, since the birth of Jake, then Skyler, and then, when they'd thought they were done, Celia.

In college, Annie's work had incorporated black scribbly lines, vivid blocks of deep color and painted slogans: her heroes were Basquiat, Holzer, Kruger. Now, it's emerging differently. Annie, tentative, is sparing with her brush but works toward interpreting the subject so that it's minimally indicated, barely recognizable. Sometimes her pieces end up having oddly focused moments of realism, an unexpectedly-detailed flower or piece of fruit, or a hand, mid-gesture.

Tim moves around the class, gesturing at one canvas or another. Those who take his advice invariably get a better painting out of it; those whose work is praised, preen. Annie watches closely as he critiques the other students' work, especially when what he's suggesting seems counterintuitive. She tries to see as he sees, the spaces, the colors, the forms. He spends a good deal of time with the Squad guys, then Maria, until Phoebe clamors for his attention, and then back to Maria. Annie waits for him to comment on hers, but perhaps he's idea-ed out by the time he gets back to her part of the classroom. He gives her work a glance and a nod or once in a while a little shrug. She tries not to take it personally.

One week, Tim has arranged for a model, a Rubenesque older woman whose luxuriant folds of skin are echoed by those in the thick red drapery she's posed on. Annie is scrutinizing the subject, deciding on her approach, when her hip buzzes. She slips her phone out of her pocket to check; it's a text from Madison's mom, Lori. She looks up to see Tim's scowl, and quickly steps out to the hall. Lori is stuck at Ninja Warrior class with her younger son. Can Annie pick the kids up from ballet? *I know u have class, but u can leave, right?* But luckily, Annie reaches Kaitlin's mom, who will save the day. Annie ducks back into class with a little half bow and a mouths a *Sorry*.

"A reminder, guys. You all know the rule—absolutely no phones in my classes," Tim takes the opportunity to state, and Annie's cheeks warm.

A few days later, Annie is taking a short break between work assignments, lingering at her local coffee shop, The Bean Tree, for ten minutes with her latte instead of rushing back to her desk. She sees a girl in line with hair like Phoebe's, platinum tipped with purple and green, but this one has on a baggy sweatshirt and patched jeans, unlike the girly stuff Phoebe wears. She turns and it is Phoebe; she gives Annie a little wave and walks over.

"I almost didn't recognize you," she says to Annie. "Coming from someplace special?"

"No, just my job; I work around the corner from here."

"That sucked when your phone buzzed in class. Tim hates that," Phoebe adds.

"I noticed," says Annie. "My daughter was stuck and needed a ride."

"You have kids? That's so cool, I love little kids. How old?"

"The boys are seventeen and thirteen and Celia's eleven." Phoebe's eyebrows go up and she looks closely at Annie. "I didn't realize you were . . . you had kids. Wow." Annie's often mistaken for younger; she's petite and slender, and her hair style, unchanged since college, seems lately to have come back into vogue.

"Do you live around here?" Annie asks, to change the subject.

"Nope, I'm up in Peekskill. I'm just stopping in at The Crafty Fox to pick up some supplies," Phoebe replies. Her fingers idly play with the end of her ponytail. "Tim recommended it." She says his name like she likes the feel of it in her mouth. "You should have stuck around after class last week. We were having such a great conversation we took it to the Wayfarer and continued over drinks. It was awesome—Tim hung out with us all night."

Annie has noticed that at the end of each class the three Squad guys and Phoebe cluster around Tim. They interrupt each other to pepper him with questions—What was his take on a recent article in *Hyperallergic*? How did he feel about a show a bunch of them had gone to at a gallery in Beacon? Should they apply for a residency at Haworth or Charrington? They're all fluent in art-speak and display insider status by employing the latest buzz-words, *speculative, rupture, transverse,* each gunning for his attention, his wisdom. They clearly understand the benefit of having a mentor to give them a helping hand. Annie gets it. In college, her senior advisor, Benoit O'Reilly, had approved of her then-style of painting. He'd became something of a mentor to her, recommending her for a group show and an Art Department prize. His mentorship of the good-looking guys in the class was of a more intimate sort, and he'd cycled through them, dispensing favors and close companionship.

The students here hang on Tim's every pronouncement. Annie, who hasn't been up on the gallery scene, who doesn't even subscribe to art magazines anymore, would have liked to have been part of these conversations, but isn't confident or knowledgeable enough to venture an opinion or formulate questions. After the second class, she'd lingered, but didn't push herself forward, and finally left; at her age, she'd felt ridiculous acting the acolyte. And the following week she'd been half embarrassed, half piqued at being chastised for cell phone use. Anyway, she usually has to get back to check on what her own kids are up to, or finish an interrupted work assignment, or pull together dinner for the family. Matt's stuck at the office late most nights and somebody has to hold down the fort. Annie has noticed that Tim isn't in any hurry to escape; he seems to enjoy the conversation and perhaps isn't immune to the admiration.

One week, the Squad is more interested in arguing about an exhibit they'd seen over the weekend than in getting down to paint. "It's pandering!" says Brian, one of the guys who works big, of the new show by an artist they'd previously all admired. "Sad," says Niles, the minimalist guy. "He used to do good work. Now it's *decoration*."

"I thought it was kind of modern," Quinn said.

Tim runs his hands through his hair, which makes the spiky front part stand up like a feather. "Okay, you all want to do this? Right. So tell me. What is art?" He takes the time to look at each student in turn, his eyes narrowed.

"Making," says Jinx.

Phoebe speaks up. "Nope. That's craft."

"Statement," says Brian.

"Nuance," Niles puts in.

"Design," states Quinn. The third Squad guy makes a rude sound.

"Imagination!" Phoebe.

Maria raises her hand. "To me, it's the intersection of intelligence and emotion."

It's seeing, thinks Annie. Seeing and sharing. And maybe having what you saw be seen.

But Tim is already on it. "Art," he says, "is two-headed Janus. It acknowledges the past and gazes out toward a future. It's a marriage of the personal and the universal. It's primal—beauty and horror, creation and ruin. A window, a microscope, a mirror. But bottom line . . ." and he gazes over the heads of the listening students to some point in the far distance, "it's what someone else will pay for." The Squad nods sagely. Maria slowly shakes her head.

Phoebe looks crushed. She puts such stock in Tim, Annie thinks. But it's more than that. Each week she comes to class with an expanse of skin exposed. A plunging neckline over which peek twin half-globes of small, high breasts, or a crop top revealing a milky plain of stomach. Annie finds herself remembering her own first job at the ad agency. She'd get plenty of attention when she wore skimpy clothes (in fact, had been wearing a particularly short skirt the day she'd met Matt). But Annie knew from experience that it can backfire, the subject considered an object, fun to flirt with but passed over for advancement. Annie thinks about saying something to Phoebe, but stays mum. It's her right to wear what she likes.

"Tim, help!" Phoebe tosses her long platinum hair, ends tipped purple one week, pink and green the next, like the pastel creatures she likes to paint. She flutters curled, super-long black eyelashes (false?) and employs an inelegant giggle, a series of short snorts, at Tim's every *bon mot*. Phoebe contrives to call him to her easel several times each class. "Tim, look!" She sounds like a kid going high on a swing, seeking parental approval. Annie feels sorry for the girl, dangling herself like ripe fruit without garnering so much as a nibble. There had been one or two times in her own past she'd paraded before indifferent reviewing stands; she recalls the pre-meeting excitement, the rationalizations. She's glad her youngest, Celia, hasn't reached this stage. Tim smiles politely at Phoebe, but his gaze drifts. Toward Maria.

Maria is the one whose work he notices. He acts the firm taskmaster, chiding her on a misplaced brushstroke, a too-easy or expected shape. She seems to be nothing but professional with him, nodding and taking instruction and executing under his watchful eye. But Annie sees that blue, assessing eye travel to the girl's rich dark hair, to the small hollow at the base of her long throat in which nestles a tiny silver crescent moon on a thin chain, visible at the deep V of her faded chambray work shirt. He always finds a way to circle back to Maria's easel. Once or twice he lectures from that vantage point, his large hand resting lightly on the girl's ballerina-straight back.

Unfortunately, Annie has to miss one class entirely, but it can't be helped. Just as she's about to leave work, she gets a call from the school nurse. Skyler, chronically ill with diabetes, had practically passed out in Science. Annie rushes to the school; one look at his pale face, hair plastered to his forehead with sweat, and she whisks him right to the ER. Annie is relieved to see a nurse she recognizes from a period before Sky was diagnosed, when he'd been repeatedly hospitalized with similar symptoms; in such a situation, it's always nice to have someone who sees you as a human, rather than a case. Annie spends the better part of the afternoon in the cubicle with Sky as he naps fitfully, while she alternates worrying and idle wondering what Tim had set up for the class to paint. She texts Matt, who's in a meeting, says his away message. At last they get the test results. It turns out, to her relief, to have been a minor episode, and Sky, by then feeling better, doesn't need to be admitted. They can go home.

In class, Annie is trying not to find Tim irritating. Cynical definitions of art aside, he loves to tell long, name-dropping stories about the art scene back in the day. Worse, he offers the students gems of advice from the perspective of the wise elder, about the pressures of having a family—he has one middle-schooler, a super-gifted kid. "The sweetest thing in the world, being a parent. Wait till you kids experience it. But it's relentless." So hard to keep the kid adequately stimulated. How difficult to balance going to openings and art events, which he has to for his job, his career, and being there for the soccer games, the science fairs. How tricky to juggle art's irregular income with the influx of bills, inexorable as the ocean. "When you're older, you'll see," he says sagely to the class, and Annie, likely several years his senior, feels invisible.

During a slow afternoon at work, Annie browses on the computer and chances upon Tim's social media profiles; she finds his pictures from college and his first gallery show. He'd been handsome then, golden, athletic, the type she'd have gone for when she was that age, before she'd met Matt.

The next time she sees him, she acknowledges to herself that Tim is still a good-looking man. Then he starts with another of his anecdotes, starring Damien, or Cecily, or Cindy, or Takashi, artists whose names make the students perk up like puppies shown a treat. Annie rolls her eyes and glances over at Maria, who appears absorbed in her work. Hair gathered up in a messy bun, her work shirt paint-spattered and a streak of blue on her cheek and she still manages to look elegant. When she was that age, Annie hadn't had Maria's confidence, her composure. "All right, enough of that. Let's get back to work kids," Tim finally says.

Annie finds herself curiously unsettled on the mornings when she's to have painting class. She packs a nicer shirt and takes more care with her eyeliner. One night she has a strange dream. She's with someone; someone's hands are on her, not Matt's. She wakes, still in the glow of the dream, to Matt in bed beside her, gently snoring, cocooned in the quilt.

Annie gets to the studio earlier than usual and finds Maria alone there. The girl turns to Annie. "So how 's the class going for you?" Annie, happy to be chatting with the usually reserved Maria, answers quickly that she's had so much fun. "Yes, quite a teacher, our Tim," says Maria. "He can be a pain in the ass sometimes, but he's a really good painter. And he definitely takes an interest in his students. The personal touch," she adds, with a little smirk. Does Maria know Tim's interest in her may be . . . more than professional? Were they, possibly, seeing each other? If so, there wouldn't be anything wrong with that, right? Maria's young, but an adult. Annie hopes she'll go on. But Phoebe bounces in, calling out, "Guys, I had the best idea for a painting. Wait till you see what I'm doing today!" Annie feels a small prick of disappointment as Maria turns back to her own easel.

Too soon, the final session arrives; class is ending for the summer. The others will be off, interning in galleries or for arts organizations, teaching in summer camps or waitressing or bussing at a beach resort. For Annie, it'll be the usual, working and trying to make sure her kids are productively occupied; maybe a family week at the shore, if Matt can get away. Phoebe, to everyone's surprise, has won a fellowship to a prestigious art institute on the Pacific coast. "Yay, you! But to be honest, I'm jealous," Niles says, as he hugs her. "Everyone wants to be the one to get picked." Tim himself has been awarded a residency in Wisconsin and has proclaimed himself eager to go and paint cows, eat cheese, and drink beer. He's set up a still life for the last session but for once Annie isn't going with it. She doesn't even bother sketching, but picks up her brush and begins whisking pigment on, filling the empty white.

She works quickly, with her customary light hand. She renders the hard-edged precision of Quinn's canvas of battling robots, the romantic lyricism of Phoebe's dancing unicorns, Jinx's photo-realist phallic stones, the Art Squad's revolutionary slogans and ironic depictions of crushed plastic water bottles and rude cartoon characters. Actually, she's come to differentiate among them; the tall, ex-quarterback-looking guy who styles himself Brian Orange (né Orenstein) does stuff that's inventive, a cut above the others'. And in the center, like a heavenly queen surrounded by lesser saints, Annie paints a woman, using the most economical of brushstrokes, rendering out of the air a river of hair, the delicate flared nostrils, dark eyes and curve of the lips, the long throat, the tiny points of nipples beneath the chambray shirt, soft from many washings. Annie paints her bathed in light. Tim makes his way around the room, critiquing and kibitzing. Annie doesn't watch for him; her brush flies, layering tiny embellishments of the main figure, each feathery incursion elucidating more of its beauty, setting it in the canvas as a jewel, un-ignorable.

She feels a prickle at the back of her neck, hears a soft intake of breath. It's Tim, behind her. His eyes on her painting, transfixed by the figure. "You're doing something interesting here," he says, quietly. "That central figure. It looks like . . ." and he trails off. He's in love with the girl, Annie thinks. He can't even say her name. Phoebe jumps over to see what's going on. "Annie, this is amazing. Maria, she got you perfectly!" Maria rises and weaves her way to Annie's easel in the back. Annie sees the line that etches itself between the girl's brows, the tight downturn at the corners of her pretty mouth. "I don't know," she says. "I'm pretty sure my boobs aren't that big. Right, Tim?" Something twists in Annie's stomach. "Maria, I'm so sorry, I didn't mean . . ." Maria gives her a crooked smile. "No worries!" but Annie still feels terrible.

Later, when everyone's packing up and saying goodbye, Annie dawdles in hopes of apologizing again, but Maria's in close conversation with Brian. The two of them stroll out together, and it's too late. Annie is gathering her things when Tim, surrounded as usual by students, looks up and says, "Um, Anna? Can you stay a minute? I'd like to speak with you." Annie waits, wishing she could vanish. What could he want? She's afraid she's going to get scolded for objectifying Maria. That's what it looked like, right? But she doesn't think she had been; she was just seeing, trying to see her in a certain perspective. After the students finish an interminable round of "goodbye" and "have a good summer" and "catch you in Beacon for the

Kramer retrospective," after the last of them has trotted out the door, Tim motions her forward.

"Anna. I wanted to talk to you," he says. "You've been doing some good work lately. Your painting is strange. Intense." That isn't how Annie would have described her style. Interesting. He rests a big hand on her shoulder. "So. An artist I know, a friend, gives a summer class down in Soho; two days a week, a six-week session, extremely competitive. He's offering a fellowship to one of my students who'll do it as a work-study, come early and stay late to assist in the studio. Might you be interested? To work with . . ." and he drops a name that makes Annie catch her breath. Tim goes on, "I'd planned to recommend . . ." he surprises her with, ". . . Phoebe, but she got the Sandhill fellowship. But today it hit me—how your work has progressed here. How much you've gained from my instruction, the class. So I thought, hell, why not Anna?"

"Thank you, Tim." His name feels awkward in her mouth. Even if it sounds like it was something of an afterthought, he'd chosen her. Annie tamps down her rising excitement, calculating. How could she manage to fit in two days a week down in lower Manhattan with her job, the kids? What if there's an emergency and she and Matt are both in the city?

"Wow, thank you so much. It sounds wonderful," she stalls. A chance to work with an artist whose work she's admired forever, a genius, really. What would that experience let her see? How might her own style, whatever it was, articulate? She'd have to take more control of her work assignment schedule. Celia could go to camp; maybe a day-trippers program for Sky? Jake would be home the summer before college, able to be called on if Sky needs help. Come summer, Matt might even have more flexible hours . . . .

Annie becomes aware of Tim's hand, still on her shoulder, the warmth and weight of it. Has the pressure increased, or is it her imagination? Is this the price of being seen? After another second of pretending it's not there, she shifts her feet and the hand is quickly retracted. Tim raises his arms, palms facing Annie, as if in benediction or to show blamelessness, like perps when they're caught or contestants in TV baking contests when they're told time's up. Annie backs up another step; gives him a steady look.

"Yes," she says. She allows herself to feel a little thrill. "Yes, I'd love to." She has the sudden impulse to press on further with the day's painting, maybe scratch some scribbly lines into the canvas or add more vibrant color. Maybe something she hasn't even dreamed of yet.

Drop / Tonissa Saul

Leaving the Farm

Elizabeth Gauffreau

Maggie's house was the last building standing on a farm in Vermont that had not been worked since Calvin Coolidge was president, the barn taken down when she and Tom bought the property, the various outbuildings, afterthoughts to the barn, now gently collapsed onto their shallow foundations and covered with vines.

Across the road stood a small hay barn, open in the front and close to the road. For years, the barn had received no maintenance, its rough boards weathered gray, its tin roof streaked with rust, yet it had stood straight and sturdy all those years, keeping the hay dry through the winter. It was not until Tom's death that Maggie noticed signs of deterioration, boards coming loose, the tin roof peeling back at the corners.

No one knew she was alone in the house, alone and a widow. Her niece did not know, her neighbors did not know. None of Tom's family knew. Overnight, Maggie had become a different person, a person without Tom, a different person for the rest of her life and *no one knew.*

The coroner knew. He had come and taken Tom's body away. One of the men who came with him had stripped the soiled bedding and taken it with him to be disposed of, opened the windows to air the room. The windows were open still, two hours later, the dank November chill now settled throughout the house.

Maggie herself did not know how long she had been alone. She and Tom had gone to bed together at ten as usual, talked for a bit, read for a bit, kissed goodnight. He had died in his sleep. Peacefully, so she would say when she finally roused herself enough to make the phone calls, having no way of knowing it had been otherwise. If it had been otherwise, she had not awakened, and he had died alone.

She wondered if the house looked any different, now that there was a widow living in it instead of a couple, just as it would have looked different if she and Tom had been a family, with children and a large mongrel dog. Was the yard suddenly unkempt, chokecherry bushes covering the downstairs windows, the driveway overgrown with weeds? Was the paint peeling, the wood rotting, the shingles on the roof tattered and useless against the rain? She herself must be different now, too, the unfathomable emptiness inside her manifesting itself in her face, her eyes, her legs, her hands. Would she recognize herself in the mirror now? Would she dare look in a mirror now?

She had to make the calls. There were so many people to call. It was not right to withhold Tom's death from them. But she could not call them now. How could she call them without knowing how Tom's funeral would be staged? They would ask about the arrangements, and if she had nothing to tell them, Tom would be disappointed.

Tom expected it of her, to stage his funeral for maximum impact, to stage it as he himself would have staged it, so that each person in attendance would take home only one image, the defining moment of the scene. The moment when all in attendance celebrate a life lived to its fullest and ended at a fitting time. The moment when the widow takes solace in the discovery of how many of his students' lives her husband had changed for the better. The moment when the widow realizes that she never really knew her husband at all. The moment when the widow acknowledges for the first time that she is truly alone.

Would the scene be melancholy, tragic, suffused with irony? Would the weather be sunny, overcast, raining? Would the defining moment take place in the church or graveside? Would the mourners be dressed in black or in their ordinary clothes? Would the casket be ornate or plain, open or closed? Would there be flowers? Would a wind be blowing? Would the mourners be leaning on one another for solace or standing apart in their grief? Would their heads be covered or bare? Would the minister have a deep voice or a reedy voice? Would he wear vestments or a suit? For that matter, would the minister be a man or a woman? Would there be music, poetry, elegy, eulogy?

She did not know. Above all, the funeral could not be ordinary. Tom would be so hurt if his funeral were ordinary.

Betty Archambault guided her LTD slowly down Snyder Road, the tiny container of aspirin Norman had sent her out to buy at nine o'clock at night because his arthritis couldn't wait until the drugstore opened in the morning tucked into her coat pocket. The car felt unsteady on the icy road, and Betty drove with both hands tight on the steering wheel, the radio turned down to an indecipherable rise and fall of background noise.

Two feet of snow had fallen since morning, and the village crew had given the road their customary lick and a promise. While they had cleared the worst of the accumulation by noon, they had not put in another appearance until nearly four o'clock, when Johnny Erno roared past Betty's house in the village truck with his brother Jimmy standing in the back tossing out random sprays of dirt as he struggled to keep his balance.

The LTD skidded, and Betty sighed as she eased it back into the tracks left by the few cars which traveled the road. Even after living on Snyder Road for most of her life, driving it in the winter made her nervous. The snow leveled the landscape so that she could hardly tell what was road and what was ditch and what was her own front yard.

As Betty approached Maggie Sebastian's house, she thought she saw a light in one of the upstairs rooms. She looked up at the house as she passed it, but the car skidded again, and she could not be sure. Her rearview mirror showed nothing but the faint red glow of her own tail lights. By the time she reached her house with Norman's aspirin, she told herself it had been a trick of the light, headlights flashing against window glass. The Sebastian house was empty.

Maggie awoke with a feeling of anticipation so strong she had to open her eyes to ground herself in place and time. She was lying comfortably in her own bed, crystalline winter sunlight glittering through the bare windows of her bedroom, the house perfectly still. Her nose felt cold, and she took her hand from under the covers to touch it. As she slipped her hand back under the covers, its spotted skin and graceless shape quickly dispelled the sense she had had upon waking of being a young woman about to set off on an adventure—a young woman who, before the day was out, would have suddenly, inexplicably fallen in love.

Maggie was not one for summer romances. A summer romance was distracting for the participants, not to mention annoying for any unfortunate observers. Maggie had no time to be distracted when she played summer stock, not when there were lines to learn and props to obtain and, most of all, atmosphere to absorb.

Nevertheless, that summer, in the three short months before she was to begin a graduate program in drama in the fall, Maggie developed such a crush on the man who played George that she could not stand to be in the same room with him. Everything about him flustered her: his fine, handsome face, his soft, faded clothes, his lithe body, his sardonic humor. He had a beautiful speaking voice, an actor's voice, deep and warm and charmingly disingenuous. When it was her turn to paint flats with him, she would work with her head down, never taking her eyes off the brush in her hand, dreading the moment he would speak to her, leaning back on his heels and smiling.

The first time he spoke to her, he asked the usual questions: *Where are you from? What do you do? Where did you go to school?* and when she answered with three rudimentary facts of her life, he appeared as satisfied with her answers as if he meant to make use of them some day in a context which had nothing at all to do with her, his smile making creases in his face, just below the eyes, the muscles of his arm undulating beneath the skin as he passed the paint brush back and forth across the canvas.

The next time he spoke to her, to comment upon their director's infuriating lack of temperament during a rehearsal, she thought perhaps she had imagined it, pulling his wonderful voice from his throat herself, to linger warmly in her ear as she prepared for bed three hours later, wondering as she stood at her makeshift closet, three hooks and a clutter of wire hangers, if she dared wear her favorite outfit that summer, a peasant blouse, full skirt, and sandals, in front of him.

At the first cast party of the season, held at the pretentiously quaint cottage where the director was staying, Tom threw himself at her feet (she was sitting on a chaise lounge on the patio nursing a glass of rather bitter red wine and he plopped himself down on the foot of it) and announced, "I failed boilers." Maggie gaped at him and drew her feet up.

Tom reached for her hand and took the wine glass from it. "That's usually my best line. Piques their interest and all that."

Maggie tried to think of a clever rejoinder. "I'm not much interested in boilers."

"Neither am I. That's why I failed the course." Tom grimaced and handed the wine glass back to her.

"Oh." Maggie clutched the glass by its stem. Tom had made no move to change his position on the chaise.

"I changed my major to English," he said. "My father was terribly angry. He thought I would become a teacher. Those who can do, those who can't . . . you know."

Maggie inched her legs into a more comfortable position, a mere six inches from Tom's hand. "I tried teaching for a year after I graduated from college. My mother told me no good would come of it."

"No good would come of it," Tom intoned, his voice dipping low on *good*.

"That's right. No good came of it. The children told their parents they were frightened of me."

"Why would children be frightened of you?"

"I'm not sure." Maggie paused. "They were too frightened to say!"

Tom threw his head back and roared, reaching forward to grasp her ankle, where his smooth burning hand remained, for a mere moment or the rest of her life, Maggie could not say.

Maggie lay in bed a few minutes longer, waiting for the feeling of anticipation to return. Now that the furniture was gone, the room had taken on a different smell, which in her exhaustion the day before she had been unable to identify. For forty years, her bedroom had had its own distinct smell of winter: a musk of cedar, wool, and furniture polish. But now, the room had taken on the smell of the house itself, of wood and plaster, the way the air outside took on the smell of bare trees before it snowed.

Having movers in the house had tired her terribly, and she had spent most of the previous day in bed, reading and napping, relieved at last to be left alone, free of the movers' questions *and this? and this? and this too?* and free of Betty's hustling her out of the drafts that swirled into the house as the movers carried out a mattress, then a bureau, then a cardboard wardrobe filled with summer dresses.

Maggie reached for her bathrobe and shuddered as she got out of bed. The room was painfully cold. She turned on the warmer light in the bathroom and chose wool slacks, a turtleneck, and a thick sweater from the closet. As she waited for the bathroom to become warm enough for her to dress, she stood by the window looking out at the beguiling radiance of sunlight on new snow.

Later, sitting on the window seat in the study with her breakfast, Maggie wished she could fix herself a nice fire in the wood stove. She had not built a fire since Tom's death, and the stove had remained cold, its stale smell of ashes fading as the weeks passed. Looking out the window to the end of her driveway, she noted without alarm that she was snowed in. Tommy LaRose would more than likely come to plow her out before the afternoon light faded. He generally did her driveway at the end of his regular rounds, after the others, the ones who had children to get to the bus stop and jobs to get to.

As she looked back into the room, the empty bookshelves gave her an unexpected jolt of sadness. She had not gone through Tom's books after he died, keeping them on the shelves where he had left them, until she went through her own when she made the decision to leave the farm, a few passed on to relatives, some donated to the College, most to the public library. The only book of hers that she held back for the remainder of her time at the farmhouse was a thick anthology of women poets.

The travel mementoes that had been scattered among the books were gone, too, given to the Sebastians—the kylix from Greece to Tom's brother, the bright wooden menagerie from Mexico to a grandnephew's son, the dish of mismatched pewter buttons of forgotten origin to Tom's sister. For a brief moment Maggie regretted having given them away. Their absence reminded her of all those summer trips abroad with Tom and her inability to stop herself from envisioning the forest reclaiming the farm because they weren't there to stop it. They would be standing by a lake in Switzerland or watching a play in London or taking photographs in Rome, and suddenly she would see before her eyes the approach to the farm as though coming upon it from the road, and the pasture would be gone, the meadow gone, their driveway gone, maples and pines and brambles growing there instead, all access to their house blocked, the house itself unrecognizable, a lichen-covered mass under the trees.

Setting her breakfast tray on the floor, she leaned back and rested her head against the cold window glass as she looked out the opposite window, her vision unable to see past the for-sale sign hanging askew in her front yard, its painted yellow post having been barely driven into frozen ground.

The telephone rang, and she rose without hesitation to answer it. She was, she quickly assured herself, neither a misanthrope nor a dotard. If she could get to the phone without falling and risking broken bones, she would answer it. If not, whoever it was could call back.

"Mrs. Sebastian?" A female voice, ingratiating and overly familiar.

"Speaking."

"Mrs. Sebastian, Maggie, this is Carol, Carol Rollins. I've been trying to call you all morning at Brookfield Commons, but there was no answer. I had no idea you were still at the house. We have a prospect."

"A prospect for what?"

"For the house. A prospective buyer."

"I see."

"He's already ridden by the house with me, and he seems interested, *very* interested. He's eager to see the inside. I have every expectation that once he sees it, he will offer our asking price."

Carol, a thin blonde in her forties, struck Maggie as somehow feline, her voice in particular. As she gave Maggie a synopsis of the prospect's financial status, Maggie envisioned a cat with a dead bird in its mouth: carrying the bird into the house, laying it proudly on the carpet at her master's feet, looking up expectantly for praise—but meeting only revulsion.

"I'd like to bring him by today, if possible," Carol continued. "What time would be good for you? It's best to do it while it's still light; before three o'clock would be best."

"I'm sorry, I can't do it today. I'm right in the middle of something, and I can't be interrupted."

"Oh, but you won't be! You just make yourself scarce, and I'll show the house."

"Yes, of course, but today is simply not convenient. Why don't I give you a ring tomorrow to set up a time? Good-bye now!" Maggie hung up before Carol had a chance to say anything else and, shaking her head at how much of the morning had passed, made her way through the empty living room to the spare room.

This room was now filled with cardboard boxes, the packing tape peeling off, brittle with storage and age. Jack Archambault had carried all of the boxes from their storage places—from the top shelves of closets, from the shed next to the kitchen and the loft over the garage—and arranged them so she could begin at the door and work her way to the back of the room, going through each box and disposing of its contents without having to lift anything heavy.

As she stood in the doorway, she recognized some of the boxes, easily visualizing their contents and the day she had packed them. The others she would stumble into unprepared. She wondered if she would find anything of Tom's, throwing back the flaps of a box to reveal a jumble of wire, model train pieces, and chunks of quartz, the sort of junk a boy would keep in the bottom drawer of his bureau and a man would keep in a box in the garage so he would never forget what it had been like to be a boy.

The first box she opened contained fabric, some stained tablecloths she could throw out, and a picture her grandmother had painted. The fabric would go to her niece Gwen, even though Gwen hadn't sewn in years. Maggie packaged the fabric securely in brown paper and enclosed a note: The rose print is from Austria, one-of-a-kind, according to the shopkeeper we bought it from, Tom haggling in German out of one side of his mouth and grumbling in English *You don't sew!* out of the other. The red cotton is from Guatemala—it's vegetable-dyed, so it will bleed. The green gingham my mother Mary bought before the First World War and never made up—it is only thirty-six inches wide, so watch your layout!

The painting, a vase of flowers on white velvet, would also go to Gwen. Maggie's grandmother, Gwen's great-grandmother, had done the painting the year before she married: it had hung in her bedroom all her life. Maggie wrapped the package and addressed it without telling Gwen that for the last thirty years, the painting had remained packed in a box in a closet because it was not very good. It was the sort of thing that young, well-to-do Victorian women did for lack of something better to do, and Tom in particular thought the top shelf of a closet was the appropriate place to keep it.

The telephone rang as Maggie was carrying the two wrapped packages into the kitchen. She hesitated only briefly before deciding not to answer it and returned to the spare room to break down the box she had just emptied before taking it to the shed.

When the telephone stopped ringing, Maggie thought she heard the sound of an engine straining. She looked out the kitchen window but couldn't see anyone at first, the smooth expanse of white snow unbroken except for the for-sale sign. The engine sounded close. As she continued to look out the window, she saw a jeep at the end of the driveway, pushing at the hard bank of snow the village plow had left. That would be Tommy LaRose coming to plow her out now that the snow had stopped. He seemed to be having a hard time of it, and she wondered why. He didn't usually have that much trouble, even after a big storm.

Looking more closely, she saw three people sitting in the jeep. She watched as it backed up and strained forward, making only small progress against the snow bank. As she continued to watch, the jeep finally broke through and quickly pushed the rest of the snow to the side. It backed up again and began inching its way up her driveway, clearing as it went. When it reached the study window, she saw who was driving: Jack Archambault.

His parents were the two passengers, Norman in the front, Betty in the seat behind him, leaning forward with her hand on Norman's shoulder.

It did not surprise Maggie to see them. One of them must have seen her light on last night. She sighed. She should have expected it. Well, at least they had not brought the sheriff. And since they had come, she could ask Jack to take the packages for Gwen to the post office.

The jeep stopped, and the three Archambaults came stomping through the snow to the ell by the kitchen. Maggie greeted them at the door. "Well, hello. What brings you out today? You didn't have to plow my driveway. You know Tommy LaRose does it."

Betty peered anxiously into the room. "Are you all right, Maggie? What happened? I didn't mean to just up and leave you here."

Maggie closed the kitchen door behind Norman, who had lagged behind his wife and son. "You didn't. I have a few things left to finish before I move. It shouldn't take me much longer."

"But I thought you was leaving the day the movers was here. You had it all planned out."

Norman was looking uncomfortable, already making motions to his wife that he wanted to leave. "Is there anything we can do for you, Maggie?" he said. "Is there anything you need?"

She picked up the packages on the counter and held them out to him. "Why, yes, Norman, now that you mention it, there is." Jack laughed at this, but Norman stood impassive, his farmer's mouth set in a thin, firm line.

"What is it, Maggie?"

She opened a cupboard by the sink and took down her purse. "I just need these two packages mailed, if you wouldn't mind." She took a bill from her wallet. "Twenty dollars should be enough. Please insure the larger one for two hundred dollars."

Norman made no move to take either the money or the two packages.

Betty took the twenty-dollar bill from Maggie's hand and reached for the packages. "I'll take them when I go to town." She tucked the twenty-dollar bill into her purse. "Maybe you should stay with us while you finish your things, and I could help you."

Maggie shook her head. "No, thank you, that's lovely of you to offer, but I'll be fine."

Norman nodded once and cleared his throat. "We'll be going then." He opened the door, and Jack followed him out to the jeep.

Betty stayed behind. "I didn't mean to just leave you here. I thought somebody was coming for you. I had no idea there was nobody coming for you."

"There are things I need to do," Maggie said.

Betty nodded. She turned the collar of her coat up before reaching for the doorknob. "You shouldn't be staying here alone."

Maggie folded her arms across her chest as Betty opened the door and cold air scuttled across the room. "I know."

Standing at the window watching the jeep back out of the driveway, Maggie marveled at how easily and naturally the truth had slipped out of her.

Over the next week, the weather stayed clear, and Maggie was interrupted by at least one telephone call each day, sometimes two: from Carol Rollins, from Brookfield Commons, and of course from Gwen, pleading with her not to stay in the empty house alone in a misguided attempt to organize the past for the future. After the second or third day, Maggie tried leaving the receiver off the hook, but late that afternoon the sheriff appeared at her kitchen door. She invited him in, assured him that she was all right, and sent him to the post office to mail a package. Betty Archambault stopped by twice with casseroles, which Maggie gratefully accepted. Her task was taking longer than she had originally anticipated: after she emptied each box, wrote an explanatory note, packaged its contents, and took the empty box to the shed, there was another box to go through, and another, and another, and another.

Now she had found a box of silver—chafing dishes and candlesticks and serving spoons, wedding gifts to an untold number of long-dead brides. She had to carry each piece to the kitchen, rub off the tarnish, decipher the monogram, and polish the piece to a shine before she could decide who should get it and begin writing the notes and wrapping the packages. She had just begun working on her great-grandmother's serving spoon, the silver worn thin and fragile from years of use, when the telephone rang.

"Mrs. Sebastian, Maggie, I need an answer. We don't have any other nibbles right now. It's very difficult to sell during the winter."

Wedging the phone between her ear and her shoulder, Maggie reached for a towel and wiped her hands, staining the towel pink and gray. "You're calling about the prospect."

"Yes! Are you ready for me to show the house?"

Maggie took the receiver down from her ear and wiped the towel over it. "When did he want to come?"

"Any time, Maggie! We've just been waiting for you."

Maggie set the towel down on the counter. "I suppose you could come this afternoon. In fact, you probably should, before it snows again. We're due for another storm."

"That's wonderful!" Carol said. "Mr. Webber will be so pleased. Will one-thirty be all right? How's the road? I haven't been out there in a couple of weeks."

"The road is fine. You shouldn't have any trouble with my driveway either. I shall expect you at one-thirty, then."

"One-thirty it is!"

Maggie went back to the serving spoon and thoughtfully rubbed the bowl. The sale of the house was her biggest decision, and if she continued to put it off, someone else—Gwen, or more likely, Gwen's lawyer—would make the decision for her. Even so, she didn't know how she could bear another showing. The peering eyes, the mud tracked across the floors, the intense discussions of Williamsburg colors.

Maggie set the polished spoon on the counter. "Tom," she said aloud, "it's not our house anymore. Just remember that."

It was after three o'clock before Carol and the prospect pulled into the driveway in Carol's black Jaguar. Carol got out first, her scarlet coat bright against the snow. The prospect emerged from the car in a camel's hair coat, with a paisley scarf tossed around his neck. His head was bare, his hair carefully blow-dried. His fingernails, when he graciously extended his hand to Maggie in greeting, would be manicured.

Maggie stood at the kitchen door watching Carol gingerly pick her way through the snow in leather boots with three-inch heels, her gloved hand grasping the prospect's arm. When they reached the ell and stood stamping the snow from their feet, Maggie noticed that the prospect was wearing boots—rubber boots with leather tops from L.L. Bean.

"Maggie, this is Michael Webber from Hanover."

His pants were right, gray wool with a sharp crease, but to go with his camel's hair coat and fine wool scarf, he should have been wearing lawyer's loafers or wingtips safely encased in black rubbers.

"How do you do, Mrs. Sebastian?" He extended his hand and shook hers before she had a chance to offer it. She looked up from his feet and withdrew her hand. "Fine, thank you, Mr. Webber. I'm glad you could come on such short notice."

He smiled. "Not at all. Thank you for having me. I've been very eager to view the property."

View the property? Who would call her house *the property*? Who would come to her house dressed like a lawyer with L.L. Bean boots on his feet? She flashed a look at Carol, the carrion real estate agent.

"Well, now!" said Carol. She took off her gloves, loosening each tight leather finger before pulling the glove over her knuckles. "Well, now! If you need to get back to what you were doing, Maggie, I'd be happy to show Mr. Webber the house."

Maggie made no move to leave. She turned to Michael Webber. He had loosened his scarf, she noticed, but he had not unbuttoned his coat any further than the top button. "This is the kitchen," she said. "The floor, the moldings, and the ceiling beams are original to the house. Everything else is not.

"All the appliances convey," Maggie continued. "Tell me, Mr. Webber, are you married? Does your wife like to cook? My husband and I used to cook lovely meals in this room." She took Michael Webber's arm. "And right through this doorway is the dining room. It has a built-in china cabinet"—she pulled the doors open and closed—"and a *delightful* view of the woods. You'll notice the patio through the French doors here—or maybe you won't—it's buried in snow. But once summer comes, you and your wife can dine al fresco on the patio and barbeque for your friends and colleagues. Or, Mr. Webber, are you more of a family man? With children, Mr. Webber? And what you're really looking for is a big eat-in kitchen and a den for the television and wall-to-wall carpet for the little ones to play on. Tell me, Mr. Webber, is that what you're looking for?"

She abruptly stopped speaking and looked out the French doors at the yard. The mid-afternoon sun cast a cold pink light over the snow. She felt light-headed and strange, as if she were no longer in her own body. Carol's voice buzzed behind her. *I'm sorry . . . so sorry . . . .*

Maggie spoke as Carol continued her apologies. "If you will excuse me, I have work to do. I'm sure Mrs. Rollins can answer any questions you have about the house." She left the room as quickly as she could, gathering up her silver polish and rags and taking them into the spare room, where she shut the door firmly behind her.

As she lifted another newspaper-swathed bundle from the box of silver and set it in her lap, she could hear Carol and the prospect leave the dining room and go back into the kitchen. A door creaked open and closed; Maggie had neglected to show him the pantry. Then Carol's heels sounded across the living room, each step leaving a tiny indentation in the hundred-and-fifty-year-old floor. The heels paused by the fireplace—fieldstone hearth, original mantle—and again by one of the windows—original muntins, original glass. They continued out into the hall, paused again by the closed door of the spare room, and resumed past the bathroom, up the stairs, and into the study. Maggie wondered why Carol was bothering to go through with it. She knew as well as Maggie did what Michael Webber was after, and it wasn't pine floors, built-ins, or fireplaces.

After she heard their footsteps creak up the stairs to the old wing, where the bedrooms were, Maggie continued to hear their voices, but no more footsteps. They must be discussing price. She reached for a clean rag.

Tom had found the house one hot summer night in mid-July. They had just gotten back from a trip to Scotland, and even with all the windows open, the air in their Hanover house was unbearably close. After changing their clothes and unpacking their bags, they ate a late supper and left town.

Tom drove with no particular destination in mind, crossing the river into Vermont. Coming on an unpaved road, which looked the same as the other unpaved roads he had already passed by, he said, "This looks good," and turned.

Woods lined both sides of the road, and the air felt cooler than it had in town. There was a smell of water beyond the trees, and they passed a sign for a summer camp. Cabin lights glimmered through the trees, and they could hear the distant sound of girls singing. Tom slowed the car, pulled as far off the narrow road as he could, and turned off the engine. The girls' voices sounded young and clear carried on the night air with the smell of trees and water.

"'Simple Gifts,'" Maggie said.

"What?"

"'Simple Gifts.' The song they're singing."

"Oh." Tom leaned his head back on the seat, his angled profile sharp. "Yes, you're right. You must have gone to summer camp when you were a kid." He fingered his chin. "We all did, I suppose."

"Yes, we did." But not like he thought, not like that at all. Not the rented cabin in the Adirondacks, middle class cousins spending two weeks tanned and disheveled, wrestling on the grass, swimming at will, while their mothers fretted over lunch and their fathers sat on the porch with their shirt collars off and books turned over their knees, on vacation. "I went to Girl Scout camp."

"Girl Scout camp?" Tom's hand came down from his chin. "You were a Girl Scout? How Fascist of you."

"I know. I loved it." The uniform, the salutes, the songs, the pledges. "I loved every bit of it. I was an avid Girl Scout, a *fanatic* Girl Scout. I even won an award from the President."

"Of the United States?"

"Yes. I went to Washington, and he presented it to me. I have a picture of it, of Calvin Coolidge shaking my hand. Haven't I shown it to you? I was very impressed with myself."

Tom shook his head. "Uh uh. How about Calvin Coolidge?"

"Oh, he was impressed with me, too."

"I'm sure. I meant were you impressed with him?"

"No, not really. I think I made him nervous. I was bigger than he."

Tom smiled at that, and his hand went back to his chin. Even after twenty years of marriage, Maggie felt a quiver of insecurity pass through her. In middle age, Tom's body had turned tough and sinewy, while hers had softened, broadened. She had never been slender; even as a young woman she had had a healthy, sturdy body, with large breasts and thick ankles. Sometimes, in the summer, when Tom sat on the edge of the bed in his pajama bottoms before turning out the light, she would look at his belly for signs of thickening or sagging and feel a twinge of betrayal.

The girls were singing a different song now, one she didn't recognize. Tom said, "I wish I'd met you sooner, when you were still a girl."

"Why? Don't you know enough about me already?" The girls' song continued, high and sweet and out of reach. "I was very self-righteous. And athletic. It's a bad combination in a girl."

Headlights flashed in the rearview mirror just then, and Tom pulled back onto the road. After a few miles, the trees cleared, and Maggie smelled hay. It smelled good, strong and musty. Crickets chittered in the tall grass on both sides of the road. An owl hooted from an unseen tree or fencepost. There were no human sounds anywhere, no houses, no lights, just their car, the engine loud and steady, the tires crunching gravel, the heavy chrome bumper deflecting stones, the headlights cutting two small swaths through the immense summer darkness.

"There's a house over there," Tom said, slowing the car and pointing through the windshield. "Do you see it?" He eased the car to a stop. "Let's go look at it."

"How do you know no one lives there?" Maggie said. "You don't want to go nosing around some farmer's house in the middle of the night. You could get shot."

"No one lives there. No one's lived there for years." He opened his door.

Maggie got out of the car and slammed her door, loud enough, she hoped, to wake whoever was in the house so that he would not be taken by surprise. As soon as they had stepped away from the car and started toward the house, she knew Tom was right. There was no driveway, just grass and weeds. Her canvas espadrilles were soon filled with stones, her skirt wet with dew. When they were about halfway there, close enough to see broken windows—not all of the glass Carol had pointed to was original—and a collapsing front porch, Tom turned back. "I'm going to get a flashlight. So we can see inside."

Even in the dark, Maggie could tell the house had not been lived in for years. Tom returned and played the flashlight over mottled wallpaper, crumbling plaster, and a crust of bird droppings on the floor. When they had looked through as many windows as they could reach from the ground, Tom clicked off the flashlight, and they headed back to the car. "Let's live here," he said. "We can come out tomorrow in the daylight and find out what town we're in; then we'll check the records to see if anyone owns the place. I'll bet we can get it for back taxes."

Maggie had agreed without hesitation. They had lived in the same house in Hanover for fifteen years, within walking distance of the College and the shops, the same house the other faculty lived in: three bedrooms, oak floors, kitchen updated every ten years, wallpaper and paint done every five. A box hedge in front and a clothesline in back, where the neighbors couldn't see it.

Maggie heard footsteps above her head; the stairs creaked. The footsteps came closer, followed by a rap on her closed door. She rose stiffly and opened the door on Carol's thin, satisfied face, Michael Webber standing several paces behind her, buttoning his top button and arranging his fine paisley scarf around his neck. "Did Mr. Webber see everything he wanted to see?" Maggie asked her.

Carol was drawing on her gloves. "Yes, thank you, we'll be on our way now." She drew Maggie aside and said in a stage whisper, "I should have an offer for you in a couple of hours."

Maggie whispered back, "Don't bother. I'm not selling."

"I'm ready to see the rest of the property now," Michael Webber announced.

Maggie frowned and said to Carol, "I thought you showed him the entire house."

Michael Webber interjected before Carol had a chance to respond, "Yes, she did, it's very nice, but I came to see the property."

Maggie gestured toward the nearest window. "There it is."

Michael Webber's smooth brow creased slightly as he turned to Carol. "You said this property includes fifty acres in addition to the three around the house."

"Oh, yes," Carol said, "it does. Wooded."

"I'll need to see the acreage before I can make an offer."

"Indeed," Maggie said. "And how do you propose to do that?"

He looked down at his rubber L.L. Bean boots with the leather tops. "Don't you have—?"

She shook her head. "Not in the winter. There's no way to get back there. You'll have to wait until spring."

Both Carol's and Michael Webber's eyes widened at the thought of their profit melting away in the spring runoff. "Don't you have—?" they cried in unison.

"There was an old pair of snowshoes in the shed," Maggie said, "but the movers should have taken them."

The three of them marched single-file into the shed. The snowshoes, simple bear paws, were still there, hanging on a nail on a stud. Michael Webber looked dubious. "Where are the bindings?"

Maggie pointed to two crumbling rawhide laces draped over the nail. "It was nice to have met you, Mr. Webber."

She went back into the kitchen, locking the door behind her. Standing at the kitchen window, she watched the shed door open onto the ell as Michael Webber tried to exit the shed with the snowshoes laced to his feet. When he had gotten himself to the driveway, he straightened his back, tucked his scarf inside his coat, and set off for the woods, blond hair whipping around his head, camel's hair coat flapping, arms and snowshoes flailing. Carol Rollins stood forlornly in the driveway next to her Jaguar waiting for him to return, his hands cold but still limber enough to prepare a purchase offer.

The following day, Maggie awoke at first light and could not go back to sleep. She tried closing her eyes and breathing deeply, but her irritating wakefulness did not pass. She could tell by the muted quality of the light in the room that it had snowed the night before. Waking to the dull light of snow had always given her an odd feeling, a kind of restlessness that brought with it the sense that something was about to happen if only she could articulate it in time.

She got out of bed and went to the window. An expanse of new snow stretched from her house to the edge of the woods. There had been another storm. The room was unimaginably quiet, as if the snow that encased the house were muffling its customary creaks and groans. She was snowed in.

Looking down from her window, Maggie felt her throat constrict, and she had the anxious feeling that she could not remember where anything was under the snow. Tom used to have a garden—a big one covering nearly half an acre with corn and tomatoes and zucchini and rows of herbs for cooking. The garden had gone to seed after his death, but, still, she should know where it was. She should be able to trace the outline of dried stalks and withered vines and crumpled weeds which marked its place. Yesterday she had been so confident as she pointed out the patio to the prospect, Michael Webber, but now she could see nothing but the smooth snow, obliterating everything.

Beyond the patio was a swimming pool, its protective cover also buried in snow, its location evident only by the mound made by the pump house. She and Tom had installed the pool for swimming laps when they both developed arthritis. As she stood at the window looking at the pump house, remembering the sun sparkling off the clean blue water and the feel of the water under her and over her and against her skin, she knew she would never swim in the pool again; her body would never feel that way again.

She did not want to go. She spoke aloud in the empty bedroom. "I do not want to go." There, she had said it, and, she supposed, Tom had heard it. "I do not want to go."

It had been the sensible decision, to sell her house and move to Brookfield Commons. She was old, damn it, and there was no denying it. She was eighty-five years old, and although she did not feel as though her body were falling apart, it had lost its strength; there was a fragility in the core of her bones that she could sense with every move she made, whether walking across a room, or getting up from a chair, or turning over in bed.

Leaving the farm was the sensible thing to do, but she did not want to go. She would be living in town. She would never again have an unobstructed view from her window. There would always be something in the way: a telephone pole, a building, a parked car. There would be no fields, no woods; the air would be filled with noise, traffic and plumbing and querulous voices, and once she left her house, she could never go back.

She would have to take her evening meal in the common dining area. She would have an assigned seat. There would be planned activities: crafts and greenhouse gardening, poetry classes taught by some woman from the DAR. The thought was too much to bear. She turned away from the silence of her window to the silence of her bedroom. "How am I going to get out of this one, Tom? Can you tell me that, Tom?"

Tom gave her no reply, so she dressed and ate a little breakfast, still waiting to hear his voice, perfectly modulated and a little sardonic. *I'm afraid not. You've caught me fresh out of ideas, baby.* After a second cup of coffee, which she knew she shouldn't have, she went into the spare room to work, the absence of Tom's voice reverberating softly inside her head.

Maggie sat on the window seat in the study wrapped in a hundred-year-old Hudson Bay blanket. The blanket, still thick and tight against the cold, smelled strongly of old wool and, faintly, cedar. Outside the blanket, the air in the house was cold enough to stiffen the skin of her face. Outside the house, the temperature was twenty below zero, the bright snow immutable under the cold winter sun.

Maggie had finished going through her things, and the spare room was now empty, the door closed, the empty boxes carted away, the floor swept clean of the unidentifiable detritus which falls from boxes that have been stored for a very long time.

The tarnished silver and yellowed linens, smudged vases and orphaned lengths of tatting, which had seemed so meaningful two months before, were gone. The special things, the things with stories behind them, Maggie had mailed individually, to family members she thought might appreciate them, the stories, if not the items themselves. But some of the things, most of the things, while still usable, had no stories, no significance associated with them at all, and Maggie had boxed them all up together and called Gwen to come and get them, Gwen accepting out of a sense of obligation, Maggie supposed, to store them in her attic, until her two children acquired attics of their own. Gwen arrived in her large station wagon with her husband, clucking over the puddles of melted snow they left on the floor as they carried the boxes out to the car, exclaiming over the farm's isolation and pleading with Maggie to leave it at last.

Maggie did not know what to do, whether she should remain as she was, unmoving inside the blanket, conserving her energy, conserving her warmth, or whether she should throw off the blanket and move around, walk from room to empty room, to generate warmth herself. For the first time since she had moved her furniture out, her house felt empty and cold, all traces of Tom gone, and few traces of herself left, just her winter clothes, some food in the refrigerator, and a thick anthology of women poets. She would leave no legacy, no recorded performances, no writing of any consequence, no plays, no poetry, just a few articles published in academic journals and hundreds of letters, if any of the recipients had bothered to keep them.

An odd feeling passed over her, like the shadow of an immense cloud overhead moving majestically across the ground, blocking out the sun where she stood, only to continue advancing, leaving her behind to stand in the sunlight once again. When the feeling had passed, she looked out the window, at the hard, packed snow of her empty driveway, the bare brittle branches of the trees which bordered it, the truncated piece of road which fronted it, the half-buried hay barn which faced it, and wondered if her staying in the farmhouse were indeed folly, as Gwen believed, the self-indulgence of an old woman who had the financial wherewithal to do as she pleased, regardless of the consequences to herself or her family—or, even worse, affectation. In Vermont, the beginning of February was when hard winter set in, when the Norman Archambaults took each armload of wood for the furnace warily, eyeing the woodpile with increasing trepidation, when the Betty Archambaults approached the pantry, the mason jars of tomatoes and green beans, with the same wary eye, just as their sons who worked construction watched their savings, praying the weather would break before the money ran out. And she knew none of it, nor had Tom during his lifetime, their relationship with the land only aesthetic after all.

The weather did not break for a week, and Maggie spent most of that time wrapped in the Hudson Bay blanket reading. It felt good to read poetry by herself in her empty house, and she marveled that she had existed for so long, days, weeks, months, years without reading the poem which at that moment she was reading.

At the end of each poem, she paused to look out the window and consider what had prompted the poet to write the poem, what experience, prosaic or profound, what feeling, fleeting or sustained, what image, intense or barely perceived, and to wonder how the poet had felt when she knew the poem was finished, to imagine her laying down a pen, cranking a piece of paper out of a typewriter, leaning back in her chair and exulting aloud to an empty room.

As she read, Maggie slowly began to feel herself again, to feel Tom's presence in the house again. The house did not seem as empty, the prospect of spring so unimaginable. Maggie heard the sound of a car engine in her driveway. She was not surprised to see that the engine belonged to Carol Rollins' black Jaguar. Maggie had not heard from Carol in days, after she had refused to sell her property to the developer from Hanover. She was in for it now, she supposed. Poetry was no defense against a real estate agent.

Carol's coat today was a blazing royal blue. The high-heeled boots were the same. The briefcase, a feminine white leather, was also the same. Maggie opened the kitchen door before Carol had a chance to knock. "Hello, Carol, won't you come in."

"I took a chance on coming out here without calling. I hope you don't mind."

"No, not at all."

Carol stepped inside, and Maggie closed the door behind her. "Let me take your coat," Maggie said. "We'll have to talk standing at the kitchen counter. I have only one chair."

Carol tugged off her tight leather gloves more quickly than Maggie would have thought possible and handed Maggie her coat. When Maggie returned from hanging it up, Carol had her briefcase open, a neat pile of papers on the counter in front of her, and a Mont Blanc pen balanced delicately in her thin, manicured hand. She looked up, smiling, as Maggie entered the room. Maggie stood next to her, also smiling, and ceremoniously placed her clasped hands on the counter in front of her.

"I thought now would be a good time to assess where we are with the sale of your house," Carol said, gesturing with the pen, "to see if you want to make an adjustment to the price or have any work done before the spring buyers come out. Although that's still a couple of months away, of course. Now, I believe Michael Webber is still interested in your property, if you would like me to contact him. I'm not sure where he would stand on price right now, but I would certainly be willing to discuss it with him."

Maggie nodded and said, "Nice pen. Mont Blanc?"

"Yes, it is, thank you. I received it as a gift. At a closing, as a matter of fact. Now, what do you think about my approaching Michael Webber?"

Maggie did not respond, watching as Carol fiddled with the pen. Then she said, "I wonder what kind of poetry someone would write with a pen like that."

Carol looked down at the pen in her hand, nonplussed.

"As for your contacting Michael Webber," Maggie went on, "it won't be necessary. I've decided not to sell."

Maggie watched as the pen slipped from Carol's hand and rolled across the counter and onto the floor, where it continued to roll until it reached the baseboard on the opposite side of the room.

"As you can see, the house has settled some," Maggie said.

Carol retrieved her pen from the floor. When she resumed her place at the counter, her face was flushed. "I don't understand. You've bought into an assisted living community. You don't even have furniture here. You signed a six-month listing!"

"True," Maggie said, "however, since I'm not going to sell the house, the listing is moot." Maggie picked up the pile of papers, straightened their edges once, twice on the counter, and replaced them in Carol's briefcase. "So! There we are. I'll get your coat."

After Carol had pulled away in the black Jaguar, the tires spinning petulantly in the snow, Maggie fixed herself a cup of tea and went into the study to sit on the window seat, where she could have a little chuckle with Tom and look outside for a harbinger of spring, however slight.

What would she have to do to get her furniture moved back to the farm in time for spring? she mused, blowing gently across the hot tea. And her clothes. She had to get her clothes back. She couldn't very well wear wool through the summer, now could she?

Come spring, she would plant a little garden, just a little one, a corner of the one Tom had abandoned, the corner closest to the house, with tomatoes and herbs and Bibb lettuce. She would have the pool cleaned, and keep it blue and sparkling throughout the summer. Although she no longer trusted herself alone in the water, she could sit out on a chaise by the pool and wait for the handsome young man who played George to throw himself at her feet.

Who would have thought it?

Epilogue

Maggie looked out the window at the leaves of a maple tree. From her propped position on the bed, she could see into the crown of the tree, where heavy black power lines twisted through the leaves and branches. Judging from the dark green of the leaves, she thought it must be summer, but she could not be sure. The window she was looking through did not open.

If it were indeed summer, Gwen's children might come around for a visit, with their spouses and young children, staying for an awkward half hour or so before escaping back to the suburbs whence they came. Maggie turned from the window and said aloud, "The suburbs whence they came." She listened closely, reconsidered the full stop, and said it again, this time with an ellipsis: "The suburbs whence they came . . . ." A very nice line. Tom could not have said it better himself.

Gwen came regularly, the last weekend of the month, her speech halting, her hands smelling of soap. She would not enter the room without something to leave for Maggie, a box of flavored teas, scented hand lotion, the latest *New Yorker*. Sometimes her husband came with her; more often he did not. Betty Archambault also came to see her once a month, until Norman passed away, when she began coming every week, after Sunday mass.

For quite some time, Maggie had been aware of a need to move her bowels, which she finally acknowledged as futile to ignore. She managed to get her legs out of the covers and sit up but was unable maneuver herself off the high bed to stand on the floor. She tried one last time, cursing herself for being so fearful of a fall, reached over to her pillow, and pressed the call button. Within moments, an aide appeared, who shouted as she approached the bed, "What can I do for you, hon?"

"For a start, stop calling me hon. I don't like it."

The aide laughed as she always did, and said, "Sure, sweetie, what can I do for you?"

Maggie sighed. "I need to use the bathroom."

"You want a bedpan?"

"No. I just need help getting off the bed."

"Okay, sweetie." The aide helped Maggie off the bed and led her to the bathroom, with Maggie trying and failing to shrug the aide's hand off her shoulder. "Okay, sweetie, there you go."

Maggie made no move toward the toilet. "Could you please shut the door?"

"Sorry, sweetie, can't. If you call for help toileting, I gotta stay with you. Sorry, hon."

"Please."

The aide turned around but left the door open. Maggie lowered herself onto the toilet and closed her eyes.

Once back in bed, pillows arranged, covers tucked, hand patted, Maggie heard a voice crying from down the hall. "No," it cried, "no, no, no!" The voice paused, gathering enough strength to shout, just once, "I don't want to!" before it resumed crying "no" once again. Maggie was unable to determine whether the voice belonged to a man or a woman. The voice was cracked with age and distorted by desperation, and her own hearing had dulled. There was no pattern to when the voice would cry out; it did not seem to be tied to any of the daily routines of the place, the giving of medications, the changing of bed linens, the serving of meals.

The voice stopped, resumed, then stopped for good. Maggie looked out the window as the leaves of the maple tree swayed to a silent, unfelt breeze. She had become accustomed to the tree's slow, random rhythms and could watch them for hours, the leaves' shape and movement evocative of pleasant things just beyond memory.

Paradises / Lara Chapman

Chasing the Dragon

Kathy Hoyle

'Con Rong, Chau Thien'
Vietnamese proverb: Children of Dragon, Grandchildren of Gods

TJ

That summer was one of the hottest on record. Mama's radio piped out Tammy Wynette, and she would sing along. Then afterwards she would cuss, "Hell, Tammy, why you always tellin us to stand by that shit-for-brains man?"

Mama sliced watermelon on the counter, but that was the first summer she didn't two-step us around the kitchen table.

"It's too goddamn hot to live," she said.

Nothing but heat, crawlin out from under the porch every morning, spreadin down past the hog field and the wiltin corn crops, all the way out to the dyin pecan tree that sat on the county line. It scorched our arms and left us parched and breathless. Mostly we just put on the hose and let the water soak us down or we had spittin contests under the shade of the haybarn roof. There was no hidin from it. It sucked the air right out of our lungs, made the world slow down till we were all wilted and sleepy, like belly-filled possums.

"You boys gotta stay cool an' make sure you drink the water. Gotta drink the water," Mama said, wafting at her flushed cheeks with an old lace fan.

When we'd had our fill, she'd wipe the sweet watermelon from our chin with a cold cloth and give us an ice cube each from the freezer out back. Cal would try and fit the whole cube in his mouth, just like us, opening his jaw wide and shoving at it with his chubby fingers and Mama would flick him on the ear with a towel and cuss.

"God dammit, Cal, why'd you always gotta try and choke yourself? As if I ain't got enough on my mind without having to worry about you."

Me, Jacob and Richie would push our cubes into our mouths as we ran past him, back out into the heat, and Cal would trail behind, ice cube melting into the palm of his hand.

There were four of us that summer, Richie, Jacob, me and my baby brother, Cal. I was always complainin to Mama 'bout havin to drag Cal around, and she would always give me a look that would freeze the sun when I did. In the end, Cal got to hang with us anyways, even though none of us wanted a nine-year-old kid in tow.

Richie cussed about it.

"Why'd you gotta bring a baby? What the fuck we gonna do with a baby?"

Jacob just shrugged and said, "One more won't make no difference, quit whining," and Richie shut up, cos it was Jacob had told him. I was glad. I fought Richie once, last winter, and still had a chunk of tooth missin that Mama said would need fixin up when I was older. After Jacob had told him to pipe down, Richie sat in the yard chewing his lip, looked like he was swallowing cuss words right down into his gut. But he would never fight Jacob, we all knew it, Cal especially.

Jacob was smart, like his Pa, I guess. Mama said Jacob's Pa was the smartest guy she ever knew, went to one of those fancy colleges and everything. I guess all that knowin was just too much for Jacob's Pa. He was kinda wasted in this place and maybe he knew something about the next life that us folks don't. Maybe he was needed up in heaven. I don't know why he did what he did. But Jacob don't talk of it none. He don't like guns none either. He says he's a pacifist. That he don't like hurtin no one nor nothin. I guess that's just how my mind would be too, if my daddy had blown off the side of his head with a shotgun.

Jacob stood head and shoulders above all of us. Big and smart together meant Richie knew Jacob could crush him into mush if he took a mind to it. Richie never was the type to take on someone bigger an' him. I guess Richie was just like his pa too.

Anyways, once Jacob told Richie how things were gonna be, Cal took to following Jacob like a dog on a leash. Mama never had to worry no more 'bout where he'd be. Always sittin in Jacob's shadow.

"Mary-Lee done got herself a pure angel when she got that boy," Mama would say, every time Jacob came to call.

And Jacob was all good manners and *yes Ma'am no Ma'am* and letting Cal stick by his side, like a fly on a turd. I could barely stomach it. Richie mostly stayed out on the porch, scuffing his heels against the timber post, scowling at nothin in particular and Mama never really paid him any mind. But she sure did love Jacob.

Me? Well, I knew I was nothin special. Just plain old TJ. Or Thomas Jefferson Scott, when Mama was hollerin 'cos I done something bad. Mama never spoke too well about my Pa. Mine was a no-good son of a bitch accordin to Mama. I got a letter once or twice a year with a New York stamp on the front, that's about it. I still remembered him, bouncing a wailin Cal on his knee in the kitchen, fixin up the truck with Granddaddy. He was here, but he always seemed to be somewhere else in his mind. He would stare out over the prairie and write and write in that notebook of his. Seems he wrote so much about this place, he needed to find somewhere new to write about. One day I'll ask him why he left. And why he never came back. One day, when Mama don't need me to take care o' her.

I like to write too, maybe I am just like him, a no-good son of a bitch. I sure feel like it ever time I look at Mama's worn face and her sad eyes. But writin out all that happened that summer eases me somehow. I can't never make it right, but I guess if I can put it out on the page, it don't stay inside, eating up my guts.

That day we first heard about Cousin Willy, was a midmornin' in July, and hotter than hell's furnace.

"The phone done broke again," said Mama, as me and Cal wandered into the house after a mornin's chores.

"Cousin Willy's got the withdrawals. I saw Aunt Claire down at the store this mornin buying up all kinds of pills. She's tried everythin. Told her I'd be right on over. TJ, ride your bike out to Aunt Maggie's and tell her she needs to get to Aunt Claire's soon as she can."

Claire and Maggie were Mama's sisters. They'd stuck by each other through most things. Mama says 'kin is all we got an' all we need' but even so, I wasn't fixin to get burnt to a crisp that mornin, so I whined.

"Aw Mama."

"You do it," hissed Mama, picking up her purse and keys, "Willy's family and he's ridin a tornado to hell right now boy, so git gone."

I sighed, no use arguin' with her.

"Here take this," she said, giving me an old soda bottle filled up with water, "you make sure you drink it."

Mama dragged Cal up from the table by his scrawny arm and I followed them outside as they hurried to the pickup. I'd heard 'bout the withdrawals from Richie. His Pa had 'em when he first came back, but seems he took to hard drinkin just as well. I knew Willy musta been in pretty bad shape to get Mama out into that heat.

Mama screeched off towards Willy and Aunt Claires, as though the devil himself was on her tail. I stood there choking in a cloud of dust, shading my eyes from the blinding sun.

Willy

You go right ahead and ask me why, Mama. Again, and again, you keep askin me why. But when I tell you, it's like you don't hear me. You just see what was and not what is. I'll tell you again, Mama. This time you gotta listen good. I gotta make things right. Unlock that door, Mama ... please. You out there?

You can put me in here, Mama, you can put a man in a box, but you can't stop his mind from seein.

I seen things. I followed a dragon, followed him down, down into that shit-stinking water, followed him through hell. And you wanna know what else, we came out of that water, him an' me, we came out together. I am him and he is me. I'm one of his children now. Me an' that dragon, we go together.

I got a chance now, a chance to make it right. 'Cos there weren't nothing right about that place. Nothing, except that goddam beautiful golden dragon.

When I go down with him, down into that place, Oh Mama! It's like the sweetest dream. The water ain't so bad down there and the noise, the noise it's all gone cept for his voice, whispering, tellin me what I gotta to do.

Gotta save the boy.

Mama, please....

What you think is good ain't good, what you think is bad ain't bad. Mama?

TJ

By the time I reached Aunt Maggie's, I was wrung through with sweat, panting like a fevered dog. Chester, Maggie's son, was swinging in a hammock wearing just his scuffed boots and a straw hat, blowing sweet-smelling smoke rings up to the turquoise sky. Johnny Cash was mumblin' through a beat-up radio, hung up by a wire above Chester's head.

Chester was kinda mean lookin, and creepy as hell, thin and wiry, like an old rattlesnake ready to strike. He had him these yellow eyes that seemed to burn right through you. He always spoke real low too, like his words were as thin as his body. Even though I'd known him my whole life, I never once had a mind to spend time alone with him. Mama used to say he and Willy were "like two peas in a pod, always runnin' around together" when they were kids. But seemed that since the war had turned Willy, Chester liked bein alone.

I shook him by the boot, and he squinted out at me.

"What?" he rasped.

My throat was dry from the ride, I guess, 'cos the words stuck hard to my tongue.

Chester was fixin' me with those mean yellow eyes o' his, when Aunt Maggie came out onto the porch, hummin and pullin at the thin strap of her top. She looked up and threw her hand to her chest.

"Good Lord child, you gave me a goosebump. What the hell you doin' all the way out here? Come on, come on now, get in outta this goddamn heat."

I followed her through the porch door into the cool kitchen, glad to get away from Chester, and sat on the chair she'd kicked out for me. Glugging down the ice water she handed me, I held fast while she rubbed at my forehead with a cold cloth.

Aunt Maggie smelt like fresh lemons. She was always real easy to talk to. I never worked out how she an' Chester could be kin. She was the nicest person I ever knew, like she was made of spring sunshine or somethin. Seems a lot of folks thought so too, well menfolk, anyways. She always had some guy or other helpin her out. I never knew Chester's pa. Mama said she'd rather spit than talk about him and Aunt Maggie didn't seem to miss him none.

"Mama sent me," I said, when she'd finally stopped scrubbin at my head.

"Your Mama told you to ride on over here, in this?"

I nodded. "Phone's broke."

Aunt Maggie picked up her purse and took out some dollars.

"Here. You give her this. Should be enough to fix it. Tell her she gotta tell me next time. Those fuckers just cut you clean off, you even miss one day."

I took the dollars and stuffed them into my shirt pocket. She lit up a smoke and folded her arms eyeing Chester, who'd wandered into the kitchen wearing just the suit God gave him.

"Y'all might wanna cover up that peanut, boy. Damn thing gonna shrivel up an' drop off."

Chester opened the fridge, drew out a cold beer and glugged it down, smacking his lips and driving out a great belch.

"I like my freedom, Mama. I earnt it."

He sure was weird. I became awful interested in Aunt Maggie's tablecloth.

Maggie shook her head and blew out smoke.

"What in the hell did I raise?"

Chester ignored her and walked over to me. I looked up at him. He stared me down.

"Well? You gonna tell us why your Mama sent you, boy or we gotta wait all day?"

"It's Willy. He's real bad with the withdrawals," I stammered.

I looked to Aunt Maggie. "Mama said Aunt Claire needs you, right now!"

I needed Aunt Maggie to hear the worry I had seen in Mama's eyes.

Her face turned pale as milk.

"Again? Goddam it."

She nodded to Chester who shook his head, and gave a low whistle then went out back.

"TJ, you wait here," said Aunt Maggie, "there's ham and watermelon in the fridge if you get hungry. Don't ride home till after six, cos you gon' fry to a crisp if you do."

Maggie went out back and got a cube from the freezer and shoved it into my hand. "Here. And you make sure you get plenty water."

Chester strolled back into the kitchen wearing cutoffs, pulling a Vipers T-shirt over his head. He plucked a cigarette from Maggie's pack on the table, lit up and nodded to her.

"Let's go, Mama."

Aunt Maggie grabbed her purse and ruffled my hair.

"Willy's gonna be just fine, don't you worry." She turned to Chester. "I don't know why those bastards sent him back like that. Ain't no better than in a goddamn body bag. At least then he'd be some kind o' hero and Claire could hold her head up in town."

Chester slammed his hand against the counter, eyes blazin. "You wanna help him or you wanna whine and bitch about what you think you know, when you don't know shit, Ma?"

I held my breath.

Aunt Maggie turned and stormed out, the porch door slamming behind her. Chester gave me one last scowl before he followed her outside. I sat for a second sucking on the ice cube, then I pushed back my chair and wandered out onto the porch. I looked out across Maggie's farm wondering what the hell I was gonna do with that long old stretch of time left before supper . . . then my eyes came to rest on the wood.

Willy

"Troop! Don't you drink that water. That shit will kill you stone dead."

First thing I heard from Harvard when I got in-country. I remember thinkin, if alls I had to worry about was the water, then things sure were gonna be a hell of a lot easier than I thought.

I was dumb as shit.

I mean, there was water everywhere in that goddamn place. Ain't like home, Mama, miles and miles of dust and dirt, ain't like anywhere I'd ever seen before. Seemed like most of the time, I could hardly breathe. If we weren't walking through water, leeches suckin at us, the water was rainin down on us. You talk about hellfire, Mama, but hell ain't fire, it's one giant shit-stinking river of water.

And all that noise, burnin a hole in my brain. I needed to get aways from all that noise. The rain rapraprappin, bam, bam, bam, guns popopin, and there ain't nowhere to go, you just gotta move. Move! Popopop! Move! Get down, troop, get up, troop! See, Mama, without the dragon, it's just noise. Guns, blades, and screams . . . boys like me, screamin out for their Mamas.

Y'all told to think of 'em as gooks, as dinks. They don't mean a thing to nobody. But the dragon, he made me see. Made me see, we all his children. Grunt like me ain't supposed to ask why? Why we killin? What the hell did we do it for, Mama? Ain't nobody won nothin. Y'all think Chester's some kinda hero. I used to think so too.

Now I know, there ain't no such thing as a hero.

I tried, tried to turn my mind to the killin. Chester, he loved it. Got him a man's scalp hooked to his belt like he's some mean motherfucker. I ain't no coward, ain't no pussy but you can't just kill a man, or a woman, or a goddamn kid for nothin.

You go on point, rain ratatattin on your helmet all night long, just waitin and waitin, knowing either you or the man next to you gonna die, and it's just goddamn pot-luck if you make it back to the hooch next mornin. Chester had him a scalp, but all I had me was a rabbit's foot from Granddaddy. And I was scared, Mama. I ain't never told you that before, but I was so fucking scared.

Then I found Thùy Linh. And her voice, it was so soft, felt like a velvet cloth wrapped all around me. And her hands, her mouth, all over my body,

"Relax, GI. Thùy Linh take care of you now. Take the pipe. Close your eyes, lay back, I tell you story of sacred dragon."

And Mama, I did, I lay down on that mat and I took that pipe with the golden dragon curled around and around it and I went someplace so beautiful, it was like Jesus took my hand and gave me a goddamn tour of heaven itself. For the first time I didn't hear no screams, didn't hear that popopop, didn't hear the blades coming closer, ready to take those boys home in boxes.

See you can put a man in a box, Mama, but what you think is good, ain't good.

You got to let me out, now. Open that door. 'Cos I got a chance, I got a chance to make it right. I see Thùy Linh', I feel her hands on me. Only now she ain't soothing the itchin' that's crawlin' all over me, Mama. And the dragon, he ain't whisperin. All I hear is Chester's voice. Rising above all that noise. I see him pushin away that friend of Thùy Linh's, the one with the long black hair and those real small titties.

Chester hissin, "I don't want me no gook bitch."

Those yellow eyes of his, searchin' that hooch till he found what he wanted hidin' in the corner.

And those words, Mama. I hear those words that changed everythin between me n him...

"How much for the boy?"

TJ

I filled up an old soda bottle with water and set off.

Whenever we visited Maggie's farm, Mama had always said no 'bout goin to the wood. She said we would have to be done with chasin the hogs and chickens out back 'cos she couldn't trust us not to fall down the ditch and be dumb enough to drown. Trees. A great clump of cool, shady cottonwoods, magnolias and oaks, all sat beyond Maggie's farm. The wood had always been off-limits, but here I was, with no Mama to stop me, freedom fizzin in my gut. I was gonna go see what I could find.

It was cool, almost damp, like stepping into a whole different world. I could breathe for the first time in what felt like months. I left my bike flat down in a clump of ferns and picked my way across the spongy ground under the cool shade of the trees. Birds were singin overhead as I kicked at leaves and pulled up a clump of switch cane to swipe at the flies. I could smell that real sharp stink of wild garlic mixed up with sweet magnolia, and I found myself hummin as I walked through the shady wood. It sure felt like I was on an adventure, just like Huck Finn.

It was the noise that stopped me. Trickling water. Maybe a creek that lead to the ditch Mama was always warning us about? But something else too, kinda like a motor running, but high and whiny, the pitch all wrong. I ain't never been what you'd call real bright, so I walked towards it. I came to the edge of a sloping, mossy bank and looked down. At the bottom was a pool of dark, sludgy water and all around, there were frogs. I could feel a vibration underfoot and that sound was so goddamn hypnotic, it drew me closer n' closer. Man, they were ugly suckers. All brown and lumpy, amber-eyed and slash-mouthed, slick and squelchin in the mud, and I ain't exaggeratin when I tell you, they were bigger than my granddaddy's hand. I reeled back, falling straight onto my butt. There were so many of them all hollerin out that weird noise. I ran. My breath caught in my belly. Heart hammering. I was scared, but kinda excited too. I couldn't wait to show Jacob and Richie those ugly-ass toads. I ran all the way to back to my bike, pushed it through the trees and jumped on, ridin out into the burning sun.

Mama and Cal got home long after the sun was settin. Mama flopped onto the couch and wafted her face with a fan while I ran to fetch her an iced tea, sure to make it just how she liked it, with extra lemon. She looked like all the cares of the world were beating down on her shoulders. When I asked

Cal about what happened, he said he didn't know 'cos Mama had thrown him out at granddaddy's on the way to Aunt Claire's. He had rabbit's foot curled in his hand.

"Granddaddy says its lucky."

"Not lucky for him when Mama finds out he let you at his shotgun."

"She won't find out," said Cal, stuffing the foot in the pocket of his shorts, "me and Granddaddy know how to keep a secret."

Cal held that rabbit foot close all night long, strokin his cheek with the fur.

Next morning, Mama found it stuffed down the side of his bed.

"That man and his goddamn guns," she hissed, whipping up the foot and tossing it in the trash, "I told your grandpa, over and over, I don't want my boys near any goddamn guns. Jesus H Christ, My own Pa."

Mama was so angry.

That was when she said Cal gotta stay with me, instead.

Guess I was right. A rabbit's foot ain't so lucky after all.

Willy

It burns. Shit, Mama the truth, it's burning a hole in me so big that no matter how I look at it, I can never fill it. Not with praying, not with drinkin, not even the dragon can stop the burnin.

Mama, I gots to tell it, so I can breathe easy again. I think maybe if I tell it, if I do somethin, maybe the dragon, he might set me free.

Mama, what I did out there, that ain't the worst of it...

I shoulda stopped him. I know what he's doin'. I seen that boy runnin round town with Chester's stink all over him. Ain't nobody to stop it but me.

All that hate, it sticks in my throat like that shit-stinkin swamp water and its's choking me up, choking me up and I'd be happy to take my last breath, but the dragon, he weaves his way through it all, he always finds me no matter what. And he takes me down, down away from the noise and the guts and the blood. He's the only one can take me, Mama. He whispers, oh, I can hear him saying, *Willy, now you can be something more, someone better.*

Mama, I hear you out there, don't think I can't hear Y'all. I hear Aunt Maggie and Aunt Sarah. Y'all think you know what's good for me. But what's good ain't good, what's bad ain't bad. You think you can stop it? You can't stop the dragon, Mama. Only the truth can stop him.

I hear Chester out there too. I knowed that voice my whole life, it's like when we speak, we are ringin the same bell. He is my kin, but he ain't like no brother no more. I hear him. Mama, don't you let him in here, don't you dare.

Jesus, Mama, I'm so goddam cold, they're all over me. Rats, runnin all over my body.

Mama, please...

TJ

"Toads," said Jacob, peering through his glasses over the edge of the slope.

"Huh?"

Richie had a stick, mottled with moss, and was swiping at the air with it.

"Let's go down and kill 'em," he said, grinning as he hopped and jabbed. He caught Cal in the side with the stick and Cal fell to his knees, tears threatening.

"Baby," hissed Richie, catching a look from Jacob.

"They're cane toads," said Jacob, stepping back from the edge, "not frogs. Don't normally get 'em here. Must be the heat that's brought 'em. I read about 'em once. They kill all kinds of bugs n critters, to help the crops grow."

Richie started to slide down the slope toward the pool, stick in hand, face full of menace.

"Get back Richie, you goddamn idiot!" shouted Jacob.

"Why?" shouted up Richie grinning, "gonna kill me some stinkin toads."

"Richie, I mean it, get outta there. They're poisonous," Jacob hollered down the slope.

Richie dug his nails into the mossy bank to stop himself from sliding down. He was stuck a halfways up and a halfways down. He looked down at the toads then back up at me Jacob and me kneeling on the edge.

"I mean it Richie. Get your ass back up here!" shouted Jacob.

I held out a hand as Richie crawled to the top. He grabbed it and I yanked him back over the edge, losing my balance when I took his weight. We tumbled to a halt by the log where Cal was sitting.

"Goddamn idiot," I said, giggling at Richie as we rough n tumbled a little more.

Jacob came and parked on the log next to Cal, took the rucksack from his back, unpacked cans of soda, and handed them out.

"You sure are a dumbass, Richie," he said, shaking his head. Cal sniggered, and took a can from Richie.

I popped the top off the soda and slurped it down.

"Got any smokes?" asked Richie popping his own can open.

"Sure, like you smoke," snorted Jacob.

"Do too. I tried it last week, Chester showed me how. I smoke all the time now."

"Chester?" I asked, "why's he hangin' with a scrawny ass kid like you?"

"Cos I ain't a dumbass like you, TJ . . . . He's pretty cool. Showed me his medals and somethin else too."

"Yeah? What?" asked Jacob

"Aw, you wouldn't believe me even if I told you."

"What'd he show you?" whispered Cal, eyes wide.

Richie smirked. He had us eatin from his hand now.

"Chester got him a gook scalp. Keeps it in a jar. He done brought it over to my house and showed me. Still got gook hair an' blood an' everythin."

"Fuck you Richie, that's a downright lie," said Jacob, shaking his head.

"Ain't no lie!" shouted Richie, "I saw it true. An' Chester, he says I'm in his unit now. Gave me two dollars, just for takin a grocery bag to some buddy o' his."

Jacob shook his head again

"You sure are dumb, Richie. Chester got you runnin around for him. You gonna end up in real trouble. Chester's a mean-ass snake. You should stay the hell away from him. If you had a Mama, she'd tell you that straight."

"Oh yeah? Well I got Pa, and he says it's just fine! Him and Chester got big plans."

Richie walked over to the edge of the mossy bank and swiped at the air with his stick. We all left off a him then, knowin the only plan Richie's pa had was to drink himself to death. He had a medal from the US Army hangin on his wall, but he never had no job, and Richie's mama left bout three seconds after his pa came back from Nam to go and live with some guy out in LA.

Cal was leanin back in the grass next to me eyes closed. I was staring up and the wisp of cloud floatin over the yellow sun.

"Goddammit those calm toads sure do make the worst noise," said Richie, breaking up my daydream.

"Cane toads," said Jacob sitting up and shading his eyes.

"How they poison anyways?" I asked, "do they bite?"

"No," said Jacob. "Glands."

"What's glands?" I asked.

"Well, they got these bumps full of poison right behind the eyes. If you touch 'em you get poisoned. Some folks say, if you lick 'em, it makes you higher than a cloud. But mostly it can kill you stone dead."

"Jesus. Cousin Willy would make a soup outta those guys," I laughed.

"I'd take a lick," said Richie jumpin up and swipin at a clump of fern with his stick. We all laughed.

"Quit it now," he scowled, "I would. You yellow bellies wouldn't dare. But I would. Chester told me what it's like. He said it's like you swallowed a rainbow, all colours an' music and warm inside. Like the best dream you ever had in your whole goddam life."

Cal's eyes were wide as he jumped down from the log, puffing out his chest.

"I would do it too," he said, "I ain't no pussy." Then he scowled at Richie. "Ain't no baby either."

"Siddown, Cal," I said, grabbing his arm. "You ain't to go near, y'hear. Mama would strip the skin from my hide if she knew I'd even brought you out past Maggie's farm, let alone getting all rainbowed up on some crazy toad juice."

Richie clutched at his stomach, laughing so hard, "Ha ha! Baby lick the toad, baby lick the toad."

He pulled his mouth into a hard, thin line and cuffed Cal around the ear. Cal steadied himself but when Richie jumped forward, Cal lost his footing, staggering back and falling into a patch of stingers.

"Get up, pussy," said Richie.

Jacob pulled Richie away. I put out a hand for Cal, but he pushed himself up and shoved me away. Angry patches of red were spreading across the back of his thin legs and Cal couldn't hold back the tears this time.

"You always spoil it, Richie," Jacob said, quietly. "Why you gotta be so mean?"

"You hate him too!" Richie shouted. "You said it. Said it was just until his mama can take him back and all we gots to do is ignore him. He ain't one of us. He ain't never gonna be one of us."

Richie's knuckles were white around his stick as he pointed and jabbed it toward Cal.

Jacob had turned beet red.

He turned to Cal, "I aint never said I hated you."

But Cal was already gone, stridin toward the clearing, arms wrapped tight around himself, tears coursing down his cheeks.

Willy

You let him in, Mama? Why?

Alls I see now is that dragon. The water it's so blue down here. Dragon scales shimmering like sunlit glass. It's so quiet Mama. Let me stay here. Wait now? There's something I gotta do?

I'm swimmin, Mama, swimmin through that water. I'm following that dragon's tail, swirling and curling around and around. The colours, like rainbows, I'm swimmin through rainbows Mama, don't never wanna come up.

Shhh now, Mama, no more noise.

Shh now, Mama, stop hollerin.

Y'all can leave me now. It's peaceful here, Mama. So quiet.

Don't cry. Shh now.

TJ

Mama looked dead tired, her face all creased and pale, with dark hollows for eyes, like one of my comic-book ghosts.

"Ya'll gotta take care of yourselves for just one more day," she said, setting out bowls of oatmeal.

She splashed milk into the bowls and slammed down spoons. Some of the milk had spilt onto my shorts but Mama was angrier than a wasp in a jar, so I kept my mouth tight shut.

She was slammin and bangin, opening and closing, the cooler, the cupboards, the porch door. We'd barely finished, when she snatched up our bowls and slammed them into the sink. She almost scrubbed them invisible, and all the while, she was muttering.

"Goddamn Willy. Always had shit-for brains, always full o' the goddamn jitters. Claire shoulda sent him on up to Canada. Even when he was a little kid, he couldn't cross the road unless he was hangin' off Chester's shirttail. What goddamn use was a boy like him to the Army."

Seemed like Mama was workin' herself up to blow. I sat at the table, too scared to move. Cals eyes were wider than a racoon. We'd never seen Mama so spittin mad. She banged those bowls and knives and spoons onto the drainer so hard I thought they might smash clean through the counter.

"And now lookit! Like a goddamn horror movie, hollerin, eyes poppin outta his head, sweatin an' shakin, three of us holding him down. In this heat! Where's the army now? I ask you? Cos they sure as shit ain't takin care o' him. Thank the sweet Lord Maggie had the good sense to bring Chester. Only one to get Willy calmed. Chester always had to look out for that boy."

Mama was breathing real hard.

"Mama," Cal whispered. "Is Willy sick?"

Mama whipped around from the sink.

"Sure is. Oh, he's sick alright and lemme tell you boys now. I ever see or hear about you takin' them mind-bendin drugs, you better hope you die right there n then, cos I will whip you into next spring if you ever touch that shit, you hear me? They can put a man on the goddamn moon, but they sure as shit can't fix our boys once they've broken them."

Mama looked like Reverend Johnson, eyes all bulging, an ungodly demon swelling in her chest. I almost peed my pants.

Cal trembled a little but held fast. I think he always knew, deep down, Mama would never take a whip to him, but I wasn't so sure. A memory still burned deep, the day I told her she must have driven Daddy away on account of her bein so mean, and she hit me with the hog bucket so hard, I thought I'd lost an ear.

Mama picked up her purse and took my chin in her hand.

"You're a good boy, TJ. You're the eldest and you need to take good care of your brother again while I'm gone. I know it ain't what you wanna hear, but I can't take him. Claire done some readin bout how to help Willy, she says this'll be the worst day. Then it'll be done. You understand? I'll be no more than a couple hours. You drink the water."

"Don't worry, Mama," I told her, proud to have her trust me. I pulled Cal to me and put an arm around Cal's bony shoulders. "I always take good care o' him."

Mama smiled, then kissed us both on the top of our heads and rushed out leaving only the faint scent of her lavender cologne.

I let go of Cal's shoulders and he sat down on the kitchen chair and began picking at the welts on the back of his legs. They'd scabbed to a crisp in the heat.

Willy

"Do it Willy, fucking do it, man. He ain't one of us, he ain't never gonna be one of us."

Moonlight on metal. Chester's yellow eyes, brighter than all that fire lightin up the sky around us, my heart, pounding like it might punch straight outta my chest. He looked more alive than any person I ever saw, laughing real hard when I drew that knife across Harvard's throat. I see it over and over Mama, Harvard, fallin face first into the mud and Chester's boot on the back of his head, twistin and twistin until the mud and the blood and Harvard all became one rain soaked, shit-stinkin lump of nothin.

"Eat dirt motherfucker. We don't take no orders from no pussy college boy."

I was strung out, Mama, is all I can tell you. Took me something made my mind swirl and my heart pump. Voice in my head saying, *It's okay, it's okay, do it, Willy. Do it for the unit.*

Harvard was a short timer too, been crossing off the days on his calendar, and I killed him. He never got to see his girl back home and he ain't never gonna go to that fancy college of his.

Mama, I killed one of our own men and that ain't the worst of it. I did it and it can never be undone. I could maybe even learn to live with a thing like that if I had a mind to, I could convince myself that I done right, that it made it easier for all of us. Those suits, they was gonna stop the boy bringing in the bag, and I knew, Mama I knew, I couldn't face another night in that rain, with the noise, and the blades, without those two dollars' worth.

"I ain't no pussy," I told Chester, "I ain't no pussy."

I'm ashamed to say it, Mama, I cried. And Chester, he told Harvard.

"Let the kid through. Give these goddam men what they need."

But Harvard, he stuck fast. Scared to break the rules that some suit put in place. Some suit that never walked one goddamn step in-country.

Harvard was just a dumb college kid. Playin at bein a hero. All that blood bubbling outta his throat. It wasn't my fault.

But the boy. God forgive me, Mama He was just a kid. He had a name, Binh. Chester had him runnin for him and the kid was too goddam scared to say no. That night, the whole sky was lit up like the goddamn fourth of July. Binh musta known his village was gone. But he sat by Chester, head down, with that sack between his knees. He never moved, not one inch.

They threw Harvard's boots on the fire. Got it goin real high. Then Binh brought it out of the sack. A King Cobra.

They were chantin my name and Chester's too. Willy! Chester! Willy! Chester! Yayayaya! Screamin an hollerin like a bunch of goddamn Red Indians. Chester took that huntin knife o' his, grabbed that motherfucker and sliced it clean open. Tore out that snake's heart and shoved it in his mouth.

There was so much blood, Mama. So much blood. It was rainin blood that night. Chester's mouth, dripping with it when he bit through that snake-heart, and the boy holdin that dead cobra with blood all over his hands. Harvard's blood on my knife and the fire and the noise, chanting my name Willy! Willy! Willy!

Mama, it's in my head. Ever goddamn day.

I watched them. Watched them disappear into the darkness, Chester's arm slung around those thin shoulders, and the boy's tears shinin in the firelight.

And I didn't do a goddamn thing. Just sat by that fire and puked all over my own goddam boots.

Thùy Linh gave me that pipe, Mama and I sucked on it like it was goddamn air for livin' ... and the dragon, he came, and he carried me, down, down, down.

God forgive me. I shoulda stopped him.

Don't you let him in here no more, Mama.

TJ

Aunt Claire was wrong. It took more than a day to get Willy straight. Mama said it was like the Devil himself done took hold of Willy, and she and Aunt Claire and Aunt Maggie were praying so hard, their knees were as raw as skinned hide.

Mama would come home every night and fill the washbowl with ice, drag it out onto the porch. and sit with her feet in it till the sun went down. I asked her bout Willy how he was doin.

"That boy spittin up all kinds of stories. Won't let nobody near him now, not even Chester. Claire says she got God on her side. She gonna fight every day to get her boy back. I just pray she's right, 'cos from where I'm sitting, God got too many other things he needs to attend to."

Seemed to me like Willy wasn't fixin to get better any time soon, but Aunt Claire believed the Almighty would pull him through. Mama said the waitin was unbearable.

"Like waitin for death or salvation and you ain't sure which one's comin first."

I would make Mama her iced tea and Cal would sit next to her on the on a little wooden stool that granddaddy made. I'd long outgrown my stool, so I helped Mama best I could, by making sure the chores were done and the hogs and chickens were fed. It seemed like I was doing all the hard work, comin back to the house with sweat drippin down my neck, while Cal got all the hair-strokin and Mama hummin sweet songs into his hair.

I kinda liked Willy. I thought it sure was nice of my Mama and Aunt Maggie to try and help him. He sometimes gave me a dollar here an' there, and once he took me and Cal to a movie, but that was before Nam, before he ended up with his head like a box full of jigsaw pieces.

Sometimes, I lay next to Cal in bed and said a prayer for Willy. I would ask God to make him better, so Mama could come home, and we would get her to ourselves again, before school started. Cal said that was prayin for us and not Willy and that was a selfish kinda prayin. I felt bad after that and gave him a dead arm for making me feel that way. Then I felt bad again, when the bruise spread gold and green above his elbow and Mama asked him what happened, and he said he slipped on the hose water. Cal could make you feel bad about most anythin.

With Mama over at Claire's, we could do as we pleased, so every day, we took an old corn bag filled with jello sandwiches and rode our bikes, out past Aunt Maggie's, to the toad wood. Jacob and Richie were usually close behind and in the cool shade of the cottonwoods, we hung a rope that Richie had found in his Daddy's pickup. We took turns to swing across the ditch, our hearts in our mouths, for fear of fallin down, down, down, into that nest of toads, eyein us, all menace and hate, in the ditch. They seemed to get bigger each day, some as big as alley cats, but as Mama says, boys sure are stupid. We would whoop and holler as each one of us made it to the other side. Even Cal got so good at the swinging, he joined in the jump, letting go of the rope midways across and hurling himself onto the bracken on the other side.

One day, we built a hooch, Richie was CO of the unit of course, but we all knew it was really Jacob and eventually Richie let up on Cal a little ways, since Cal was the best at tyin knots and lightin a fire from the magnifying glass Aunt Maggie got him on his last birthday. Jacob said that Richie must never, ever get a hold of that glass, otherwise we'd all be burnt like sinners, cos Richie got no sense at all. Cal was always careful and built a good fire, with rocks all around, to stop it spreadin, and he made sure it was all doused out every day before sundown, just like Grandaddy had taught us. Cal said, when he grew up, he would live all alone and cook rabbit on an open fire and sleep under the stars. Richie said he probably would, 'cos he wouldn't have no friends, 'cos nobody liked him, but Cal just laughed, and Richie went and hacked at a tree with his stick for a good while after that.

Richie sure was set on catchin him a toad. Ever day he would sit at the top of the slope, giving those ugly critters the stink eye, thinkin of ways to do it. He tried his daddy's old net for fishing, but it had too short a handle. They were too mean and slippery for a snare wire, lowered down on a piece of old rope, and the rocks we threw just seemed to plop into the creek, scattering the toads every which way, causing 'em to holler even louder.

"One day, I'm gonna get me one of them suckers," said Richie, "an' I'm gonna make Cal lick it and then I'm gonna slice it's belly open eat its heart. Chester told me if you eat the heart of something you catch, you take on its power. I'm gonna be the biggest, meanest critter in town. An all you pussies gonna bow down to me!"

"Sure, Richie," I said, laughin, and Jacob chuckled, his back resting against an old tree stump, head tilted toward the sun.

"You wait, pussies. Chester told me I can be king of the world if I want to!"

"Ha! and my Mama told me I could fly me a rocket like Neil Armstrong," chuckled Jacob.

Richie scowled at Jacob then turned to Cal. Seems his belly was full of vinegar and he just needed somewhere to spit.

"Baby," hissed Richie, as Cal sloped off to his spot on the log.

He took a few steps toward Cal, swinging his stick to and fro.

"Hey guys," Richie shouted, his voice echoing through the forest, "how long you think till Willy's better now?"

I shrugged. "I dunno. Aunt Claire thinks he's through the worst."

Richie had that sly smirk on his face. He was itchin for trouble.

"So, your Mama'll be home real soon, then?"

All the while he was snakin closer and closer to Cal.

"I guess so," I answered, standing up. The air got real cool and I swallowed hard.

Richie stopped in front of Cal who was fiddling, head down, with a blade of grass.

"Well goddamn hallelujah!" shouted Richie, right in Cal's face, causing him to jump up like a scolded cat.

"That means baby here, can go back to his Mama and we can all go back to bein how it should be. No Fucking New Guys. No goddamn babies!"

Richie jabbed Cal with his stick, but Cal stood fast, his little hands curling into fists.

"I told you I ain't no baby. You quit sayin' that, Richie."

I ain't never seen Cal like that before, eyes black with temper.

But Richie was outright laughin now

"Pussy boy, baby boy," he sang, darting around Jacob, who had hurried over to stand in front of Cal.

"Shut up, Richie!" said Jacob, giving Richie a shove.

"Leave him, Richie," I said, moving toward them, but my words came out kinda stuck and my legs seemed to be filled with sand. Richie turned on me like a rattlesnake.

"You shut up. You hate him. We all do. You gotta drag him around cos your Mama says so, you dumbass."

He spat on the ground and wiped his mouth with his sleeve.

"I ain't no pussy!" screamed Cal and ran at Richie, his little fists balling into his back, cuffing his head and ears with all he had.

Richie turned and shoved Cal away. Cal staggered backwards but Richie strode towards him again with the Devil in his eyes. Maybe I shouted out? Maybe Jacob tried to pull Richie back. I don't know. That moment seems like a blur, like a picture that ain't quite in focus, me and Jacob, frozen in time.

Richie took Cal down with one blow. Smacked him hard, right on the side of the head and Cal folded to the ground as though his bones done turned to mush. Richie gave him a kick in the stomach for good measure and Cal whimpered but made no mind to move.

"You're a baby," Richie hissed, then glared at me, "and you're a pussy, ain't both of you a pair o' dumbass pussy boys. Your just like your no-good Pa, a pair of goddam yellow-bellies."

I came unstuck and ran at him then, rage burning in my throat, but he was ready. He caught me a good one in the gut and the air rushed outta me. I curled over, panting hard, throat stingin, and Richie kicked me hard in the ribs.

Jacob yanked him away, pushed up his glasses, and squared right up to Richie. Jacob was shakin so hard, his fists balled up real tight. Richie sucked at his teeth for a moment then it seemed like the fight just drained clean out of him. He stuck out his chest, shook his head and picked up his stick. I heard the swish and whoosh as he walked away, hacking at the ferns, as he made his way out of the wood.

Jacob helped Cal up. He spat out a little blood, then staggered as if a hard wind were blowing at him. Leaning against a thick oak tree, he took some deep breaths. I was down on the floor, tryin to catch some breath. I looked up at the sun, burnin through the flickering leaves, then closed my eyes against the glare. I felt the vibrations of the toads through my body, their dull hypnotic drone soothing the pain in my gut.

"I ain't no pussy." Cal broke the silence.

I opened my eyes and sat up, pulling my knees tight to my chest.

"I would lick that toad and see the rainbows, and I would fight Richie again," Cal said, "Any goddamn day or night. I ain't scared of him."

Jacob made his way over and pulled up me and Cal. The three of us slowly wheeled our bikes home, the hot sun beatin down on us the whole way, with Cal in the middle, and me and Jacob righting him, whenever he stumbled.

It was almost dark when Mama came back from Claire's. When she saw Cal's face, she let out a noise I only ever heard from a cow, keenin through a birthin.

"My God, baby, what happened to you?" she asked, scooping Cal up tight.

"You were supposed to take care o' him," she snarled at me. I backed up to the counter and steadied myself.

"Goddamnit, TJ."

Mama pushed Cal down onto a chair and came at me.

I took the beatin, made no attempt to cover myself. Mama ran out of steam, pretty quick. She shoved me away and I leant my face against the cooler. I never told Mama that Richie had got me real hard too. I guess Cal had some pride, and I had a mind to let him keep it. Nobody wants to fess up they got a beating. Not even to their own Mama.

I looked on while Mama bathed Cal's jaw with an ice cloth, then she rubbed some arnica on the side of his head, where the swelling was pretty bad. She soothed and crooned, until finally he fell flat out asleep in her arms and she carried him up to bed. A low rumble of thunder shook the house. A storm was comin.

I lay on my bed listening to the tap-tap-tap on the windowpane. The rain had started. A sharp flash of light lit up the whole room, then another deep rumble shook my bed. I began to count. One one-thousand, two one-thousand, waiting for the next flash. The door opened, and Mama peeked around the frame, her face pale in the dusk-light.

"I'm sorry," she whispered, careful not to wake Cal.

"Me too," I whispered back.

"C'mon,'" she nodded, and I crept from my bed.

She let me sit with her on the couch till real late, snuggled up warm and tight watching a cop show on T.V. Outside, the thunder yelled, and the lighting sparked.

Willy

Bambambam! Guns popopop. Get down! Get down! I can't breathe. Mama get the pipe! Please, I'm beggin you. Make it stop make it stop It hurts so bad itchin' it hurts so bad. I'm so cold so cold I can see that fire flashin outside I hear them guns, Mama.

Let me out!

I hear you I know you're out there Mama. Let me out. I'm scared. The noise. Get down, troop get down troop move! Move! Move!

... need to save the boy. Save the boy Mama please Rats everywhere. So cold.

TJ

The lemon-pine perfume from the purple sage drifted through the open window. I winced as I turned over, the bruisin on my rib was tender. Richie was right, I was a pussy. I shoulda socked him hard. Shoulda got him first, before he even got to Cal. Like I said, Cal always made me feel bad. I'd dreamt all night bout how I woulda done things different. Now, eyes full of grit, I knelt up on my bed and looked out of the window. The clouds looked bruised, like their bellies were still full of thunder. It was spittin rain. I watched as a mockingbird sat on the fencepost, singing out an early morning hymn to me, just like he was in church, or something.

"Sure is dark out there," I said, keeping my voice low.

I yawned and rubbed at my rib. I poked my head through the window and let a little rain fall on my tongue. It felt good to suck in some of that that cool air. I looked up at a cloud dragon forming in the sky.

"Look, Cal. A dragon," I whispered.

Cal was silent.

I sighed.

"Cal, I sure am sorry 'bout what happened."

It hurt my gut to say it. But I was just as mad at that fool Richie as he was. And I took a whipping off Richie AND Mama for it.

"C'mon, Cal," I whined, sore at him for being so stubborn.

I turned and looked across at his bed. His sheet was rumpled up against the wall. Cal's old bear was limp on his pillow, one eye squinting at me, but there was no Cal.

A twist of worry curled in my gut. I slid the window shut and made my way across the landing to Mama's room. She sat up when I creaked the door open.

Rubbing her hands through her hair, Mama glanced at the clock. "What?" she croaked.

"Cal's gone," I said and gnawed at a hangnail as Mama stumbled from her bed.

"What?" She made her way across the landing and into our room, staring blankly at Cal's empty bed.

"Cal?" Mama called, yanking at his bedsheets.

She looked under the bed and in the wardrobe then she went all around the house checking each room faster and faster like a spinning top, until she was red-faced and breathless. She shoved me out into the yard. Rain pounded my face. The storm had turned again. I shivered as Mama shouted from the porch door.

"Check everywhere, I mean everywhere. You don't come back till you have him!" Then she disappeared, leaving the porch door swingin in the wind.

I did as I was told. I made a real show of checkin the yard and the barn, the hog house, even inside the pickup. I wanted to look like I was helpin Mama. Wanted her to think it wasn't my fault. I was drenched through and breathing hard when I finally came back into the kitchen. Every cupboard was open, boxes and buckets pulled out onto the linoleum. I stepped over the debris and peeked into the den. Mama was heaving the old couch from the wall to check behind it, all the while shoutin for Cal to quit hidin. Looked like everything we owned had been pitched across the floor. A crack of thunder shook the house and I turned to Mama, shivering in my wet shorts and T-shirt.

Mama lifted the phone from the kitchen wall and jabbed at the buttons. She waited a second, then I retched a little, as she smashed the receiver, over and over, against that wall.

"Goddamit! Goddammit! I paid, you motherfuckers, I paid it yesterday."

I put my arms around her as she slid to the floor, the fight seepin from her body.

I knew there was no place in hell good enough for me, but I fessed up anyway.

"M-, M-, Mama," I said, teeth chattering with cold.

She looked up and I wiped her hair from her face.

"I think I know where he is."

By the time we got to Maggie's farm, Mama was no longer crying, just real quiet, her lips a tight thin line, her knuckles white on the wheel of the pickup. She screeched to a halt as Chester came onto the porch, fixing his cap over his dirty blonde hair. He sucked on his stokie and squinted at me as Mama ran past him up the steps shouting.

"Maggie! Maggie!" she pushed open the door and disappeared inside.

I got down from the pickup and waited. I'd only told Mama to head to Maggie's. No more. After that, she'd grabbed me by the collar and threw me in the truck.

I knew Mama would get to it soon enough, but I sure was scared by now. I knew I would get a whoopin when I told her I thought her baby was wandering the woods all alone. That he was maybe even rollin around high like Willy, after licking the meanest ugliest critter she would ever see. Only thing I couldn't get to thinkin straight was why he would go alone?

Chester walked over and rested a hand on the pickup door. I pushed myself back as far as I could. He leaned in real close and blew smoke in my eyes. I coughed and tried to get by, but he pressed me hard against that door, yellow eyes narrowin.

The grey clouds parted, and the sun streaked through blinding me. I put up a hand to cover my eyes.

"Seems like ever time I see you there's some kinda trouble," he said.

I hung my head.

"Why you here, kid?"

I looked up at him.

"I need to go tell Mama--"

He gave me a shove

"Why you here? Willy shootin' his mouth again? My Mama's already done enough for him--"

"No. No sir ... its Cal."

"Your daddy done come and took him? Goddammit. Thought that piece of shit was gone for good."

I shook my head. Chester leaned back and pulled on his cigarette and squinted at me then turned as Mama and Maggie came running outta the house.

They stopped in front of me and Chester, Maggie was tugging at her bathrobe, Mama's face was white with worry.

"Well?" she asked, "you said Maggie's."

I looked down at the ground. I wished Jacob was here. Maybe I wouldn't get whooped so hard if she knew Jacob had been to the wood too.

"He ain't here, Sarah. Why would he come here?" asked Maggie. "Do you know what the hell's going on?" she said, turning to Chester.

"I don't know shit," said Chester. "Spit it out dumbass. Where's your brother?" he asked, shoving me in the chest.

The clouds were slidin across the sky thin as a whisper and the sun was rising higher now, seems like it was hottin' up ready to burn me like the sinner I was. I pointed, out across Maggie's backyard towards the woods and heard Mama gasp.

"Shit," said Chester. Then he set off, faster than a rabbit from a gun.

Willy

Mama I

... are you there
It's okay, Mama.
It's me Willy.
I'm so tired, Mama.
I know what you done was to save me.
I know I done broke your heart, Mama.
I gots to go,
Can't stay here. You know that.
Chester gon' get around to killin me someday
Ain't no doubt
gon kill me   kill me   kill me

I thought I could do somethin bout him.
But see
how see how my mind   it don't work right
See how I'm all broken.
Tiny
tiny
pieces

TJ

We buried Cal in early fall. Reverend Johnson spoke quietly. Aunt Maggie and Aunt Claire held onto Mama while she keened for her baby.

The sun had lost its heat and the leaves were fallin across Maggie's yard when we all got back to her place. Jacob had gone on home and I was scuffing my heels against the porch, not knowing what the hell I could do to help fix Mama's heart.

I sat on the steps and slowly read the letter Pa had sent. He said he real was sorry he couldn't come to bury Cal. That he was fixin to write about what happened to men like Chester and Willy. He'd been working hard to find the truth about the war, and he was gonna tell folks what really happened. I hated him then. I knew nobody cared 'bout that goddamn war. He shoulda come. Shoulda come and said goodbye to Cal.

I wandered into Aunt Maggie's kitchen wipin the tears off of my cheeks. The counter was filled with home cooked pies and at least four pots filled with stew we'd never eat. Folks from town had called in and out all day long, and now the last of them had gone, it was just Aunt Claire and Aunt Maggie, sittin at the table with Mama. She was starin at nothin but the wall, her hands folded in her lap, and she was still wearin her church hat.

"TJ. Sweetheart," said Maggie, her voice soft as ice cream, "Come and sit down, I'll bring you some water."

She stood up and pulled out her chair for me. She wandered out back to get some ice and I sat down next to Mama. I put my hand on hers and squeezed. She pulled it away and tucked it into the folds of her black dress.

I looked to Aunt Claire who was scowlin at something behind my back. She was angrier than a wasp in a jar.

"Jesus Christ, have some goddamn respect."

I turned around to see Chester grabbin a beer from the fridge. He was naked 'cept for his vipers cap and boots.

Mama looked across at him frowning under her the shadow of her hat.

"This is my home, Claire," hissed Chester, drunk and full of the devil, "I can do whatever the hell I want in my own goddamn house."

Maggie came from out back. She slammed the water onto the table in front of me. The ice cubes rattled in the glass.

"Chester! Jesus H Christ! Put some clothes on. Go on now. Git."

Chester walked right on up to her and pushed his face into hers. "I told you before, Mama. I like bein' free."

He smirked at her then nodded in my direction,

"Besides, TJ here been side-eyeing me all afternoon, trying to get him a look at what a real man got, ain't that right, TJ?" He winked at me and my cheeks flamed like hot chillies.

Aunt Claire stood up and narrowed her eyes. She spoke real quiet.

"You better take yourself on outta here, Chester, I mean it."

Chester swigged at his beer. His was swayin back an' forth, slurrin and mumblin. He looked at Claire and narrowed his eyes.

"How's Willy, Claire? Couldn't make it out here, huh? Not even for the kid.? Y'all give him my love next time you visit."

"Get out!" screeched Aunt Maggie, rushing at Chester and shoving him hard. Chester stumbled. Aunt Maggie looked over at Aunt Claire who was standing now, holdin on to that table like she might faint. Chester wandered toward the door, chuckling to himself. Maggie came towards Claire,

"Claire, I'm sorry, I--"

"He ain't worth it, Maggie," whispered Aunt Claire. She was cryin kinda hard now.

"He ain't worth me an' you--"

"Oh hey, TJ!" Chester interrupted, he was leanin by the door fixin me with those yellow eyes, "you come on over anytime now."

I felt the air seep outta the room.

Chester winked again and cupped his hand around that corn dog o' his and started wavin it around, laughing like he'd just told the world's best joke.

Mama was out of her seat like a streak of lightenin, lettin out a roar like the fiercest dragon I ever heard.

My glass fractured on the kitchen table. One half lay belly-up against Aunt Maggie's fruit bowl. Ice water dripped onto the shoes I'd shined up for church.

Aunt Claire grabbed at me then, tryin to pull me into her, it seemed. I buried my face in her black dress, my heart poundin like a jackrabbit ... 'cos it was too late. I'd seen it. Seen it all.

Aunt Maggie, leanin over a screamin Chester, his hands pushed between his legs,

Mama, white with rage, the other half of that jagged glass in her shakin hand,

... and blood. So much blood.

Willy

Help me

    need to find me someways to getting wired up right again.

    Dragon he done left me   left me all alone in the water
        Mama.
    Popopop   bambambam

    Take me to that fancy clinic you and grandaddy been savin for, Mama.

    See if them suits can't fix me.

    Rats   comin

TJ

We ride our bikes over to the new arcade in Gainesville. Jacob is king, his high score flashing bright, at the very top of the list of names. Sometimes, we buy cokes and candy and sit on the wall at the skatepark, watching older kids flip and spin. They bust some real cool moves. We never go to the woods by aunt Maggie's, we never talk about toads and no one ever talks about why Chester left town.

Sometimes we see Richie at school, but he hangs with a new crowd now. Older boys with greased hair and a likin for cars and swiggin booze.

These days Mama sits on the porch sipping iced tea, gazing out toward the county line as if she's expecting someone, or somethin. Ain't no talking to her and ain't no getting close. I watch TV alone. The black suit I wore in the courthouse hangs in the wardrobe, next to Cal's good shirt and pants, his church clothes. Mama said I ain't to touch a goddamn thing. Cal is gone and there ain't no bringing him back but sometimes, when Mama is sleeping, I lay on his bed and he is there. I can smell him. I can feel him. I can hear his breath in my ear.

I tell him he's the bravest brother anyone could have.

They said he would have been confused. A blow to the head that hard, the swelling, it most likely would have made him woozy. He still rode all the way out to the toad wood, though. There were scratches on his legs and back. They said he musta fallen so many times. But seems Cal was determined to get there.

They asked us over and over. Which one of us did it. But if you don't say, if you bite your lip real hard to stop the words spinnin out, then they can't blame anyone of you. We already lost Cal. Couldn't let em take Richie too. So, we stuck tight and sweated it out in those black suits with the bible burning our palms. I know I'm going to hell. Probably Jacob and Richie too. I see it in Mama's eyes, every day. The way her mouth slams tight when I try to talk to her, the way Aunt Maggie and Aunt Claire only look at me side on.

But Cal? He's some place good. Some place real sweet, where Mama will go too, to stroke his hair and sing her songs. Just as soon as it's her time.

They said when Cal licked the toad, he would have taken in so much of that poison as to cause him to hallucinate. When Jacob explained to me what that meant, I was real happy. I like to think Cal did see rainbows when he took his last breath, in that cold wet ditch, covered in those mean-mouthed cane toads. I like to think he heard their strange, hypnotic song, lulling him to sleep, soothing the pain in his head, from Richie's blow. I like to think he was surrounded by colors and music and felt so warm inside, like it was the best goddamn dream he ever had.

I sure do like to think that, cos, in the end, Richie was right about Cal all along . . . . He was just a baby.

Michelin Boy (With Rabbit Ears)
/ Gabriel Embeha

Review of *Idiot Wind: A Memoir* by Peter Kaldheim

(Published by Canongate, August 2019)

Review by Neal Lipschutz

This readable memoir of being down and out (and eventually restored) in mid-1980s America has an unusual publishing history. As recounted in the book, its writing can reasonably be said to have been about thirty years in the making. Its appearance marks the full-length authorial debut for an enterprising seventy-year-old.

The moniker "Idiot Wind" is borrowed from a 1974 Bob Dylan song title and wailed refrain. To Peter Kaldheim, the idiot wind is a siren call to immediate gratification and a weakness of will. For him, it's a gust of addiction and self-destruction. It blew through his Ivy League education and promising start in book publishing. It knocked down a marriage and transformed him into a small-time New York City cocaine salesman, one so fond of his own product that it flummoxed any attempt at profit or even solvency. If Mr. Dylan's song lyrics more broadly nod to the misconceptions created by popular culture and the corrosive cult of celebrity, it's of no moment. Mr. Kaldheim successfully adopts the phrase for his own purposes.

The story told is of one man's fall and redemption, though Mr. Kaldheim concedes some guilt about past actions and broken relationships won't completely fade. Indirectly, it's also a paean to the vastness of the American road and the reinvention and second chances buried in those open spaces. Those opportunities may harken most to the collapsed with the already established skills and erudition enjoyed by the author, who understands his predicament and has a keen sense of the world around him. Throughout his travails, Mr. Kaldheim invokes the spirit of Jack Kerouac's "On the Road" as a cosmic marker to his own journey. He states his admiration of great writers known for their alcohol consumption as well as their art. "By romanticizing their excesses, I suckered myself into believing I could do the same . . . ."

After scamming a cocaine wholesaler in the winter of 1987, Mr. Kaldheim exited New York to escape the gangster's wrath, asking a Greyhound bus clerk in time-honored tradition to put him on a bus as far as his meager dollars would allow. That's followed by his hitchhiking odyssey across the nation. The goal is to get to San Francisco, where an old friend has dangled a job in construction. When that opportunity fades while the author is already on the road, circumstance leads him instead toward the Pacific Northwest. There's a double past tense in this journey for the current reader. The US of 1987 was a far cry from the post-World-War-II years that set the stage for the highs and lows of Keruoac's "On the Road" characters. The saga of writer as down-and-out misfit with thumb in the air had by the mid-1980s already run its course, though Mr. Kaldheim does bring it new life as a next-generation fan of the beats. Read now, in an age of social media permanence and virtual as well as physical existence, the distance between coasts doesn't seem nearly as great and the ability to simply disappear and wind up three thousand miles away as a new person is seriously hard to fathom. One small example of the very different time: a homeless Mr. Kaldheim has to track down a place he can receive mail and then await references to arrive courtesy of the US Postal Service when he applies for a job.

Nothing truly outrageous happens to Mr. Kaldheim as he traverses penniless across America. That fact enhances the book. The path, while certainly difficult and at times scary, feels real. It's no doubt trying on his soul and his soles (he hobbles through most of his travels in ill-fitting boots). Interspersed with the road narrative are glimpses of the author's earlier life and a rehashing of another nadir, time spent in jail at Rikers Island that led to a split with his parents. But little is written about the author's inner throes as he shakes his previous constant thirsts for cocaine and alcohol. Once on the road, he doesn't seem tempted to indulge, even when in the company of regularly swilling down and outers. Except for a long ride with a judgmental Vietnam veteran (to whom the author is generally sympathetic and ready to lay blame on himself for the fraught relationship), Mr. Kaldheim is regularly the fortunate recipient of the good will of a fellowship of the road. Whether its advice on successfully hopping freight trains or managing the generous shelter and welfare systems of Portland, Ore., the author usually finds a helping hand. Even potential enemies—train brakemen and police officers—are less than heavy-handed. And then there's the American West, in its natural beauty and boundlessness, offering an awe-inspiring landscape for the author's personal transformation.

Inception Contest Winner & Finalists 2019

The Lungs are the Seat of Grief

Winner, Inception Contest

Novel by Elizabeth Marian

When she thinks back to that night much later, she will wonder if it was the hinge upon which her life turned, and if she could have changed things, how much else might have turned out differently. And then she will make herself another vodka martini and light a Salem because that's useless now, all the imagining, and she has always prided herself on being a practical person.

But no, that isn't true—she has always been eminently a dreamer, head in the ether. Or now am I thinking of myself?

Her name is Joann Frakes, and in December 1949 she is the publicity director at the Camelback Inn when the Shah of Iran, Mohammed Reza Pahlavi, comes to visit the United States for the first time. This is the story the newspapers will print: The Shah sees Joann across the room, red rose in her blonde hair, and sends an aide to ask her to dinner. They eat and dance into the night, and then she goes to bed, pretty head abuzz with the events of the evening. He stays for three days, playing tennis, swimming, riding horses, attending receptions, and then he is gone. A royal encounter, over as swiftly as it began.

The Shah of Iran's first American date, Time *magazine will say,* a willowy blonde from Oak Park, Illinois.

Citrus Sinensis

First Runner-up, Inception Contest

Essay by Cynthia Belmont

Down in the wash, in the chalky railroad bed at the bottom of the canyon, we laid pennies on the tracks. No trains rolled the slick black rails. Smashed eucalyptus leaves cracked in the dust everywhere. We were small but we knew how to get back, by the path through the sudden oranges like fruit trees in a tapestry, to where the yucca started at the foot of Nanna's hill. Glowing Valencias clustered around us, walking together up the quiet dirt rows, don't eat, don't touch, watching for snakes.

Our mother lived in the San Bernardino foothills above these Redlands orchards in the 1940s, and she was a ringleted blonde, a single child, she was never allowed down here alone. She told us the farmers used to fumigate the orange trees and tent them to keep the mist in. One time some children lifted a tent like a skirt to see underneath, and they were asphyxiated. The end . . . .

Magnets

Finalist, Inception Contest

Poem by Barb Reynolds

>Your coat is dusted
>with magnets, aphrodisiacs
>sewn into your hems.

Cheonjimun

Finalist, Inception Contest

Novel by Kat Lewis

천지문 | *Cheonjimun*

In Korea, they call me *Jeoseung Saja*. They say that I appear in black *hanbok* and a wide-brim *gat* hat, that I hunt down ghosts and send them onto the next place. In the west, there is no traditional clothing, no hat with a brim as wide as a crow's wing. There is only a scythe and the bleached bone hand wrapped around it. In some corner of your internet, there is a comic about how Life gives gifts to Death—her lover—and Death keeps them forever. None of these interpretations of who I am are completely wrong, but neither are they right.

Now, I can't tell you everything that happens when you die, but I can tell you this: you will meet me in the last place you lay, and what I will look like depends entirely on you. Sometimes, I am your mother, your father. Sometimes, I am the childhood dog you still dream about at night. Other times, I am a swing set, a park bench, the door to your childhood bedroom. No matter who or what I am, you will know what you have to do: take my hand, take a seat, take a step through the doorway to pass on, and in your passing, your thoughts become my thoughts, your memories my memories, your fears, hopes, and dreams all mine. But it won't feel like a betrayal or a violation. It will feel like your gift to me, the final gesture to a friend before leaving.

The Mad Scientist's Husband

Finalist, Inception Contest

Novel by Eric Roe

His name was Charlie Rabin. He was a photographer for KBHI News Portland, but his lazy-afternoon dream was to make an epic feature film of St. George and the Dragon. He believed that the lush forests of the Tualatin Mountains, near where he and his wife lived, could serve as a surrogate for the woods of England (he'd never been to England), and on solitary hikes he imagined the dragon crashing through the old-growth trees in its furious attempt to devour St. George and his white horse, who were impeding the dragon's intended meal of the lovely Princess Sabra. But Charlie Rabin would be remembered for something else entirely: He was the husband of Catherine C. Rabin, MD, PhD; he at first collaborated with her on the project that would make her infamous and then, after he changed his mind, tried and failed to stop her.

They met courtesy of a paper mill mechanic whose arm was caught in a machine and turned into a gory horror movie prop. Charlie's news team covered the story when the accident occurred, and they came back for a miracle-of-modern-medicine follow-up. "First doctor wanted to amputate, all the way up at the shoulder," the mechanic said. "I wasn't having that. They finally sent me over to Marquam. They bring in Dr. Rabin, and I tell her, Look, I need my arm for work. I can't lose my arm. She just gives it a once-over and says, Okay."

Before and After

Finalist, Inception Contest

Prose by J. Brooke

If I did in fact utter those words she swears I did, it would have occurred just after my father died, just after I ended that dreadful relationship I never mention, just after she told me she was divorcing the depressed man who no longer slept in her bed. This was before we travelled to Paris and never left the hotel room. It was before we gave a real estate broker fake names to disguise our identities. It was before the wedding in another country. It was before some of the children fell apart and before we glued them back together. It was before we made a lot of money and spent a lot of money. It was before her middle daughter stopped speaking to us. It was before we wrote checks to 12 therapists and 5 lawyers. It was before the "Happy Hanukkahs" and the strained Thanksgivings. It was before I started getting published. It was before we started fighting and before we stopped fighting. It was before 3 kids went to six boarding schools. It was before we were interviewed sometimes and misquoted always. It was before we started using moisturizer on our necks. It was before I stopped and started and stopped and started and stopped and started drinking. It was before we installed the alarm system. It was before we went to the Bronx zoo -- just last Summer -- and saw the gorillas in their habitat napping tenderly endlessly effortlessly intertwined...and I burst into tears.

Maddie Wants a Man

Finalist, Inception Contest

Prose by Kim Diaz

Maddie wants a man. He has to be tall, good-looking—no weak chins, bad teeth, or thinning hair. In good shape, muscular, and he's got to have some smarts. He doesn't need a college degree if he's a self-made man. He should be worldly, well-traveled and well-heeled. He needs to be the same political party but she says it's not polite to talk about politics on the first date. I'm thinking when the Amazon and president's pants are on fire what else is there to talk about?

Maddie keeps changing her profile username and photos. Right now it's BrainyLady and the picture is from her college graduation. When I asked her why the old photo, she said, "I still look pretty much the same." Thirty years and thirty pounds seems pretty different to me.

In Maddie's profile she says it's important to her that the man "share her faith"—which happens to be a very old, well-established religion that's been getting a fair amount of bad press lately. I'm more about the Law of Attraction but Maddie dismisses it, calls it "Magical Thinking" while her religion relies on an intermediary and a busload of saints.

She wants a man but needs a reality check. She's an unemployed teacher with anger management issues and three cats. I know, because she talks nonstop about herself. Mostly about how unfair it was that she got fired after saying, "For God's sakes, just shoot me," and walking out during a faculty meeting.

Single Word Contest 2020

Aloha

Stephanie Launiu

Single Word Contest 2020 Finalist

"Live *Aloha*" is a common phrase seen all over Hawaii. It's on t-shirts, bumper stickers, posters, in store windows, and in many public and private places. It's an important reminder that *Aloha* doesn't just mean "hello," "goodbye" or "love." It is a universal principle that is meant to be lived. *Aloha* is the single word that is most important in today's world, and if each of us were to "Live *Aloha*", the world would be transformed.

The indigenous people of Hawaii, the *kanaka maoli* or Native Hawaiians, had no written language. All of their knowledge was passed down orally from generation to generation for thousands of years. When the Christian missionaries arrived in Hawaii in 1820, they worked closely with the natives to put their oral language into writing. Even with the best of intentions, a written language designed by foreigners will never completely capture the intimacies and emotions of a society's history, religion and culture that are entwined into a language. And so it was with `olelo Hawai`i – the Hawaiian language.

Ancient Hawaiians used the word *Aloha* whenever they greeted someone and when they parted company. So, the missionaries thought that it was a way to say hello and goodbye. The Hawaiians also used *Aloha* when they presented gifts and when they became emotionally close to someone. So, the missionaries thought that *Aloha* also meant Love. What exactly does *Aloha* mean? And why is it so important in the 21st century?

The word *Aloha* is a combination of two words – *alo* and *hā*. *Alo* means "face," "front" or "presence." *Hā* is the breath of life that the ancient ones believed came only from *Akua* or the Creator. When a baby is born, it is the divine *hā* that brings that soul to life and leaves a portion of divinity within each of us alive today. There are no English words that can properly translate *Aloha,* but the closest meaning perhaps is that you and I are in the presence of God. In the word *Aloha,* we meet each other humbly as equals.

So, what would the world be like if we all knew and believed that the Creator was present and watching us? I think most of us would become the best versions of ourselves.

What would the world be like if we could recognize the spark of divinity in even the rudest person on the subway? Or the homeless woman with the shopping cart clogging up the sidewalk? Or the rude driver who just missed hitting your car while cutting in front of you on the highway?

If there were more *Aloha*, national leaders would think twice about declaring war in the world. Decisions about war are made behind closed doors, and not with the humbleness that *Aloha* requires. *Aloha* is a partner of diversity, because when equals come together, prejudice and discrimination fly out the window. If we knew the Creator was present and watching us, how often would violence of any kind really occur? Domestic violence, random shootings, and small inhumane acts like purse-snatchings. Don't you think *Aloha* would make these acts rarer than they are today? They're often so common they don't even make headlines anymore. The cruelty of social media can be erased with *Aloha,* so that cyber and in-person bullying are conquered by kinder days while keeping the miracle of technology. The political and racial divides that have come to characterize the 21st century can be tamed with more *Aloha* in the world, while those who struggle for human and civil rights could experience more victories with *Aloha* beside them. If *Aloha* were widely recognized as a universal principle, the Me Too movement would not be needed.

Aloha is about the dignity and equality of being human in an imperfect world. *Akua* may be watching us, but he's not controlling us. So those 'Live *Aloha*' signs that I see everyday in Hawaii remind me that we are in charge of our futures. Living one day at a time, with *Aloha* . . . .

You're Mine You

Valyntina Grenier

Single Word Contest 2020 Finalist

A person of many solitudes
they give valediction
they give from instinct infinitesimal selves
they keep pained expressions out of the household
they disregard infinitesimal selves

Unceasingly they aren't public
unending under unending another not subconsciously
They aren't alike parallel to some center
They aren't unalike from some surface equality

They stay

They unberth haters w/ difficulty
They wake apart/ untethered/ boundless
They forget waking apart and then they begin
They make w/ infinitesimal selves

They aren't stable tethered
They aren't wild apart
They are revealed
They yes longer possessionless

Equanimity became a nest
they created

Burning

Olga Gonzalez Latapi

Single Word Contest 2020 Finalist

burn the pink petals within the clouds as paws made of wood and velvet tongues lick whiskers on my face because all the future accidents of the world scratch the heavens as wooden demons made into cats destroy firehouses full of spirits looking at pianos full of scrunchies made of flesh from flowers burnt to a crisp just as pillows of heaven leave chests to become mist

Self-Quarantined

C.W. Buckley

Single Word Contest 2020 Finalist

The good news is, we're all sick
                                        Your scent in scentless rain
Incurable obstacles to cut off on the way to Bartell or the bus
                              Morning biker spreads a county fair petrichor
In the way, virally entangled
                          Alfalfa and manure, Spring round-up on the ranch
We are in respiratory distress
Work from home
Wash your hands
                            Ferment steeps through Pike Place Market bricks
Particles arrayed like a halo or crown
I am your face
                    Don't touch me
                          The boy skunks of peanut butter and pot
Enveloped virus
                            Old man smell, dog and sweated wool
I am medicated
                                A tang of forbidden grapefruit
I am vulnerable
                    Isolate me
                      Fish in a midnight dumpster off NE 75th
I translate into protein in your host cells

A positive-sense, single-stranded RNA strain
                                   In the absence of wine: lavender and ammonia
Your mantle entwined in formline design
Our Lady of Seattle, Undoer of Knots
                        Denature me
                                           The smell of burning wax
I am a lingering cough
                        Cover me
May I never be far from my people
                                 A hearty crock of onion and cumin chili
Let them never claim me as their own
                         We are not well, and have been infectious all along

The ה Meanings

Omer Wissman

Single Word Contest 2020 Finalist

The above written fifth letter of the Hebrew alphabet presents several facets which make it uniquely important, now more than ever. These include its use as greeting, then in questioning, as defining/honorific, in laughs and breaths, the latter related to the biblical function, which in turn is linked to its most zeitgeist context, which I term the meaning equation. This letter is pronounced as a letter "hey", the standard greeting of our times. In Hebrew it is written identical to a command to be. In critical theory, Althusser put forth his concept of interpellation, turning and saying something to some other which positions him in a particular role within the systems of society. Althusser used the example of a police officer turning to a citizen, bringing him within a law & order mentality. The hey greeting, as common in my native Israel as it is in English speaking countries, has dethroned, symbolic of globalization and global turns to the right wing, our Shalom (peace) greeting. To me, if not for Althusser, any *hey* greeting in Israel turns the interpellated subject as well as his interpellator into objects in globalized hyper-subjectivity, whose parts greet mainly to maintain their place in national-global Wittgensteinian language game, saying in subtext we care nothing for each other but are linked as similarly essential to the hyper-subject of society. This unspoken edict tempts me to contrast it, discussing utilities of this letter in questioning, wherein it is put at beginnings of sentences to present a question polite yet emphatic. The sound of such phrasings calls to mind the very current mood communication modality of passive-aggressiveness. But I suggest we disrupt this rote play to call upon the role of this letter as our "The", in order to question everything we think believe and take for granted. In English, this might be expressed as a move from "I am depressed" to "The I is depressed" through "The I is the Depressed" and finally "The I is the depressed?" Thus achieving a critical distance which allows one to doubt if it is really he who feels depressed, or a more global I role which has become the depressed part of subjects such as him. In this same position of our "the," I'd like to explore a rather new Israeli Hebrew turn of phrase, translating as "This is one the best X if not *The*." Such a colloquialism goes so far as to eventually omit the X object which was set out to be defined in honor, and leaves merely our need to restore aura to the singular instances, in a world of digital reproduction and the love of swiping. This leads me to the letter as put into play in a "Ha Ha Ha," an exaggerated non-laughter rebelling flagrantly against the cultural need to always be amused. On the other end of this spectrum stands this letter as pure breath, of meditation, relaxation, of deep being beyond quotidian, and of course also as exhaled cigarette smoke. This letter of deliberate conscious breath is more than a concentrated pause of our rat race. It is the first and final utterance of crystallized living language, before and after all words, in birth as at death. What letter then more suited to denote in the Old Testament, the Hebraic holy bible, a name of god? But god uses a nifty trick, attaching to the letter an apostrophe, calling upon the believer to say not ha or hey but something quite different, "My Lord". This is what I call a meaning equation. It started out in this sacred religious text as a way of saying to the faithful, you can never know the one true name of god, and more than this, you can never grasp with human faculties the full nature of this god who grasps and encompasses all being, the way a breath allows all language wings. This line of thought sheds an interesting light on the meaning equation X=X', or verbally a variable which is equal to that variable modified, something of the same but a bit different nature. In the light of the above interpretation of the divine meaning equation, our more earthly and even atheist concern with a search for meaning seems to become, in my eyes at least, exposed as a lost cause, a chain of signifier variables which leads one nowhere, or rather, to his start as lonely, non-apostrophe x. People still are trying to make sense of existence utilizing such equations, Stating I am me the lover of Y, or I am me the father of Z. But all these attempts at redefinition of terms appears to me doomed to fail, as requiring to be replaced with an identity question, I=?. As long as subject X has not consciously found out his identity separate from the varying roles of this or that X', he cannot take on any social-subject positioning with authenticity and unshakeable core knowledge of thyself, leading to all manner of friction, tension, explosion even. An I has to use his question to find out who he really feels himself to be, in order for him to not take on things he does not really want and therefore will struggle to bear, choosing in its stead to make a life true to the admittedly partial understanding of his own identity, not interpellated by society into a function equation too large or narrow for his authentic identity. In such a way we may do away with a zeitgeist of imposter syndrome, endless YA moratorium, broken/cracked homes, toxic polyamor, depersonalization-derealization, and a general malaise of feeling, meaning lost in the everything-is-not-what-it-seems way of X' problematics, solved superficially b identifying with variable fictional characters, more than with real & dear as a self-determined, true-to-self solution of I equaling constant Y. So, ask not where in the world is Waldo, but why is Waldo's I there, and more importantly, should *The* Waldo I be the There?

VIRAL / CLAIRE LAWRENCE
SINGLE WORD CONTEST 2020 RUNNER-UP

Ubuntu

Ethel Maqeda

Single Word Contest 2020 Runner-Up

U*buntu* is a Nguni[1] word derived from the philosophy "*Umuntu ngumuntu ngabantu*" (a person is only a person through and because of other people). In other words, we can only be fully human when we acknowledge, accept, appreciate and nurture other people's humanity. In practice, *Ubuntu* fosters group solidarity, compassion and respect for others and encourages and enables individuals to continually expand their circle of humanity to embrace and celebrate diversity.

Growing up in a township in a small Zimbabwean city, I was content that my humanness was complete and affirmed by my friends, family and the community around me, although my world didn't extend beyond a thirty-kilometer radius until I was nine. *Ubuntu* for me then meant respecting everyone, especially my elders, and sharing food, home and clothing with the less fortunate. The Shona saying *Avirirwa*[2] (dusk has surprised him/her) was one I heard often then. It meant that strangers could

---

[1] Nguni people are the Zulu, Ndebele, Xhosa, Sotho, Swati, Phuthi, Nhlangwini, Lala and Ngoni speaking peoples of Southern Africa who share a similar culture, traditions and beliefs.

[2] "*Avirirwa*" and "*mainini*" are Shona words. Many Zimbabwean children grow up in multilingual households.
The Shona people of Zimbabwe share a similar worldview to that of Nguni-speaking people and other African cultures.

knock on any door on an evening and ask for shelter for the night before carrying on with their journeys. They then became an aunt/uncle, a relative for life. *Ubuntu* also meant you weren't to stare or point at people that looked any different to you or make them feel different. We played netball with a feminine boy we called *mainini*, a term of endearment meaning "mother's young sister," and didn't think anything of it. It has apparently become unacceptable as the boy became an adult and someone decided that his femininity made him subhuman.

Nobody is born with *ubuntu* . . . these are communally accepted and desirable ethical standards that a person acquires throughout his/her life, and therefore education also plays a very important role in transferring the African philosophy of life.[3] Family, community and school education all played a role in the development of my *ubuntu*. Just before the end of the War of Liberation from colonial rule in 1979, I turned seven and the tips of my fingers could finally reach my ear over my head. This meant I could start school. This extended my understanding of my circle of humanity to include children from other villages and communities, from the mining communities around the city whose families were usually migrant laborers from Malawi and Zambia. I became aware that the world was a much bigger place, not just peopled by black people and white Rhodesians; that there were other Christianities, other religions, other ways of thinking and being. I began to understand that people from the same clan could support different political parties, that not all black people were agreed on what independence from colonial rule meant. I learned that some black people had fought on the side of the Rhodesians. *Ubuntu* is about accepting such painful truths.

In the following year or two after I started school, an uncle, who I hadn't been aware existed until then, came home from exile, a place I didn't know existed either, and brought me a beautifully bound and illustrated copy of *The Arabian Nights*. As I gradually to read, I became enthralled by the tales of peoples in far-flung places, who in so many ways were so alien yet in so many other ways were also familiar. By the time I reached secondary school, the insatiable appetite to explore as many different ways of being as there are in the world had so taken over my life that I had read everything I

---

[3] M. Letseka, "African philosophy and educational discourse," in, P. Higgs, N.C.G. Vakalisa, T.V. Mda & N.T. Assie-Lumumba (Eds), *African voices in education* (Juta: Lansdowne, 2000), p 186.

could lay my hands on. I also learned about the importance of being a good listener.

At twenty, when I travelled beyond the thirty-kilometer radius and went to university, my understanding of humanness was further enriched by meeting people from other parts of the country and the world. I lost my first family member to HIV/AIDS, moving it from my science textbook to real life, and I fell in love with a Japanese boy called Ken. I also continued to be interested in literature, geography, history and politics, and to feed my appetite by reading, travelling and meeting new people at every opportunity. My education not only broadened my view of what it means to be human, but also allowed me to embrace my Africanness with pride, to appreciate and celebrate human diversity and to negotiate my way through encounters with people who hold on to differences and make them the basis of their relationship with other people. I have been called a monkey a few times.

In today's world, ridden with war, displacement, poverty, and disease which put our *Ubuntu* to test, it will do all of us good to remember to be kind, considerate, and compassionate. *Ubuntu* is about the common good of society, with humanness as an essential element of human growth.[4] By deduction, anything that puts the life and wellbeing of others in jeopardy is anti-human. It means, in these challenging times, not hoarding food, toilet roll or soap. and not disregarding calls to practice social distancing or self-isolation.

Umuntu ngumuntu ngabantu!

---

[4] Elza Venter, "The Notion of Ubuntu and Communalism in African Educational Discourse," *Studies in Philosophy and Education, 23. 2-3 (2004),* 149-160 (p. 149).

The Meaning of Free

Hannah van Didden

Single Word Contest 2020 Winner

An exploration of the word in a selection of its nuances.

Definition* of "free"	Sample sentence
a. [chemistry] uncombined, unpaired.	New research is finding that free radicals may actually be good for you.
a. excluded.	Rich in polyphenols, fair trade dark chocolate can be enjoyed guilt-free when eaten in moderation.
a. gratis.	The child's meal comes with a free toy.
a. [of trade] open.	The free market is often touted as a benefit of capitalism.
a. liberal (not miserly).	The businessman's free nature extends only to his mates.
a. void of something, usually undesirable.	The despot is free of moral burden.
v. to be rid of something.	In crossing the border, they thought they would be free of any further threat of attack.
a. permitted to take a specific action.	Because it appeared to be within the letter of the law, the decisionmakers believed they were free to act without considering broader humanitarian and ethical obligations.
a. without direct cost to the recipient.	The center offers free meals, entertainment, and accommodation.
a. wild.	Flitting from branch to branch, the tiny bird was free.

Definition* of "free"	Sample sentence
a. able to act with liberty.	The woman fled from her home so that she might be free.
and easy a. unrestrained.	A sad longing accompanied the recollection of her grandmother's free and easy hand when it came to butter on fresh-baked bread.
a. able to act in accordance with one's own will.	While they were, in principle, free to look for work, the community prevented them from having safe and meaningful employment.
a. [of speech] frank; fairspoken.	The commentators continued to cast insults and slurs, arguing they had a right to free speech.
v. to liberate.	The medical professionals sought to free the man from conditions that adversely impacted his health.
a. liberated; not limited or controlled.	The woman wants her child to know what it is to be free.
v. to make available for a particular purpose.	The man frees the rope from the post for a use known to no one but him.
a. [of nations] not subject to foreign rule or despotism.	The girl longed to be accepted into a free country, not knowing that in such a place she would still be unable to leave the house alone without being held accountable for what might befall her.
a. no longer confined or imprisoned.	Far across the ocean, a grieving mother says, "Finally, he is free."
a. noble; joyful.	The woman's free spirit sees her greet each day with smiling hope.

*Definitions based on information from *The Shorter Oxford English Dictionary* (3rd edition, with revisions and addenda, 1966), the *Cambridge English Dictionary*, Oxford Living Dictionaries, Etymonline, National Center for Biotechnology Information.

$100 for 100 Words or Art 2020

In these uncertain times
In these uncertain times
In these uncertain times
In these uncertain times
In these uncertain times
In these uncertain times
In these uncertain times
In these uncertain times
In these uncertain times
In these uncertain times
In these uncertain times
In these uncertain times

IN THESE UNCERTAIN TIMES / ALICE DILLON

$100 FOR 100 WORDS OR ART 2020 WINNER

Willow Widow

Karen Walker

$100 for 100 Words or Art 2020 Winner

A willow grew unbidden in my backyard, flattering me with shade.

But the roots that crept under the fence proved insatiable. The tree's slender silver leaves sympathized, agreeing that virgin soil and a fresh spring should have been enough, and pointed which way the wind now blew. A conspiracy of branches, each one as thick as a man, soon blocked my view.

I cut the willow down when green shoots—curly-headed like my little one—appeared all over the neighborhood. Until I find another tree (this time choosing wisely at the garden center), baby and I will plant flowers around Daddy's stump.

Time a Grand and Final Judge, Grow Bravely in Love
/ Church Goin Mule

$100 for 100 Words or Art 2020 Runner-up

Guernica

S.T. Brant

"Staring" 1

Staring at Picasso's *Guernica*, Wondering What Turns Life to Art

The bull's a bull, the horse a horse. I'm dumbfounded at the locking of ideas into things. Break the things apart. Find the stable, pull out the bolt, Yeats says. What's fascinating will rise from the shapes of freed ideas. The Galateas of the mind, through the marriage of their will, incarnate these shapes. Guernica's a place—also an idea that took a shape: intellect in form. Guernica is not a canvas. A place: not a place upon a canvas, not shaped to match the canvas shape, but that canvas is a canvas named *Guernica*. We must keep these separate.

Tilting Towards Self-Annihilation / George L Stein

Rescue

Charlotte Wyatt

Do I miss the burnt-sugar smell of the red-tail's meal? Those pink intestines tossed like streamers from white rat pelts splayed across the ground? People who know me now cannot believe I scraped sundried entrails from concrete. "You worked in a shelter?" they ask, and imagine what? Gratitude? Affection? That bird was broken-winged, miserable and afraid. So was I, because he could not confirm any happiness in the life we forced upon him. Would memories of flight offer solace or suffering? It's been years; he must be gone. I still think of him. I still don't know the answer.

Keep Those Hard Times Away / Benjamin Malay

Red

Jacqueline Schaalje

Through the window where I sleep
Mars is a tab.

My mind has puzzled over other
things since.

I think
of a boyfriend, long
ago, shoving in my blank.

I couldn't tell (you) whether
he and what we did then
was something lost or stained.

When his red cabbage head
bumped away in goodbye,

I turned up
the car window, sealed
the edges, and zipped

on the freeway. He still looks
for me online. Still cross?

He wants his fluffy
bunny and I'm still hankering
after his cabbage hands.

RESIDENT LIGHT / LOUIS STAEBLE

No Rest for the Weary / Craig Anderson

Young Authors and Artists

Trailing Childhood

Sidney Muntean

I popped out dead. When I was born, I died, or at least, I tried to. Perhaps I could already sense the downsides of life: grief, isolation, people who wear socks with sandals.... Or maybe it just overwhelmed me, all of that *life* at once, the sharp birdsong outside the hospital room, the doctor's look of distaste at me, my mother's sigh of relief after the delivery; it all left me literally breathless.

Whatever the case, my arrival into this world prompted how I would navigate the rest of my life: emotional and constantly learning lessons.

As a baby, I didn't do much, but my parents still kept me around. Because at the time, coils of hair rested atop my head, courtesy of my dad. I became known among my family and their friends for my dark curls. But my father grew jealous. He too had world-renowned curls
that, with time, withered away until nothing was left except for a naked head.

On my first birthday, my father snatched me from my bed to the bathroom. There, the monstrosity occurred. A gentle buzz sounded, and I saw a razor gleaming in my father's hands. I tried to cry for help—a scream, a whine!—but it was useless. It was over for me from the moment I saw that sinister smile stretched across his lips.

That day, my own father had shaved off all of my hair so that I looked like a mini him, bald head and all. Once my mother got home and scolded him, he made up something about reading an article and how shaving a baby's head helps its hair grow back thicker. But I knew better. That was the day when I learned to be careful about where I place my trust.

Two years later, I found myself getting into a stranger's car and telling them where I lived. It was summer. A light breeze shimmied between the trees and the sun stroked the earth with just enough heat to comfortably warm it. It was the perfect day to walk to the library.

I grew up going to the library three to four times a week, either in a stroller or on my two feet. The walk was short. All I had to do was exit my neighborhood and walk up a hill. I found comfort among the towering bookshelves or between a stack of books to read.

That day, my parents were at work, and my grandma wouldn't take me. I begged, pleaded, threw a tantrum, all in vain. She still said no.

Stubborn even then, I set my mind to go to the library myself. It would be the first time running away from home and rebelling against authority (but certainly not my last). As I stepped out of my house, I felt liberated. Even at three years old, I knew that it was unusual for someone so young to venture out on their own, and I felt proud. Walking along, I started to notice. It was my first time noticing—I hadn't done so before.

I noticed the bees dipping into the flowers beside me and the muffled sounds of children giggling from the park. I noticed the grass blades quivering in the wind and the smell of dog poop drifting in my direction. I felt like I had gathered power through my observations, like I had an edge on life that I didn't have before. Like I knew myself better, knew the world better.

I was interrupted by a car that pulled up beside me. I heard a growl saying, "Hey kid, come over here! Where do you live?"

I peered into the window to see a woman. "I dunno." I pointed towards the direction I came from. "Somewhere over there."

The woman frowned and said, "Get in. It'll be fun."

The woman opened the passenger door and I hopped in. The front seat was forbidden at my age, so naturally, I was delighted. As the woman approached my home, I hummed a Katy Perry song. Right before my cul-de-sac, I sang, "This one!"

Once she pulled up to my driveway, I ran to the front door to ring the doorbell.

My grandmother opened the door and cried tears of joy. She had been looking for me for the past fifteen minutes. The woman smiled at my grandma.

"Hi! I saw her walking alone on the street and I was really concerned and she kind of looked like Alex! And I knew that his mom was pregnant a few years ago, and his sister would be around that age, and I figured that she was related to him because they look so alike!" She seemed to speak a mile a minute.

My grandma blinked and said, "No speak English,"

They settled in broken English, with my occasional attempt to translate my grandma's Romanian the best I could.

That day, I didn't learn the danger of talking to strangers, or how dangerous it is to walk alone. However, I found the magic of spending time with myself. I started to learn who I was as a person and how I could interact with the world when alone. It was the first time I had gotten to know myself and became a project I focus on even to this day.

Now, I've been trying to teach myself the art of appreciation. It's too easy to live in negativity. Stress latches to my life and never seems to let go. But I don't mind. I just do the same as I did when I was three- I observe. I observe how the sun waves between the tree branches to say *hello, welcome, you'll be okay.* I observe how some people hold the door open for others who have their hands full, how people are still capable of being considerate and thoughtful and good. It is only through appreciation that I can muster the courage to get through the day.

Untitled

Weatherall Crump-Kean

i knew it
the moment i saw
those sincere gentle brown eyes
coup de foudre
i would be in love with you until my death

The Haunted Asylum

Robert Fitzgerald Beavers, Jr.

It's been decades since this lonely haunted asylum had been filled with the emotional sounds of laughing or crying. The mackerel sky is the only light source for miles along with the shocking lightning that flashes and strikes every waking second. It's possible to fill the lifeless suffering of the rejected and the forgotten with even more horror from their daily lives. They can't even imagine life without hearing the never-ending crying and pain of the mental patients as they try to find an escape from the house of torture. Their reality is the ever-expanding darkness all around them as they are forced to swallow and inject medicines into their bodies. They are forced to live in wheelchairs while viewing hallways with blood, spit, and doctor coats. They enjoy the comforts of padded rooms while smells of rotting corpses with flies, bacteria, and decay cover all over the dead bodies. The torture tools used with the insane people are covered in blood and have a history of entering inside the patients or, in other words, unsuspecting victims. This place is the unfortunate resting place of many unlucky victims that didn't know what was going to happen to them. The outside of this madhouse is deceiving because it is filled with trees and mountains. The front door is huge with granite steps leading up to it. The moon stands guard on top of the Asylum watching anybody who dares to enter this haunted placed. The ground crumbles and breaks apart with the lack of water, overdose of waste, and the blistering heat. The grass that barely exists around the asylum sweeps and weeps the ground as sudden low winds hit the area giving a chill to anyone that even sets foot on the ground. Stairs bust and crack as winds enter through the broken windows and hits the stairs that scream every time someone sets foot on the broken wood.

Contributors

Craig Anderson is an award-winning artist whose work is represented by private and corporate collections nationwide. He is a signature member of the San Diego Watercolor Society and has served as a juror in a number of art exhibitions, and is in demand for live demonstrations and workshops. He works exclusively in transparent watercolor. Craig believes that art is a timeless expression of the beauty that surrounds us: a fossil of some piece of real life that existed in time and space, a real, living, breathing thing.

Robert Fitzgerald Beavers, Jr. is a rising junior at a private school in Fairburn, Georgia. He is also a sports enthusiast, scholar, and one who dabbles in writing to amuse himself.

Cynthia Belmont is a professor of English and writing at Northland College, an environmental liberal arts school on the South Shore of Lake Superior, in Ashland, Wisconsin. Her creative work has been published in diverse journals including *Poetry, The Cream City Review,* Terrain.org, *Natural Bridge, Oyez Review,* and *Sky Island*.

Jerome Berglund graduated summa cum laude from the cinema-television production program at the University of Southern California, and has spent much of his career working in television and photography. He has had photographs published and awarded in local papers. A recently staged exhibition in the Twin Cities area included an extensive residency at a local community center.

Robin Bissett received her Bachelor of Arts in English and Minor in Creative Writing from Trinity University in May 2020.

Susan Bloch's stories have won prizes in the *Traveler's Tales* Solas Awards and received notable mention in *Best American Essays 2017*. She has been published in a variety of magazines and literary journals such as *The Forward, Entropy, The Citron Review, STORGY, Pif Magazine, Tikkun,* and *HuffPost*.

Jack Bordnick's sculptures incorporate surrealistic, mythological and magical imagery—often with whimsical overtones—aimed at provoking experiences and self-reflections. He seeks to unbalance rational minds, and the predominant imagery deals mostly with facial expressions of both living and "non-living" beings, and things that speak in their own languages. The result is textural, metallic and mixed-media assemblages that have been assembled, disassembled and reassembled, becoming abstractions unto themselves. Bordnick invites you to come and enjoy their stories.

K. Johnson Bowles has exhibited in more than eighty solo and group exhibitions nationally. Feature articles, essays, and reviews of her work have appeared in forty publications including *SPOT* (Houston Center for Photography), *Sculpture, Fiberarts,* and the *Houston Post.* She is the recipient of a National Endowment for the Arts Individual Fellowship and a Houston Center for Photography Fellowship. Recently, she served as an artist in residence at the Visual Studies Workshop in Rochester, NY. She received her MFA in photography and painting from Ohio University and a BFA in painting from Boston University.

ST Brant is a teacher from Las Vegas. Publication credits include *Door is a Jar, Santa Clara Review, New South, Green Mountains Review, Another Chicago Magazine, La Piccioletta Barca, Cathexis Northwest Press,* and a few others. You can find them on Twitter @terriblebinth or Instagram @shanelemagne.

A published poet and essayist, **J Brooke** is the previous nonfiction editor of the *Stonecoast Review.* With an MFA degree in Creative Writing from the University of Southern Maine, publications include *Harvard Review, TSR-The Southampton Review, The East Hampton Star, RFD Magazine, Hartskill Review, Rubbertop Review,* and *Mom Egg Review.* Brooke's film work includes *The Bed,* a short documentary, and two features cocreated with partner in film and life, Beatrice Alda.

A fourth generation West Coaster, **C.W. Buckley** lives and works in Seattle with his family. He writes about precious things, and what their loss means for us all. His writing explores geek culture, conscience, faith, and fatherhood. His work is forthcoming in the anthology *Undeniable: Writers Respond to Climate Change.* He is a contributor to *Washington Poetic Routes,* and appeared most recently in *Dappled Things, Timberline Review, Camas, Image Journal,* and *Catamaran Literary Reader.* He is the author of BLUING, a chapbook from Finishing Line Press. You can follow him as @chris_buckley on Twitter.

Mary Byrne is the author of the chapbook *A Parallel Life* (Kore Press) and the short story collection *Plugging the Causal Breach* (Regal House, 2019). Her short fiction has been published, broadcast and anthologized widely. She was born in Ireland and lives in France. https://twitter.com/BrigitteLOignon www.marybyrnewriter.com

Lara Chapman is a fine art nature photographer, writer and university professor based out of West Palm Beach, Florida. Lara's photographs earned several awards and distinctions and can be found on the walls of galleries and museums throughout the East Coast of the United States as well as Florida's west coast. She has published three photography and poetry books to date. When she is not teaching or photographing nature, she loves to spend time with her husband, Patrick, and two children, Nathan and Benjamin.

Church Goin Mule is a southern outsider artist. You can find their work online at churchgoinmule.com, and on instagram @churchgoinmule.

Weatherall Crump-Kean is a sophomore currently attending the University of Texas at Austin High School. Her first book, artificial affection, was recently published and she is looking for more opportunities to be heard.

Marilee Dahlman grew up in the Midwest and currently lives in Washington, DC. Her other stories have appeared in *Cleaver, The Colored Lens, Five on the Fifth, Metaphorosis, Timeworn Literary Fiction,* and online at The Saturday Evening Post.

Rayne Debski's stories have appeared in national and international publications including *Mslexia, The Summerset Review, Fifty Word Stories, REAL, Blue Earth Review,* and *Necessary Fiction,* and have been selected by Liars League NYC and other professional theatre groups for public readings. She is the editor of two anthologies published by Main Street Rag Press.

Josie Del Castillo is a Brownsville artist pursuing her MFA from the University of Texas Rio Grande Valley. She has exhibited throughout the state, and most recently in galleries in California, Chicago, San Francisco, and New York. Del Castillo's work consists of a series of self-portraits as well as portraits of others whom she perceives as reflections of herself and a source of human inspiration. Personal and emotional connections are often symbolically made to capture the essence of her subjects. Self-worth and personal insecurities are common themes. Much of her work often deals with the subjects of mental health and anxiety, self-esteem, and growing up in the Rio Grande Valley. Instead of emphasizing the dark connotations of mental health issues, Del Castillo challenges and confronts these themes through vibrant and colorful depictions of her subjects. Many works include Mexican-American cultural iconography and people raised in the Rio Grande Valley.

Kimberly Diaz studied Creative Writing at Eckerd College in St. Petersburg, Florida. Her work has appeared in the *Montana Mouthful, Eckerd Review, Fleas on the Dog,* and is forthcoming in a couple of anthologies. She is currently working on a collection of creative nonfiction and maybe a novel.

Alice Dillon is a fiber artist from Worcester, Massachusetts. Her roots in fiber art trace back to receiving a sewing machine as a gift in middle school. Alice began actively identifying as an artist in college when she taught herself how to embroider. Her works range from highly detailed to cleanly linear. Alice has recently become interested in repeated linear imagery, which brings a modern androgyny to a classically feminine medium. Alice is a graduate of Clark University. She is one of ArtsWorcester's 2020 Material Needs Grant Recipients, and is utilizing the grant to create life-sized, full-body embroidered portraits to be exhibited in 2021.

Tessa Ekstrom is an emerging poet in Portland, Oregon, who is pursuing a BS in biochemistry. Her work has been published by *Prometheus Dreaming* and *Blue Literary Magazine*.

Renee Elton is a poet and teacher currently working on a poetry manuscript about Japanese design in response to nature and ritual. She earned her MFA in Creative Writing from George Mason University and has a biology degree from Kent State. Her recent poetry and art have appeared in *Every Writer's Resource, Every Day Poems, Snapping Twig,* and *Literary Mama.*

Through a continual mixed-media interweaving of acrylic, graphite, digital imagery, performance, film, and writing, **Gabriel Embeha** engages a diverse range of persons, places, things and ideas involved in different forms of disability and violence. His process involves an ongoing series of interrelated sacrificial acts and quasi-ethnographic confrontations with scientific representation, the state, conscience, and futility. He lives and works in Berlin.

Nicole Foran (MFA, University of Cincinnati) is a mixed-media artist and educator based out of Murfreesboro, Tennessee. Her work investigates memory, moral reasoning, and identity. Nicole's work is exhibited internationally, and she has upcoming solo exhibitions in Wyoming and Michigan. Several of her pieces are to be included in small group shows in California and Wisconsin. When she is not in the studio, Nicole is snuggling her two Boston Terriers or going on hikes with her family.

Devon Fulford is a writer and English instructor at Colorado State University. While most of her prior publication history has been in educational writing, she has been honored with poetry, nonfiction, and fictional publication credits in *Aurora: The Allegory Ridge Poetry Anthology, Inklette Magazine, the Same* literary journal, *Handbasket Zine,* Foundpolaroids.com, and others. Fulford resides on the front range of the Rocky Mountains with her partner Levi and their chocolate Labrador, The Walrus. In pockets of spare time, she can be found hiking with her family and riding her Triumph Street Twin motorbike.

Elizabeth Gauffreau is the Assistant Dean of Curriculum and Assessment at Champlain College Online in Burlington, Vermont. Recent fiction publications include *Dash, Pinyon, Aji, Open: Journal of Arts & Letters,* and *Evening Street Review.* Recent poetry publications include *One Sentence Poems, Smoky Quartz, Medical Literary Messenger, The Ekphrastic Review,* and *Pinyon.* Her debut novel, *Telling Sonny,* was published by Adelaide Books in 2018. Learn more about her work at http://lizgauffreau.com.

Olga Gonzalez Latapi is a poet and MFA candidate in Writing at California College of the Arts. Although her writing journey started in journalism, she is now pursuing her true passion: exploring the world of poetry with a mighty pen in hand. Her work has been published in *Teen Voices, Sonder Midwest, BARNHOUSE* (Box of Parrots), iaam.com and *The Nasiona* magazine. Originally from Mexico City, she currently lives in San Francisco.

An LGBTQIA+ multi-genre artist living in Tucson, Arizona, **Valyntina Grenier**'s work has previously appeared in *Sunspot*, *Gaze*, *High Shelf Press*, *Lana Turner*, *JuxtaProse*, and *Bat City Review*. Her tête-bêche chapbook *Fever Dream / Take Heart* was published by Cathexis Northwest Press, January 2020. Find her at valyntinagrenier.com or Insta @valyntinagrenier

T.B. Grennan was born in Burlington, Vermont, and currently lives in Sunset Park, Brooklyn. He received an M.F.A. in Creative Writing from the University of Virginia and his fiction has been published in *Brokelyn*, *Digital Americana*, *White Stag Journal*, *The Seventh Wave*, and *Construction Literary Magazine*, as well as *Spaces We Have Known*, an anthology of LGBT+ fiction. His nonfiction has appeared in *TIMBER* and the *Indiana Review*.

River Elizabeth Hall is a poet and naturalist. Her poems have recently appeared or are forthcoming in *Cirque*, *High Shelf*, *Into the Void*, and *Tinderbox*, among others. She was a semifinalist in the 2019 Brett Elizabeth Jenkins Poetry Award.

Russian-American poet **Stella Hayes** is the author of *One Strange Country* (What Books Press, forthcoming in 2020). She grew up in an agricultural town outside of Kiev, Ukraine and Los Angeles. She earned a creative writing degree at University of Southern California. Her work has appeared in *Prelude*, *The Indianapolis Review* and *Spillway*, among others.

Doley Henderson is a Toronto writer of fiction and creative nonfiction. Her work is featured in *The Gaspereau Review*, *The Sunlight Press*, *The New Guard* online journal *BANG!*, *Blank Spaces*, *Prometheus Dreaming*, and *The Write Launch*. Her novel *Sea Change* has been accepted in The Writer's Hotel fiction conference in NYC, June 2020. Henderson enjoys telling a story with rhythm, texture, a strong voice, wit and grit.

Anton Franz Hoeger was born 1956 in Munich, Germany. Although mainly self-taught, his artistic roots go back to the *Wiener Malschule*, where he was taught by a master student of Professor Ernst Fuchs.

Ann Howells edited *Illya's Honey* journal from 1999 to 2017. Publications include *Under a Lone Star* (Village Books Press), *So Long As We Speak Their Names* (Kelsay Books), *Painting the Pinwheel Sky* (Assure Press), *Black Crow in Flight* (Editor's Choice, Main Street Rag), and *Softly Beating Wings*, winner of the William D. Barney Contest (Blackbead Books). Her poems have recently appeared in *Chiron Review*, *Slant*, and *San Pedro River Review*.

Kathy Hoyle writes short stories and flash fiction with bite. She holds a BA (hons) and an MA in Creative Writing. Her work has appeared in a variety of literary magazines including *Spelk*, *Ellipsis Zine*, *Lunate*, *Virtualzine* and *Cabinet of Heed*. She has been both long and shortlisted in many competitions such as The Exeter, The FISH memoir prize, and the Ellipsis Zine Flash Collection Prize. She is powered by tea and biscuits.

In a past century, **Heikki Huotari** attended a one-room school and spent summers on a forest fire lookout tower. They are a retired math professor, have won two poetry chapbook prizes and published two collections. Another collection is at press.

Penny Jackson's work has been published in *The Edinburgh Review*, *The Croton Review*, *The Gideon Poetry Review*, *Story Quarterly*, *Real Fiction*, and others. Honors include a MacDowell Colony Fellowship, The Elizabeth Janeway Prize in Fiction from Barnard College, and a Pushcart Prize. She is also a playwright and a film writer.

Jennifer Judge's work has been published in Rhino, Literary Mama, Gyroscope Review, Blueline, Mothers Always Write, Schuylkill Valley Journal, Every Pigeon, Drunk in a Midnight Choir, Rockvale Review, Juniper, Under the Gum Tree, and The Comstock Review, among others. She was nominated for a Pushcart Prize, Best New Poets 2018, and Best of the Net 2018. Her work was also selected to appear in a Jenny Holzer art installation in the Comcast Technology Center in Philadelphia. Her first collection of poetry is due out in early 2021 from Propertius Press.

Candice Kelsey's debut book of poetry, *Still I am Pushing*, releases March 6th with Finishing Line Press. Her first nonfiction book explored adolescent identity in the age of social media and was recognized as an Amazon.com Top Ten Parenting Book in 2007. Her poetry has appeared in *Poet Lore*, *The Cortland Review*, *North Dakota Quarterly,* and many other journals. A finalist for *Poetry Quarterly*'s Rebecca Lard Award, Kelsey's creative nonfiction was nominated for a 2019 Pushcart Prize. She is an educator of twenty years' standing, and is devoted to working with young writers. An Ohio native, she lives in Los Angeles with her husband and three children.

Mickie Kennedy is an American poet who resides in Baltimore County, Maryland with his family and two feuding cats. He enjoys British science fiction and the idea of long hikes in nature. His work has appeared in *American Letters & Commentary*, *Artword Magazine*, *Conduit*, *Portland Review*, *Rockhurst Review*, and *Wisconsin Review*. He earned an MFA from George Mason University.

Christina Klein received a Fullbright Fellowship in 2018. She received her MFA from Florida State University in 2017.

Susan Landgraf has been awarded a $50,000 Poets Laureate grant from the Academy of American Poets. Two Sylvias Press published *The Inspired Poet* in 2019. More than 400 poems have appeared in *Prairie Schooner*, *Poet Lore*, *Margie*, *Nimrod*, and others. Books include *What We Bury Changes the Ground* and *Other Voices*. She is Poet Laureate of Auburn, Washington.

Stephanie Launiu is a Native Hawaiian lifestyle and cultural writer who lives and writes on the Big Island of Hawaii. At the age of sixty, she went to college and earned a Bachelor's Degree in Hawaiian Pacific Studies from the University of Hawaii. She loves nothing more than to write about these islands.

Claire Lawrence is a storyteller and visual artist living in British Columbia, Canada. She has been published internationally, and her work has been performed on BBC radio. Her stories have appeared in numerous publications, including *Geist, Litro, Ravensperch,* and *Brilliant Flash Fiction*. She was nominated for the 2016 Pushcart Prize. Her artwork has appeared in *Wired, A3 Review, Sunspot, Esthetic Apostle, Haunted, Fractured Nuance,* and more. Her goal is to write and publish in all genres, and not inhale too many fumes.

Kat Lewis is the author of the short story collection *In and Of Blood*. Lewis graduated from Johns Hopkins University where she held the Saul Zaentz Innovation Fund Fellowship. In 2018, she received a Fulbright Creative Arts grant in South Korea. She is currently an MFA student at the University of South Florida.

Neal Lipschutz's book reviews have appeared in a number of publications. He has also published short fiction in several digital and print publications.

Roeethyll Lunn is a lifetime learner and educator. She has a BFA in Broadcast Media from Morris College, Sumter, South Carolina, and an MFA in English and Writing from Long Island University, Southampton, New York.

Alan Lyons is an artist from Scotland specializing in drawing and painting. Landscape, nature, and human involvement in it are of ongoing concern to his practice. The color and material of oil paints or acrylics allow him to explore their organic or inorganic makeup.

Samantha Madway is working on a collection of interlinked poems and flash fiction. She loves her dogs, Charlie, Parker, and Davey, more than anything else in the universe. Though technophobic, she attempts to be brave by having an Instagram @sometimesnight. If the profile were a plant, it would've died long ago. Her writing has appeared in *Linden Ave, High Shelf, Sky Island Journal, Aurora, mutiny!, Clementine Unbound, SLAB,* and elsewhere.

Benjamin Malay works in a variety of mediums to create deeply personal images of people and places, embracing imperfect memory and fleeting life. Influenced by patterns of the natural world, he is most inspired by the spontaneous use of available materials. He is the sole proprietor of a fine art framing business in Seattle, Washington.

Dave Malone is the author of nine books, including *You Know the Ones* (Golden Antelope Press, 2017). His work has appeared in journals such as *San Pedro River Review, Plainsongs,* and *The Cape Rock*. His poem "Spring Dress" was featured on Michel Martin's NPR program Tell Me More. Dave lives in the Missouri Ozarks and hosts the weekly Friday Poems series at his website, davemalone.net.

Ethel Maqeda is a writer originally from Zimbabwe, now resident in Sheffield. Her work is inspired by the experiences of African women at home and in the diaspora. Her work has been published in various issues of *Route 57*, the *University of Sheffield's* creative writing journal, *Verse Matters* (Valley Press, 2017), *Wretched Strangers* (Boiler House Press, 2018), and *Chains: Unheard Voices* (Margo Collective, 2018).

Elizabeth Marian Charles is a recent graduate of the Arizona State University's MFA program. Her work has appeared in *Bird's Thumb* and *Fiction Southeast*, and is forthcoming in *Minnesota Review* and *Running Wild Anthology of Stories, Vol. 4*. She lives and writes in Texas.

Melanie Martinez is a BFA student at Texas State University in San Marcos. She lives in Austin and grew up in the Army town of Killeen. Her early life led her through many worlds from journalism to horticulture, then music and historic preservation. Now she focuses on interior design and painting. An interest in society and American Studies led her to examine the ways we live in the world today. Her style evokes the attractive, illustrative yet disturbing style of Rene Magritte while the subject matter places her in the world of contemporary social realist painters.

Alena Marvin is a young woman seeking the spark to light her imaginative fire. The twenty-year-old aspiring author is just about due for a quarter-life crisis, and she uses that chaos to fuel her creativity.

Ryota Matsumoto is an artist, designer, and urban planner. Born in Tokyo, he was raised in Hong Kong and Japan. He received a Master of Architecture from University of Pennsylvania in 2007 after studying at Architectural Association in London and Mackintosh School of Architecture, Glasgow School of Art in the early 90's. His art and built work are featured in numerous publications and exhibitions internationally.

Charlene Stegman Moskal is a teaching artist with The Alzheimer's Poetry Project under the auspices of the Poetry Promise Organization of Las Vegas. She is a visual artist, a performer, a voice for NPR's *Theme and Variations* as well as a writer. She has been published in numerous anthologies, magazines, and ezines, most recently in *Southwestern American Literature*, *The Nervous Ghost*, *Sky Island Journal*, *Sandstone & Silver; an Anthology of Nevada Poets* and *Other Worldly Women*. Her second chapbook, *One Bare Foot* is published by Zeitgeist Press.

Cassandra Moss was born in Manchester and grew up just outside the city. She studied English with Film at King's College, London. and subsequently worked in the film industry for Sister Films, Working Title, and Vertigo. Since 2009, she has been an EFL teacher. After moving to Ireland, she recently completed an MPhil in Linguistics at Trinity College, Dublin. Her short fiction has been published in *Succour*, *3am Magazine*, *Cricket Online Review*, *Squawk Back*, *And/Or*, *The Passage Between*, and *Posit*.

Sidney Muntean is a high school student in the creative writing program at Orange County School of the Arts. Her work has been recognized with second place in the Freedom to Read Art & Poetry Contest, and has been published in *The Phoenix* and *The Loud Journal*. When she's not writing, she's probably dancing up a storm. She firmly believes she was a ballet dancer in a past life because the routines she'll come up with in the rain feel like a distant dream.

Chukwuma "Chuks" Ndulue is a writer/teacher and author of the chapbook *Boys Quarter* (Ugly Duckling Presse). His work has appeared in *BOAAT*, *Muse/A Journal*, *Tinderbox*, *PANK*, *Brooklyn Poets* and other publications.

Nam Nguyen is a multimedia artist who explores the unexplored.

Mitchell Nobis is a writer, teacher, and adoptive dad in Metro Detroit where he lives with his family. His poetry has appeared in *Exposition Review, Hobart, The Wayne Literary Review, English Journal,* and others. His poetry manuscript was a runner-up for the 2019 Hopper Poetry Prize, and he coauthored the teaching book *Real Writing: Modernizing the Old School Essay.* Find him at @MitchNobis or mitchnobis.com.

Robert Oehl's art is very personal. He's tried to put aside vanity and intent, and let the photographs create their own subject and narrative. His diaristic self-portraits are self-deprecating, vulnerable, raw, humorous, and histrionic; they are, for him, self-examinations of identity, as well as raw material for a personal mythology. Oehl is a process-oriented photographer using a variety of rudimentary tools. He uses simple pinhole and zone plate cameras requiring long exposures. Images produced with these cameras are characteristically dreamlike, dark, softly focused (grainy), and seem better suited to a past era. In a predominantly digital world, Oehl's process is totally analog, employing film, paper, and chemical manipulation.

A confessed outsider, Chicago's **J. Ray Paradiso** is a recovering academic in the process of refreshing himself as an experiMENTAL writer and street photographer. His work has appeared in dozens of publications online and in print. Equipped with cRaZy quilt graduate degrees in both Business Administration and Philosophy, he labors to fill temporal-spatial, psycho-social holes and, on good days, to enjoy the flow. All of his work is dedicated to his true love, sweet muse and bodyguard, Suzi Skoski Wosker Doski.

Alli Parrett is a prose writer and hold a Masters in Creative Writing from University of Glasgow. Though she was born in Illinois, she's spent much of her adult life in the Pacific Northwest and Scotland. She lives in Seattle with her husband and two dogs. Her work has appeared in Issue 42 and Issue 43 of *From Glasgow to Saturn*, *The Write Launch*, and *Crab Fat Magazine*.

Hayley Patterson is a New York artist with a portfolio that displays achievements in both analog and digital media. Hayley's knowledge of art history as well as current trends is reflected across all animated and illustrative work. In the coming year, other illustrations will be published by Flying Ketchup Press and *Meat for Tea: The Valley Review*. A recent college graduate who finished summa cum laude, Hayley spends most of her time doodling and working and doodling some more, looking for the next challenge.

Ernst Perdriel was Born in Montreal (Quebec, Canada) in 1974 and lives in Eastern Townships region, Quebec, Canada. Focusing on recycled art, designer and horticulture, Perdriel's mission of life is to transmit the passion of the cultural and environmental heritage through arts, lifestyle, and sharing of knowledge. The artist has created with the waste of human civilization since 1995. The scale of the creations goes from the 2D format to interior design and landscaping.

At age twelve, **Silas Plum** won the East Coast POG tournament. The prize was five hundred POGs, small collectible cardboard circles, each with an identical red and blue design on the front. From that moment on, he became obsessed with the question of value. Why were these important? How could anything not necessary for survival be worth more than anything that was? Does artistic sentiment have value? The POG's are gone, but the questions remain. Through assemblages of defunct currency, discarded photographs, and long-forgotten illustrations, Silas Plum challenges the idea of objective vs subjective value. He believes strongly in the tired old maxim that the true value of an object is more than the sum of its parts, that the gut is a truth-teller, and that the Aristotelian notion of learning-by-doing is the best teacher around. Judge his worth at silasplum.com.

Diana Raab, PhD, is an award-winning memoirist, poet, blogger, speaker, and author of ten books and over one thousand articles and poems. She's also editor of two anthologies, *Writers on the Edge: 22 Writers Speak About Addiction and Dependency*, and *Writers and Their Notebooks*. Raab's two memoirs are *Regina's Closet: Finding My Grandmother's Secret Journal*, and *Healing with Words: A Writer's Cancer Journey*. She blogs for Psychology Today, Thrive Global, Sixty and Me, and PsychCentral and is frequently a guest blogger for various other sites. Her two latest books are, *Writing for Bliss: A Seven-Step Plan for Telling Your Story and Transforming Your Life*, and *Writing for Bliss: A Companion Journal*. Visit: www.dianaraab.com.

Decades ago, autodidact & bloody-minded optimist **kerry rawlinson** gravitated from sunny Zambian skies to solid Canadian soil. Fast-forward: she follows Literature & Art's Muses around the Okanagan, still barefoot, her patient husband ensuring she's fed. She's cracked some contests (e.g. Cago; Fish Poetry Prize) and features lately in *Synchronized Chaos*, *Spelk*, *Tupelo Quarterly*, *Across the Margin*, *Yes Poetry*, *Pedestal*, *Reflex Fiction*, *Riddled With Arrows*, *ArcPoetry*; among others. kerryrawlinson.tumblr.com @kerryrawli

Michele E. Reisinger's fiction has been featured in *Light and Dark Magazine*, *Prometheus Dreaming*, *34th Parallel*, *The Mighty Line*, and TulipTree Publishing's 2019 anthology *Stories That Need to be Told*. She studied English and Political Science at

Pennsylvania State University and received an MA in English Literature from the University of Delaware. She lives near Philadelphia with her family.

Barb Reynolds spent twenty-two years as a child abuse investigator. Her chapbook *Boxing Without Gloves* was published by Finishing Line Press. Her poems have been published widely, and she founded & curate the Second Sunday Poetry Series in Berkeley, CA.

Debbie Robson has been writing poetry since the 1990s and has performed some of her poems on radio, at Sydney poetry events, in the Blue Mountains, and more recently as part of the Women of Words project in Newcastle.

Eric Roe has won *Chautauqua's* 2018 Editors Prize and *The Bellingham Review's* 2015 Tobias Wolff Award for Fiction. Work has also appeared in TulipTree's *Stories That Need to Be Told* anthology, the Best American Fantasy anthology, *Petrichor* (forthcoming), *The Tishman Review, South 85, december, Redivider, Barrelhouse,* and other literary journals. Eric lives in Chapel Hill, North Carolina, and serves as the editorial assistant at UNC's Marsico Lung Institute.

Esther Sadoff currently lives in Columbus, Ohio, where she teaches English to gifted and talented middle school students. She has a bachelor's degree from Sarah Lawrence College where she studied literature as well as a Master of Education from The Ohio State University. Her poems have been featured or are forthcoming in *The 2River View, The Bookends Review, River River, SWIMM,* and *Marathon Literary Review*.

Tonissa Saul is a writer and photographer from Arizona. She is the managing editor for *Bodega Magazine* and an editor for Rinky Dink Press. Her work has appeared or is forthcoming in *Write On, Downtown, The Comstock Review,* and the anthology *Miles to Go, Promises to Keep Volume II*. Additionally, her artwork has appeared on the covers of Rinky Dink Press.

Jacqueline Schaalje has published stories and poetry in the *Massachusetts Review, Talking Writing, Frontier Poetry, Grist,* among others. Her stories were finalists for the Epiphany Prize and in the New Guard Competition. She has received support and/or scholarships from the Southampton Writers Conference and International Women's Writing Guild, and One Story and Live Canon workshops. She joined the Tupelo Press 30/30 project. She earned her MA in English from the University of Amsterdam.

Samantha Schlemm is an emerging writer and graduate student in the MA in Writing Creative Nonfiction program at Johns Hopkins University.

Victoria Shannon has worked as a journalist in New York City, Washington, DC, and Paris, France, and now lives in the Hudson River Valley of New York State.

Zach Sheneman obtained his BA in Writing from Grand Valley State University. He resides in Grand Rapids, Michigan with his wife and two sons. His work has been published in *The Pinch Journal, Glass Mountain,* and *Hippocampus*.

Louis Staeble, fine arts photographer and poet, lives in Bowling Green, Ohio. His photographs have appeared in *Agave, Blinders Journal, Blue Hour, Conclave Journal, Elsewhere Magazine, GFT Magazine, Fifth Wednesday Journal, Four Ties Literary Review, Inklette Magazine, Light: A Journal of Photography, Literary Juice, Paper Tape Magazine, Qwerty, Revolution John, Rose Red Review, Sonder Review, South 85, Tishman Review* and *Your Impossible Voice*. His work has been shown in The Black Swamp Arts Festival 2016, 2017 and 2018 as part of the Wood County Invitational. Web page: staeblestudioa.weebly.com Instagram@louiestaeble.

Lenora Steele's short prose and poetry have been published in periodicals in Canada and Ireland such as *Event, Cranog Magazine, The Fiddlehead, Room, Wow, The New Quarterly*, and *The Antigonish Review*. Other works have been reprinted in Monitor Books' *An Anthology of Magazine Verse* and Harcourt Canada's *Elements of English 11*. She lives where the tidal bore brings the sea upriver twice a day in Truro, Nova Scotia, Canada.

George L Stein is a writer and photographer in the New Jersey/New York metropolitan area with interest in monochrome, film and digital photography, urban and rural decay, architectural, street, and more generally, art photography and digital manipulation. His work has been published in *Midwest Gothic, NUNUM, Montana Mouthful, Out/Cast, The Fredericksburg Literary and Art Review*, and *DarkSide Magazine*.

Marjorie Tesser's poetry and fiction have appeared in *Anomaly, Drunken Boat, Exoplanet, SWWIM Everyday*, and others. She coedited three anthologies, most recently *Travellin' Mama* (Demeter Press, 2019), and is editor in chief of *Mom Egg Review*. She has an MFA (fiction) from Sarah Lawrence College, where she won the 2019 John B. Santoiani Prize from Academy of American Poets.

Pasquale Trozzolo is an entrepreneur and founder of Trozzolo Communications Group, one of the leading advertising and public relations firms in the Midwest. In addition to building his business, he also spent time as a racecar driver, grad school professor, and magazine publisher. Now with too much time on his hands, he continues to complicate his life by living out as many retirement clichés as possible. He's up to the Ps.

Hediana Utarti is a sixty-year-old API immigrant who came to the US in 1986 to study political science. Although she graduated, she felt her life had more purpose in her current work at San Francisco Asian Women's Shelter (sfaws.org).

Gabrielle Vachon is a fulltime hair and makeup artist in Montreal and Toronto, as well as part-time writer to soothe her soul (just kidding, her anxiety is Submittable's whipping boy). She has been published in *Cosmonauts Avenue, Maudlin House*, and *Corvus Review*, and has been an invited reader at Slackline Series. She holds an Honors English Literature degree from Concordia University, and lives with her beloved husband Justin and puppy Lola in Montreal.

Hannah van Didden writes where the story takes her—usually somewhere dark but truthful; often beautiful. You will find pieces of her scattered around the world, in places such as *Tahoma Literary Review, Crannóg, Southerly, Breach, Atticus Review,* and *Southword Journal.*

Karen Walker writes short fiction and flash in Ontario Canada. Her work has appeared or is forthcoming in online magazines and anthologies including *Spillwords, Reflex Fiction, The Brasilia Review, Commuterlit,* and *Blank Spaces.* People say Karen is fun and frustrating, and her chicken lasagna is pretty good.

Mekiya Walters is a recent graduate of the University of Arkansas's MFA program and lives in Fayetteville, Arkansas.

Ping Wang is a fashion photographer and art director based in New York. He graduated from School of Visual Arts with a Master's Degree in Digital Photography. Ping specialized in combining fashion and fine art with his unique aesthetics. His love for surreal and metaphysical art has inspired him to do special works. Ping's artwork has exhibited in the US, France, China, Japan and Australia, among other places. In 2016, Ping was awarded the Emerging Photographer of the Year by *Photo District News* after competing against tens of thousands of photographers worldwide. In 2018, his work was been awarded a Gold Winner of Fine Art Portfolio by the Tokyo International Foto Award.

Kim Waters lives in Melbourne, Australia. She has a Master of Arts degree in creative writing from Deakin University. Her poetry has appeared in *The Australian, Shanghai Review, Going Down Swinging On-line, Verge, Offset 16, Communion 5, Tincture,* and *Antithesis.*

Virginia Watts is the author of poetry and stories found or upcoming in Illuminations, The Florida Review, The Blue Mountain Review, The Moon City Review, Permafrost Magazine, Palooka Magazine, and Streetlight Magazine, among others. A finalist in 2020 Philadelphia Stories Sandy Crimmins Poetry Contest, winner of the 2019 Florida Review Meek Award in nonfiction, and nominee for Best of the Net 2019 in nonfiction, Virginia resides near Philadelphia, Pennsylvania.

Walter Weinschenk is an attorney by day but spends as much time as possible as a writer, photographer and musician. Until a few years ago, he wrote short stories exclusively. Now he divides his time equally between poetry and prose. His writing has appeared in the *Carolina Quarterly* and *The Esthetic Apostle.* He lives in a suburb just outside Washington, DC.

Laurence Williams writes, plays bass guitar and worked in the courts of the Bronx. He has been published in *Middle Church Literary Journal, First Line Literary Journal,* and *Read650.*

Nina Wilson is a graduate of Coe College in Cedar Rapids, Iowa. She lives in Indianola, Iowa with her family. She loves history, especially early English history, photography, traveling, fishing, and camping.

Omer Wissman; a serialized CNF; thirty-six-year-old multidisciplinary artist; degrees in psychology and music; published in most Israeli magazines. Born someplace where people go for sickness unto death, Rescued away to the nearest town, where he developed such neat capacities as object permanence, crying out every drop of vodka he'd drink, and the art of loving and hating a person at the same time. A few years ago, fell in love with writing, and the rest remains to be.

Charlotte Wyatt is a recent graduate from the University of Houston's MFA program, where she was an Inprint Fellow and a recipient of the Inprint Donald Barthelme Prize for Fiction. Her fiction may be found in *Joyland*, and her interviews of other authors are in *Gulf Coast* and *Electric Literature*.

Haolun Xu is twenty-four years old and was born in Nanning, China. He immigrated to the United States in 1999. He was raised in central New Jersey and is currently studying Political Science and English at Rutgers University. Transitioning from a background in journalism and activism, he spends his time between writing poetry and the local seashore.

WRITING A NEW WORLD

Sunspot Literary Journal believes in the power of the written word. Fiction, nonfiction, poetry and art can speak truth to power with the power inherent in all human beings. Our mission is to amplify every voice.

Four digital quarterly editions are produced per year along with one print volume. At times, *Sunspot* will produce special editions. These might be digital only, print only, or both. All will be filled with the same quality content being created by today's unique voices.

SUPPORT SUNSPOT LIT

Today more than ever, literary journals are forces of change in the world. *Sunspot Lit* is funded entirely through private means. Every donation, even ones as small as a dollar, makes a difference.

Take a moment to drop a few bucks into the *Sunspot* magnetic field flux. Your donation helps ensure that this phenomenon lifts every voice into the stratosphere.

A PayPal link on the website makes it easy to send a tip, donate enough to publish the next digital edition, or go supernova and fund the next print edition. Please visit https://sunspotlit.com/support for details.

ADVERTISE IN *SUNSPOT*

Classified ads are available in quarterly digital editions and special editions. Spread the word about your writing and arts contests, residency programs, awards, workshops, and more. All classified ads are also posted on the website's classified page. Ad rate: $150 for up to 25 words; $5 for each additional word.

Print ads are available for the annual edition. All ads are black and white. A full page is $850, a half page is $450, and a quarter page is $295. Buy two ads of the same size for the same issue or for two sequential issues to receive a 10% discount. Set up three or more ads and receive a 15% discount.

Sunspot's groovy graphic designer can set up your ad to your specifications. Flat rate of $325, and the design is yours to use multiple times in *Sunspot* or any other magazine.

CPSIA information can be obtained
at www.ICGtesting.com
Printed in the USA
FSHW020145241120
76197FS